D0113981

The
New
Book of
SNOBS

Also by D. J. Taylor

Fiction
Great Eastern Land
Real Life
English Settlement
After Bathing at Baxter's: Stories
Trespass
The Comedy Man
Kept: A Victorian Mystery
Ask Alice
At the Chime of a City Clock
Derby Day
Secondhand Daylight
The Windsor Faction
From the Heart
Wrote for Luck: Stories

Non-fiction
A Vain Conceit: British Fiction in the 1980s
Other People: Portraits from the Nineties (with Marcus Berkmann)
After the War: The Novel and England Since 1945
Thackeray
Orwell: The Life
On the Corinthian Spirit: The Decline of Amateurism in Sport
Bright Young People: The Rise and Fall of a Generation 1918–1940
What You Didn't Miss: A Book of Literary Parodies
The Prose Factory: Literary Life in England Since 1918

The
New
Book of
SNOBS

D.J. Taylor

Constable • London

CONSTABLE

First published in Great Britain in 2016 by Constable

1 3 5 7 9 10 8 6 4 2

Typeset in Bembo Std by SX Composing DTP Ltd, Rayleigh, Essex
Printed and bound in Great Britain by Clays Ltd, St Ives plc

Papers used by Constable are from well-managed forests
and other responsible sources.

MIX
Paper from
responsible sources
FSC® C104740

Constable
An imprint of
Little, Brown Book Group
Carmelite House
50 Victoria Embankment
London EC4Y 0DZ

An Hachette UK Company
www.hachette.co.uk

www.littlebrown.co.uk

For Marcus Berkmann

Snobbishness is like Death in a quotation from Horace, which I hope you never have learned, 'beating with equal foot at poor men's doors and kicking at the gates of Emperors.'

W. M. Thackeray, The Book of Snobs (1846–1847)

Of course everyone has their own personal criteria as to definitions of social success or failure . . . someone staying with Gerry Wellington [Gerald Wellesley, 7th Duke of Wellington] was unwise enough to refer to a woman they both knew as 'smart'. Gerry drew in his breath slightly. 'A nice woman, certainly. But smart? I don't recollect ever having seen her at the Sutherlands or the Ancasters.

Anthony Powell, Journals 1982–1986

I've never come across anyone who wouldn't rather have an inherited title than one bestowed by the Queen.

Eddy Sackville-West, quoted in Frances Partridge,
Other People: Diaries 1963–1966

Contents

Part Two: Among the Snobs – Sketches

Part One
Theory and Practice

In the last week of November ... ...
of the British press would have ... ...
choice of three summer ... ...
former politician. The first ... ...
episode long thought quietly ... ...
ing to its death throes ... ...

1
The Snob Defined

'I think that is everything, isn't it? Mr Prendergast?'

'*Cigars,*' said Mr Prendergast, in a stage whisper.

'Ah yes, cigars. Boys, I have been deeply distressed to learn that several cigar-ends have been found – where have they been found?'

'*Boiler-room.*'

'In the boiler-room. I regard this as reprehensible. What boy has been smoking cigars in the boiler-room?'

There was a prolonged silence, during which the Doctor's eye travelled down the line of boys.

'I will give the culprit until luncheon to give himself up. If I do not hear from him by then the whole school will be heavily punished . . .

'I should think by the look of them they were exceedingly cheap cigars,' added Mr Prendergast sadly. 'They were a pale yellow colour.'

'That makes it worse,' said the Doctor. 'To think of any boy under my charge smoking pale yellow cigars in a boiler-room! It is *not* a gentlemanly fault.'

Evelyn Waugh, *Decline and Fall* (1928)

I n the last week of November 2014 sensation-hungry readers of the British press would have found themselves offered a choice of three separate scandals, each featuring a current or former politician. The first was, technically, rather an elderly episode, long thought quiescent but now reanimated and speeding to its death–throes in a libel court as the result of an action

The New Book of Snobs

brought by the erstwhile government chief whip Andrew
Mitchell MP against the *Sun*, which had published a detailed
account of the notorious 'Plebgate' affair of two years before.
Mr Mitchell, it may be remembered, had been attempting to
cycle through the security gates at 10 Downing Street when he
was asked by one of the officers on duty, PC Toby Rowland, to
dismount. Mr Mitchell, having reluctantly left his saddle, was
then supposed to have minted the following rebuke: 'Best you
learn your fucking place . . . You don't run this fucking government . . . You're fucking plebs.' Mr Mitchell resigned his official
post not long after news of this encounter broke, but the ram-
ifications persisted and his suit against the newspaper was
followed by a counter-writ issued by the policeman himself.
After a great deal of legal manoeuvring, on 27 November 2014,
Mr Justice Mitting decided that Mr Mitchell, whom he
described as 'childish', had indeed used the words in question,
or something so like them as to make no material difference,
and ruled against him on both counts. PC Rowland was
awarded £80,000 in damages and the costs, for which Mr
Mitchell was liable, were estimated at in excess of £2 million.

Meanwhile, a second scandal had blown up, which at one
point threatened altogether to eclipse media coverage of Mr
Mitchell and his travails. This was the case of Emily Thornberry,
Labour MP for Islington South and Shadow Attorney General.
In this relatively senior capacity, she was sent by her party
managers to the Rochester and Strood by-election, caused by
the defection of the sitting Conservative, Mark Reckless, to
help with canvassing. Out among the voters on the morning of
polling day – 20 November – Ms Thornberry tweeted to her
followers the picture of a house in the constituency draped

with St George's flags and with a white van parked outside captioned 'Image from Rochester.' In fact, as several local journalists were quick to point out, the picture had been taken in nearby Strood. Such was the outrage caused, or perhaps only manufactured, by this souvenir from the campaign trail that by the time the polls closed, and shortly before Mr Reckless's triumph, Ms Thornberry was compelled to put her resignation in the hands of her party leader, Ed Miliband.

Almost immediately, Ms Thornberry's torment was cut short by news of a third incident. This was the publication of a tape-recording – obtained by the *Daily Telegraph* – of a disagreement between the former Conservative cabinet minister David Mellor, MP for Putney between 1979 and 1997, and the taxi-driver ferrying him across London over the latter's choice of route. Mr Mellor, who as more than one commentator pointed out had form in cases of this kind, not only became overbearing but insisted on his superior status. 'You think that your experiences are anything compared to mine?' he demanded at one point. Another part of the harangue included the words 'You don't need to worry about someone who's been in the cabinet, who's an award-winning broadcaster, who's a Queen's Counsel. Treat me like shit, ruin my wife's day . . . and if you think you're going to be sarky with me, get a better education . . .' Mr Mellor later told the media that he regretted losing his temper but still believed that the flare-up was the driver's fault.

The distinguishing mark of these very different episodes was the single moral failing that appeared to lie at their core and was thought to explain the unacceptable behaviour of the people caught up in them. Mr Mitchell's arraignment hinged not on the fact that he had sworn at the police officers manning the gates of 10 Downing Street, through which it might be thought inadvisable for any cyclist to proceed, however grand his rank, but that he had used the word 'plebs', a Latin term that might be translated as 'common people'. Mitchell, according to the verdict of the press, was a 'snob'. It was the same with Ms Thornberry and her resignation letter. Useless for her to protest that this was the kind of house she herself had grown up in, and that she was merely registering the continuing existence of the demographic from where she had sprung rather than surreptitiously sneering at it. No, she was a snob, a member of a lofty metropolitan elite, and the modern Labour Party could not be seen to tolerate the supposedly patronising attitudes she was thought to be espousing. As for Mr Mellor, quite apart from losing his temper, he had committed the unpardonable sin of sneering at an ordinary person who had made the mistake of challenging him and mocking him for his lack of worldly success. He, too, everyone agreed, was a snob.

Mr Mitchell had called a group of policemen by a Latin name. Ms Thornberry had tweeted a picture of a house that reminded her of her childhood. Mr Mellor had made a vainglorious ass of himself. The fact that they were all assumed to be guilty of the same crime suggests that snobbery occupies a central place in the modern demonology and that, short of calling someone a racist or a paedophile, one of the worst charges you can lay at anyone's door here in the early twenty-first century is to suggest that they happen to be a snob. But what constitutes snobbishness? Who are the snobs and where are they to be found? What are their distinguishing characteristics? How do the symptoms declare themselves? Standard dictionary definitions are, at best, unhelpful. Having noted that 'snob' is of unknown origin, the *Shorter Oxford* gives a first usage date of 1781, when the word meant a shoemaker or cobbler, then defines it as Cambridge slang from the 1830s applied to anyone who was not a member of the university, before quoting a 1852 usage of 'a person belonging to the lower classes of society'. Interestingly, this line of descent ignores William Makepeace Thackeray's memory of his time at Cambridge in the late 1820s: 'We *then* used to consider Snobs raw-looking lads, who never missed chapel; who wore highlows [a type of half-boot] and no straps; who walked two hours on the Trumpington Road every day of their lives; who carried off the college scholarships and who overrated themselves in hall.'

A final entry gets us closer to the accepted modern usage – 'one whose ideas and conduct are prompted by a vulgar admiration for wealth or social position' – but even that is not particularly close. For the fates of Messrs Mitchell and Mellor and Ms Thornberry would seem to suggest that contemporary ideas of snobbery rely on the assumption of an essentially class-based superiority: upper-class people looking down on the *petit bourgeoisie*; middle-class property owners smiling smugly at the feckless inhabitants of the local council estate; people with £40,000 a year shaking their heads over the bizarre lifestyles favoured by those with £20,000. On the other hand, it takes only the merest glance at a daily newspaper to register the multitudinous uses to which the word 'snob' is currently put, and the difficulty of arriving at a definition of a term used so promiscuously that it shows every sign of transforming itself into one of those tantalising abstract nouns like 'liberal', now employed with such indiscriminate enthusiasm that it might be thought to have very little meaning at all.

Here, for example, is an extract from a letter which appeared in the *i* newspaper sometime in March 2015, commenting on the admissions policy operated by certain grammar schools in the West Midlands whereby 20 per cent of the places are reserved for children from poor homes from whom slightly lower standards of attainment are required. What, the correspondent demands, is this 'dreadful middle-class prejudice' that enthuses whenever poorer intelligent children are given an intellectual advantage over their peers? 'If you are poor and of average intelligence, or less, what then?' The writer concluded that 'intellectual snobbery is as pernicious and ugly as any classism'. So, separating one child from another on grounds of intellectual attainment is, apparently, 'snobbish'. But so, according to one kind of social commentator, is preferring opera to Taylor Swift. On the other hand, to like opera instead of grime, or to think Proust superior to J. K. Rowling, or imagine that polo has the edge on darts is not necessarily a badge of class. Clearly, snobbery has something to do with an area that is important to class without ever dominating it, that vague but enticing abstract *taste*.

Let us extend the range of evidence with some more news stories that rest on the imputation of 'snobbery', all of them taken from British newspapers during a single week in the summer of 2015.

- The *Guardian* 'Saturday Sketch'. This finds Zoe Williams paying a visit to the Carron fish bar in Aberdeenshire, whose proprietors in 1992 invented the deep-fried Mars Bar. In defying an order to take down a sign commemorating the fact, the shop has apparently 'fought off a council's snobbery'.

- The *Eastern Daily Press* article by Lynne Mortimer enquiring 'Who knew that gardens were a sign of your class?' and quoting the 'etiquette expert William Hanson' who had suggested that 'hanging baskets are the calling cards of the lower middle class' and that 'No one, trust me, no one, of any remotely decent stock has a patio' (the correct word is 'terrace').

- The *i* comment piece by Memphis Barker, examining the *Times Educational Supplement's* list of the Top 100 works of fiction that 'every student' should read before they reach secondary school, and headlined 'Stand aside book snobs – teenagers are better judges of fiction'. Although irked by the appearance on the list of *Angus, Thongs and Full-Frontal Snogging*, Barker concludes that 'Book snobs and aspiring book snobs (a badge I claim) can relax, as such examples of respectable literature as *Nineteen Eighty-Four*, *Pride and Prejudice* and *The Catcher in the Rye* all make the top ten.'

Significantly, the conceptions of 'snobbery' conveyed in these extracts are all slightly different. To the *Guardian*, which attributes to Aberdeenshire Council a wish that its traders shouldn't 'lower the tone', snobbishness consists of trying to ban the promotion of foodstuffs thought – by whom exactly? – to be somehow plebeian. Mr Hanson is performing the very old trick of identifying a social signifier for the benefit of the status-conscious middle classes. The implication of Memphis Barker's piece is that to make a judgement insisting that one piece of art is 'better' than another is inherently snobbish, an assumption which among other things suggests that every literary critic from F. R. Leavis to John Carey has simply been wasting their time. In some ways, the letter to *i* about the Midlands grammar schools' selection criteria is odder still. It may not be good for a child's sense of self-worth to separate one eleven-year-old from another on grounds of academic ability, but is it an example of snobbery? One might as well say that awarding a BA student a 2:1 rather than a 2:2 is snobbish, or allowing a PhD candidate to pass *cum summa laude*. There comes a point in everyone's life when a judgement about their intellect, their credentials for a job or their qualifications for a relationship with another person will have to be made: they can't *all* be snobbishly arrived at, for the essence of snobbery lies in a distinction made for the wrong reasons.

A snob, all the evidence insists, is one who delights in making judgements that are based on arbitrary criteria: wanting a duke's approval of your books rather than a professor of literature's, making assumptions about a householder's worth based on the tidiness of his box hedges, assuming that to live in Yorkshire is morally better than to live in Essex. On this reading, snobbery exists in all walks of life, at all social levels and in all social categories, and is as likely to be found in a refugee camp or at the checkout at Aldi as in a moated grange or the library of a Pall Mall gentlemen's club. Most left-wing Labour MPs are snobs. Jeremy Clarkson is a snob. George Orwell, when it came to preferring beaujolais to 'colonial claret', or dressing for dinner, was a snob. The Scottish Nationalist is a snob. The Merseysider who ostentatiously talks through his nostrils and employs the stop fricative in order to pronounce 'Those' as 'Dose' is a snob, as is the non-Merseysider who moves to Liverpool and makes a point of trying to talk like the natives. The parents who, when casting a suspicious eye over their child's university application form, mutter the words 'Isn't that a former polytechnic?' are snobs. Evelyn Waugh, who as a teenager habitually walked down the road from his parents' house in Golders Green, London NW11 to post his letters in Hampstead so they should be dignified with the NW3 post-office frank, was a colossal snob. The row of council houses in Hodgson Road, Norwich, where my father lived in the 1930s was, according to his recollection, an absolute hotbed of snobbery, with each of the sixteen resident families gamely contriving to prove that they were superior to the people next door. Snobbery, it might reasonably be argued, is a key to our national life, as vital to the backstreet family on benefits as to the proprietor of the grandest stately home, an essential element in our view of who we are and what the world might be thought to owe us.

On the other hand, the absolute centrality of the snob to nearly all forms of modern social interaction is frequently hidden from public view. While some kinds of snobbery are conspicuous – the Porsche ostentatiously drawn up on a verge otherwise filled with Ford Mondeos, the one girl in the class who has been taking elocution lessons – the majority of snobs pursue their craft by stealth. The claim to social or moral distinction can be conveyed by an agency as subtle as an undone button, a gesture, a glance, an intonation, the pronunciation of a certain word – tiny signals, admittedly, but readily deciphered by anyone in the know. Two much complained about snob archetypes in the inter-war era, for example, were the debutante who, having been presented at court, went on to supper at the Ritz with feathers still in her hair, and the man on the way back from

Ascot who wore a Royal Enclosure badge in his buttonhole. In some ways this is a consequence of the snob having two audiences – the fellow snob with whom he wants to claim affiliation and the outsider whom he wants either to impress or leave trembling with a sense of his own insignificance. Public intimations of snobbishness, consequently, exist on several levels, rarely explicit, often camouflaged, seldom making an outright claim to superiority, nearly always requiring some kind of decoding. Here, for example, are four snob 'statements', the first two more or less brazen, the third cunningly disguised as something much less offensive, the fourth more or less unconscious but breath-taking in some of the assumptions it conceals.

'The kind of man who has to buy his own furniture.' The famous description of Michael Heseltine offered by his 1980s cabinet colleague, Michael Jopling, and enough to brand Heseltine for all time as a counter-jumping parvenu. Proper people, the subtext runs, come from families sufficiently well established for the younger generation to inherit the contents of their drawing rooms.

'Someone who has not set foot in a decent educational establishment.' The reaction of *Independent* co-founder Stephen Glover, a product of Shrewsbury School and Mansfield College, Oxford, to the news that the paper was now to be edited by Simon Kelner, an alumnus of the University of Central Lancashire. Even if it could be proved that the University of Central Lancashire was not a decent educational establishment, this provenance has no bearing on the ability of Mr Kelner, who by this stage in his career – 1998 – had spent several years occupying senior editorial roles in Fleet Street, to run a national newspaper.

'She was a perfectly adequate chemist. I mean nobody thought anything of her.' The Somerville College science don Janet Vaughan remembering Margaret Thatcher, sometime after her former undergraduate pupil had become prime minister. A remark quite as snobbish in its way as that of Michael Jopling in which Ms Vaughan is quietly judging a politician whose policies she disliked by the standards of a bygone Oxford common room. Note, too, the insinuation of that 'perfectly adequate'.

'I'm not used to people talking to me like that. Not because I think I'm Mr Superstar but because I'm not fucking having it. Basically, because I'm from Woking and I don't give a fuck, d'you know what I mean?' The musician Paul Weller, after having an album by his band the Style Council rejected by the managing director of the Polydor record label. This is a classic example of inverted snobbery. What does the fact that Weller comes from Woking have to do with his attitude to his music? Or with anything else?

All this allows us to move towards a definition of snobbishness that goes further than, say, the straightforward worship of aristocrats or not wanting the tone of your high street lowered by a sign advertising deep-fried Mars Bars. Snobbery, the foregoing illustrations suggest, is a matter of closed circles, exclusive groups, knowing the jargon and knowing how to behave, a perpetual keeping-up or extending of appearances conditional on the approval of people who aren't in a position to keep them up themselves. As such, it frequently declares itself to be a matter of *tone*. The critic P. N. Furbank once described the style of Anthony Powell's literary journalism, in which much is hinted but little explicitly resolved and direct statements are scrupulously avoided, as an exercise in 'refrigeration', or keeping your readers at one remove, the author, in effect saying to his audience, 'You would have to know me a great deal than is at all likely before I would be prepared to tell you what I really thought about the subject under discussion.' My own view is that Powell is not, by and large, a snob – reproached once for his fixation on books of genealogy he insisted that he would buy *Debrett's Guide to Bank Clerks* if such a volume existed. But the snob makes a virtue of refrigeration. He doesn't want the majority to know him better because that knowledge would destroy the sacredness of his own position. His greatest wish is to remain in the minority, to find whatever is the majority view and dissent from it, a construction job in which any materials will do. Richard Rees once described Orwell as 'a fugitive from the camp of victory', meaning that no triumph in the battle for progress and equality was ever good enough for his high-minded friend, that to achieve maximum results the tent had constantly to be unpitched and carried a few yards further up the track. So with the snob, who moves on continuously from one engagement to the next, always in search of an opportunity to assert himself, to prove his quality at the expense of those around him.

Slippery, elusive, never wanting to be pinned down, snobbery nonetheless has certain hard-and-fast rules.

Snobbery is ultimately reciprocal. It only exists because it is encouraged or, in certain circumstances, reluctantly tolerated. After all, you can only put on airs if you live in an environment where the putting-on of airs is a behavioural given. Most acts of snobbery, consequently, involve the striking of a bargain between the chief party to the transaction, the snob, and his or her willing or at least pliable accessory, the sub-snob, in which both sides are complicit. In the late 1960s my father was once travelling home to Norfolk from the FA Cup final with my maternal grandfather. My father worked for the Norwich Union Insurance Group, from which my grandfather had recently retired. When they stopped at a fish-and-chip shop in Thetford my grandfather insisted that they eat the food in the car rather than on a bench outside the shop on the grounds that Mr Basil Robarts, the Norwich Union's Chief General Manager, known to have been at the match, might be passing in his car. Mr Robarts may not have been a snob but this kind of behaviour was calculated to turn him into one.

In much the same vein, the 'Alex' cartoon strip in the *Daily Telegraph* once featured an episode in which its corporate financier hero is asked by his boss, Rupert, to have lunch with a rising young man who is about to be offered an important job. The newcomer has an impressive track record, and has reached his present eminence in the City by way of a comprehensive school and an MBA degree. All that is needed is a reference from some school friend or associate who knew him in this early period of his life. The final frame shows Alex telephoning Rupert from a restaurant table where his masterful-looking companion is smoking a cigar. 'He says he's rather lost touch with them,' Alex reports. 'Excellent, no worries on that score,' Rupert replies.

Snobbery is universal. No social class, intellectual category or art form is immune to the snob virus. On the evidence of his recently published letters that great liberal and free-thinker Sir Isaiah Berlin, who admitted that he preferred the company of 'distinguished people' to those less distinguished, was a snob. Eyewitness accounts of the career of Robbie Williams around the time of Britpop suggest that he was an inverted snob, an immensely talented commercial songwriter who became horribly insecure in the company of much less successful 'indie' bands whose 'edginess' he craved. The finely calibrated social judgement can be glimpsed in every branch of the media, from the *Tablet* to the *People's Friend*. Routinely commended for its anarchic spirit, the adult comic *Viz* in fact occupies classic lower-middle-class snob territory, equally keen to poke fun at such low-level harpies as Sandra and Tracey, the 'Fat Slags', or upper-class air-heads, as in 'The Totes Amazing Adventures of the, like, Kewl Chix'. *Viz*'s bugbears, it turns out, are promiscuity, vulgarity, sexism, cheating the benefits system ('Foul-mouthed Mobility Scooter Woman') and drunkenness – all highly respectable *petit-bourgeois* complaints.

The best snob-anatomists are likely to be snobs themselves. Nowhere does the takes-one-to-know-one principle work more effectively than in the medium of snobbery. Julian Fellowes's *Snobs* (2012), for example, is a classic demonstration of insider knowledge put to ripe artistic effect. Thackeray, famously, subtitled *The Book of Snobs* (1846–1847) 'By One of Themselves'. The fascination of Evelyn Waugh's novels *Decline and Fall* (1928) and *Vile Bodies* (1930), satires of the 'smart' Mayfair world of the late 1920s, stems from the author's complex relationship with his material. If not quite a paid-up 'Bright Young Person' himself, Waugh had certainly studied the Bright Young People at close hand. Half of him, consequently, stands on the outside of this cavalcade of night-long fancy-dress parties looking out, and the other on the outside looking in, and the resonance of these despatches from the Belgrave Square front-line is only enhanced by the reader's suspicion that Waugh is framing a milieu of which he himself is a part. The same point can be made of Simon Raven's connection to the subject matter of his early novels. When Jacinth Crewe, in *Brother Cain* (1959), expelled from his public school and asked by the headmaster how his parents will take it, replies, with maximum snobbishness that they are 'respectable in their locality', he is probably only echoing what his creator said when he was expelled from Charterhouse a decade and a half before. Significantly, Raven's biographer shows him to have delighted in the minutiae of upper-class etiquette, particularly when it was being explained to him by Old Etonians. As Raven himself once put it: 'the point about these chaps was that they were amiable, funny, civilised and snooty – even at one's own expense, though this was usually expressed ironically: "You know your trouble, Raven, you don't quite hold your fork right." And one never held it wrong again, you see.'

Snobs like to see their snobbishness celebrated. A special place is reserved in the snob pantheon for the great snob-codifiers – Thackeray's *The Book of Snobs*, the *Punch* cartoonist H. M. Bateman, with his remorseless exposés of déclassé behaviour ('The Man Who Threw a Snowball at St Moritz', 'The Colonel Who Talked About Horse-Riding in the Mess'), Stephen Potter's *Lifemanship*, Nancy Mitford's Eden-era compilation *Noblesse Oblige*, subtitled 'An Enquiry into the Identifiable Characteristics of the English Aristocracy', with its distinction between 'U' and 'Non-U', Ann Barr and Peter York's *Official Sloane Ranger Handbook*. Then there are the great snob heroes of fiction – *Pride and Prejudice*'s Lady Catherine de Bourgh, The Honourable Mrs Skewton in *Dombey and Son*, Mrs Sparsit ('whose husband was a

Powler') in *Hard Times*, P. G. Wodehouse's Psmith ('the 'p' is silent
as in physic, ptarmigan and phthisis'), E. F. Benson's Mapp and
Lucia . . . The list is practically infinite.

*The man who most loudly proclaims his lack of snobbishness is
the most likely to be a snob.* See in particular the people who
preface conversations with statements such as 'I can truthfully
declare that I haven't a snobbish bone in my body . . .' or 'In the
interests of equality . . .' before producing some altogether outrageous evidence of their own in-built superiority. This tendency is
especially evident in the media. It scarcely needs saying, for
example, that the most snobbish newspaper in the country is
the *Guardian*.

There is a difference between snobbishness and pedantry. The
subscriber who writes to *Harpers and Queen* to complain that the
social editor has referred to 'Lady Agatha Crisparkle' rather than
'the Dowager Countess of Crisparkle' or that the Marquess of
Loamshire's youngest son should be addressed by his courtesy
title of 'Lord Algernon Dymme' rather than 'Lord Dymme' is not
necessarily a snob.

The problem of the inverted snob. In his contribution to *Noblesse
Oblige*, Professor Alan S. C. Ross states categorically that there
are two kinds of snobs: *true snobs* and *inverted snobs*. Both kinds
respect a person the more the better bred he is. 'True snobs
indicate this in their behaviour to, and in their conversation about,
persons of good family, though they do not usually admit this. In
their conversation about (but not in their behaviour to such
persons), inverted snobs indicate that they respect a person the

less the better bred he is.' According to Professor Ross, one would expect to find a third grouping – those who really do respect a person the less the better bred he is and indicate it – and yet 'this third category does not appear to exist'. It is a mark of snobbery's development (or debasement) over the past sixty years – Professor Ross was writing in 1956 – that the concept of inverted snobbery should have undergone a fundamental transformation, to the point where many a modern inverted snob actively despises his or her social superiors. For an alternative inverted snob stance see the remarks about Robbie Williams, above.

All this raises fascinating questions about snobs' likely political affiliations, their aesthetic stance and philosophical make-up. It is, for some reason, usually assumed that the snob is a Conservative, and yet some of the greatest snobs in the history of twentieth-century British politics, for example Tom Driberg and Richard Crossman, have been members of the Labour Party. On the other hand, the true snob is rarely a democrat. Snobbery, close analysis insists, is essentially *oligarchical*, a matter of conspiratorial intimacy and highly priced admission tickets, using whatever materials are to hand to reinforce the alliances of which you are a part, in the way that Benjamin Disraeli, with a dozen bestselling novels under his belt, greeted the news that Queen Victoria was to publish a volume of her Highland journal with the flattering salutation 'We authors, ma'am.' It is also intensely *romantic* and, above all, *idealistic*. In his attitudes to the world beyond the window, the snob may, like many conservatives, look backwards to a landscape where things were better ordered and conditions more suitable for the kind of life he wishes to lead, but he will also look forward to an ideal world where the sometimes rough-and-ready principles currently on display will acquire a solidity they do not currently possess.

There is one final question to be answered before we journey off into the snob-jungle. What are my qualifications for presuming to write about snobs? Well, to borrow Anthony Powell's immortal phrase, it is all a question of upbringing. As the son of a man who graduated from a council estate to a white-collar job by way of a grammar-school scholarship, and a woman whose grandfather ran a tiny grocer's shop in a Suffolk market town, I knew all about petty social distinctions from an early age. My father, in particular, was constantly alert to the threat of patronage from those superior to him in the social scale and used to do a mocking impression of a woman he had once sat behind at a classical concert enquiring of her neighbour 'Dahs wan hev wan's years pee-arsed?' (i.e. 'Does one have one's ears pierced?'). On the other hand, he was routinely disparaging of 'yobs' and men who appeared in public without ties, read the *Daily Telegraph* until the day he died, and regarded the half-minute he once spent in the company of the Queen as the apogee of his life. The direct grant school I attended in the 1970s, though socially mixed, was snobbish to a degree, one of the principal divisions, oddly enough, being between boys who lived in Norwich and farmers' sons from the surrounding countryside, many of whom arrived at the school gates to shouts of 'Tractor!' As a bookseller's assistant I more than once assured a customer in search of some low-brow item that 'I'm afraid we don't stock that sort of book.' My Oxford college boasted a real-live viscount, on whom the other young gentlemen fawned shamelessly when they got the chance, as well as a contingent of no-nonsense 'northern' students whose contempt for the soft, decadent south in which they now had the misfortune to reside knew no bounds. And then, for a time in the 1980s and 1990s, I worked in the City of London, a world whose essential characteristics were neatly epitomised for me by the marketing partner of Messrs Coopers & Lybrand, as PricewaterhouseCoopers then was, who once remarked of his underlings' habit of wearing suede shoes rather than black Oxfords, 'We're not civil servants, you know.'

Am I a snob? I really hope not. I am certainly not of what used to be called a 'good' family, and the family tree purporting to show that my grandmother's forebears the Castells were descended from a Spanish clan named the di Castelli who 'came over' – that wonderful phrase – with William the Conqueror was long ago proved a fake. I am certainly not a 'gentleman' – a word in any case thought (by Anthony Trollope) to have no meaning as long ago as the 1870s. And yet, and yet . . . Only the other week, asked by my wife to pin down the character of a man newly arrived in the neighbourhood, I found myself, to my shame, offering the reply 'Rather minor public school.' I couldn't begin to explain the complexities of this judgement, and what it means in terms of one middle-aged man's relation to another, but the fact remains that it was a highly – no, a *definitively* – snobbish remark. All of which confirms my suspicion that, as we embark on this voyage in search of the snob, track down his and her habitats, aims and assumptions, and marvel at the idiosyncrasies they so proudly display, we are in it together.

School Parents (see page 230)

2

Heroes and Villains:
Katie Price, Lord Prescott and Others

I almost forgot – the two subalterns who went up with the farmhouse . . . Both of them, it seems, were of Downing College and the Welsh Regiment, so that's quite all right.

Simon Raven, *The Fortunes of Fingel* (1976)

Back in 2010 Miss Katie Price, formerly the glamour model Jordan, paid a visit to the Norwich branch of Waterstones to promote her latest bestselling novel. The event was widely publicised, and merited a lavish feature article in the local paper, the *Eastern Daily Press*. Miss Price, who brought her own security guards, sat signing books in regal splendour and had instructed her minders to discourage fans from conversing with her, attracted an audience of several hundred people. Most of those queueing up for their half-minute audience with the cover star of *Heat, OK!* and other publications expressed warm approval of the proud if somewhat sulky-looking author. Miss Price, one of them told the *Eastern Daily Press* reporter, was an astute businesswoman who deserved every credit for earning sufficient money to support her ever-growing family. Curiously enough, the only faint hints of disparagement came from members of the Waterstones staff. 'We looked her up on the internet,' a sales assistant confided, 'and it said that she didn't even write her own books.' The inference was clear. This was a bookshop, a temple of learning, culture and sophistication. Miss Price, with or without her nimble-fingered ghost, was a barbarian interloper, and the university graduates behind the till clearly despised her, even as they took her readers' money.

The snob, somebody once observed, is nothing if not conspicuous. Snobbery, after all, consists in the main of imposing yourself on a social situation, pulling rank, indicating, with varying degrees of subtlety, your own detachment from the people in whose presence you find yourself. Victims of snobbery, on the other hand, are much harder to establish, if only because the snob-victim often turns out to be a snob himself, worsted in conflict by a superior being, cast off from Mount Olympus and forced to take refuge on a subsidiary crag. William Trevor once wrote a cruelly ironic short story about a middle-aged woman taking a solitary vacation in a Swiss hotel. Her path through life is both governed and sanctified by a belief in her own gentility. Each brief interaction with her fellow-guests allows her to define the behavioural terms she brings to the world and bolster her self-regard, and the tentative advances of the raffish hotel chef are stoutly repulsed. If her aspirations have a symbolic focus it can be found in an upmarket women's magazine called *L'élégance* that lies on the drawing-room table; it is regarded by her as the acme of style, breeding and moral suavity. All is comfort, serenity and genteel chit-chat until the arrival at the hotel of a brace of upper-class ladies who swiftly divine that she is not their social equal. There is a particularly awful moment when one of them spots the copy of *L'élégance* and sniffs that she is surprised they take 'that rag' here. Chastened and resentful, our heroine is last seen en route to the chef's cottage in search of solace.

Trevor's protagonist is a victim of the tightly policed social world she has tried to infiltrate, but she is also a snob herself who likes nothing better than to trumpet her own social advantages over those less well qualified. The difficulty of getting to the heart of snobbery, of establishing what social or moral point is being made, what deceits are being practised and, more important, who wins or loses, becomes even more complex in the shadow of what might be called the 'snob joke', a feature of English humour since at least the early eighteenth century. Here are two examples, separated by a gap of nearly a century, the first taken from a *Punch* cartoon of the early 1920s, the second a recent photo caption from the music magazine *Mojo*. The *Punch* cartoon, to which Orwell draws outraged attention in *The Road to Wigan Pier*, shows four or five coal miners with dark, sinister faces bowling along in a cheap motor-car. A passing friend calls out to ask where they have borrowed the vehicle. The answer comes back: 'We've bought the thing.' The *Mojo* caption is attached to a photograph of the former Oasis singer Liam Gallagher and his wife, both drably dressed in parka jackets and jeans and carrying outsize carrier bags, and has one saying to the other, 'No, love, Primark's that way.'

The *Punch* cartoon, printed before the mid-1920s slump when coal prices – and miners' wages – were still high, is simply an expression of class antagonism, a mark of the very common post-1918 assumption that not only were the working classes getting above themselves but they aspired to a kind of life that their essential natures made them incapable of living: see, for example, the frequently articulated inter-war era belief that 'If you give the miners baths they'll keep coal in them.' But the real target of the *Mojo* caption is less easy to define. Is it the kind of people who wear scruffy parka jackets and loiter around the streets with their shopping? Is it the kind of people who shop at Primark? Or merely Mr and Mrs Gallagher? In fact, the snob message is a comparatively subtle one, for it seems to suggest not that there is anything wrong in dressing like a 1960s-era Mod, or even shopping at a discount store, but that people ought to behave according to the position they occupy in life and the amount of money at their disposal. As a millionaire rock star, consequently, Liam Gallagher ought to look the part, and while *Mojo* would not poke fun at a working-class Mancunian who shopped in Primark, a formerly working-class Mancunian who conforms to the popular stereotype of the Primark patron is fair game.

Something of the same confusion attends the sniffiness of the Norwich Waterstones staff over the discovery that Katie Price doesn't write her books herself and its detachment from the kind of complaints that Ms Price's well-publicised career usually attracts. The most common criticism of this much-married, philoprogenitive, cosmetic-surgery-fancying media star is that everything about her from her constant self-advertisement to her branded bed-linen and even the names of her children is 'vulgar'. A good example of the Katie Price snob joke, for example, would be *Private Eye's* caption of her dramatically tanned figure signing books with the words 'Winner of the Orange Prize'. The Waterstones sales assistants, on the other hand, were lamenting her lack of intellectual nous:

in putting her name to a book written by someone else she was presuming to a status that her attainments did not support. But why should the fact that a successful author employs a talented helper who does most of the work be so roundly condemned? The history of the celebrity ghost-writer, after all, goes back at least a couple of centuries. Thackeray's *Pendennis* (1850) contains an account of a dinner party at which the fashionable aristocratic author The Honourable Percy Popjoy is complimented for the excellence of a scene in his newly published novel that does not actually exist. Sir Winston Churchill's multi-volume history of the Second World War was pretty much assembled by a team of research assistants, while many another book by a leading politician – from the former Conservative Chancellor Iain Macleod's biography of Neville Chamberlain to Sir Harold Wilson's *The Making of a Prime Minister 1916–1964* – was put together by hired hands. Even Mrs Thatcher's two volumes of memoirs were not entirely her own work. Why should we criticise Ms Price while letting Sir Winston and Sir Harold off the hook?

And yet most of the evidence suggests that there is a deeper cultural resentment on display here, in which Katie Price, Kerry Katona and their kind are merely collateral. When, for example, an Oxbridge-educated newspaper columnist writes a brisk little article about Ms Price's latest husband or Ms Katona's cocaine habit, their annoyance is rarely based on straightforward personal dislike, or even – to go back to *Punch* and the miners – a suspicion that the lower orders are getting above themselves. Rather, it stems from their awareness that one of the great natural laws by which they were raised has been thrown into jeopardy; the complaint, in other words, is less about the personalities who decorate the cover of *Heat* than the process that grants them wealth and exposure. Modern celebrity, this argument runs, is not a reward for skill, talent or hard work but a kind of phantasmal behavioural state granted to arbitrarily selected non-entities whose subsequent careers consist simply of living their lives in public without reflection or effort. The Oxford graduates, who had it dinned into them in their youth that writing books was laborious and time-consuming only to find Katie Price producing an effortless stream of them with the help of a paid collaborator, take this betrayal very hard, but it does not necessarily mean that their criticisms are snobbish, in the sense of being based on an arbitrary distinction. After all, nearly every advanced society has tended to encourage the belief that success ought to rely on talent and/or hard work. In the end this is less a personal quarrel with Katie Price than a moral confrontation with the system that hatched her.

In any case there are more flagrant victims – real or alleged – of snobbery than Katie Price. Take, for example, the four-and-a-half decade-long political career of John Prescott, erstwhile Member of Parliament for Hull West (1970–2010), one-time Deputy Leader of the Labour Party (1997–2007), lately elevated to the upper chamber as Baron Prescott of Kingston upon Hull, towards whom supposedly snobbish insults fly with the regularity of a pile of paperclips obeying the magnet's call. Zealously unpicked and reconstituted by the nation's journalists since the arrival of the Blair government, endlessly crawled over by ideologues of right and left, disparaged by feminists, acclaimed (sometimes) by the mysterious entity known as 'the ordinary working man', Prescott's progress has all the elements of a modern myth, in which each episode is capable of proving some salutary moral about the age we inhabit, and each supplementary character eventually declares themselves as a figure of altogether gargantuan significance. There is old Bert Prescott, the railway signalman who began it all, first estranged from his thrusting young son but eventually brought to reconciliation. There are the teachers of Brinsworth Manor School and their failure to secure him the grammar school scholarship he craved. There is the stewarding job for Cunard, and – less picturesque, perhaps, but testimony to Prescott's burning ambition to make his mark – there is the trip to Ruskin College, Oxford, and the Hull University economics degree. H. G. Wells, of all early twentieth-century novelists the one who knew the most about snobbery, might not have liked the reality of the member for Hull West, but he would have understood the world he came from and relished the spectacle of his ascent.

And, taken in the round, Prescott has always borne an uncanny resemblance to a Wells hero: come from nowhere; barrelling on to no one quite knows where; moody, prejudiced and impetuous, but also bonhomous, modest and mundane, acclaimed and despised in equal shares, as loyal to his party as to himself. Like the family described in Hilary Mantel's memoir *Giving Up the Ghost*, he had aspiration but no aspirates. No one could deny the upwardly mobile class warriors of the post-war era their materialism, modern historians tend to suggest, given the crucible of debt and deprivation in which it had been forged. There was a poignant symbolism, consequently, in this tribune of the people deploying two Jaguars (one of them admittedly government-issue) in a movement where one would sometimes have been considered too many. With Prescott, socialism was not only moving down the road – that famous 250-yard dash to a conference hall where he was booked to discuss public transport policy – but also, indisputably, with the times.

But then symbolism has woven itself through every aspect of Prescott's career like bindweed through a lawn. The most obvious mark of his larger-than-life quality is the extraordinary number of nicknames he attracted. Most senior politicians make do with one, or at most two. James Callaghan's were 'Sunny Jim', because of his supposedly equable temperament, and 'Farmer Jim', on account of the rolling Sussex acres where he spent his weekends. Prescott, on the other hand, accumulated at least six: 'Prezza', to begin with; 'Two Jags' (a reference to the car fleet); 'Jabba the Hut' (*The Return of the Jedi*'s outsize villain); 'Two Jabs' (after attacking a protesting farmer who had thrown an egg at him); 'Two Shags' (a discreditable incident in his private life); and even 'No Jobs', coined by the *Independent* after he lost his department in a cabinet reshuffle of 2006 but contrived to retain both the residence and the perquisites associated with the title. There are probably others.

Only an ingrate would suggest that the soubriquets came in inverse proportion to the political achievement. Certainly, the outsize portfolio he was handed in 1997, as head of the newly created Department for Environment, Transport and the Regions, produced surprisingly little return. There was talk – but only talk – of something called an 'integrated transport strategy'. A scheme for regional assemblies had to be abandoned. But he was an indefatigable critic of the rail companies and an assiduous lobbyist for the Kyoto Protocol relating to climate change, and later worked with the Miliband brothers on the government's post-Kyoto agenda. And then there is the unarguable fact that throughout this period the responsibilities with which he was invested were much less important than what he was supposed to represent. What he was supposed to represent was New Labour's link with 'Labourism', those (metaphorically) cloth-capped traditionalists appalled by the modernising line being taken by the party's new leaders but prepared to lend support (and funding) if power could be delivered. Even greater than this, perhaps, was the responsibility of keeping Gordon happy with Tony and vice versa.

Power was duly delivered, but the price was considerable, not least to Prescott himself. To browse the political memoirs of the 1990s and early 2000s is to appreciate just how much he was disdained by the people he came up against. Even quite nice politicians detested him. 'A terrible man, absolutely awful and a hypocrite,' John Major pronounced, shortly before the 1997 general election. Coming across him at a *Spectator* party at around this time, the former Labour MP and Murdoch crony Woodrow Wyatt and his daughter Petronella found him practically lachrymose. 'He got very drunk,' Wyatt informed his diary. 'He said he hated Blair and the people around him. "They insist on coaching me to talk grammatically and 'posh' and I don't want to speak grammatically."' Wyatt assured him that 'You do it like Ernie Bevin [Clement Attlee's rough-hewn Foreign Secretary in the Labour government of 1945]. It's all pretty coherent.'

And this, alas, is to ignore the tortured syntax of *Private Eye*'s 'Let's parler Prescott' column, and the story – no doubt apocryphal, but these things stick – of applicants for jobs on

Hansard being required to listen to one of the Deputy Prime Minister's speeches and see if they could understand what he was saying. It gave rise, at any rate in Labour Party circles, to what journalists christened 'the Prescott Defence'. Last used by supporters of the former speaker, Michael Martin, after his enforced departure from office, this consists of declaring that any criticism of politicians with working-class origins on grounds of articulacy is simply an expression of class prejudice. Prescott's detractors, alternatively, declared that class prejudice had nothing to do with it, and that ministers of the crown, from whatever social class, who presumed to address millions of people on television should be able to do so coherently. My father, for example, who came from a very similar background to the railwayman's son, disliked Mr Blair's henchman and enforcer almost as much as he disliked Mr Blair, on the grounds that he was 'a yob'.

My father's complaint about Labour's then deputy leader was that he had not brought off the feat that other working-class tribunes sent into Parliament had managed to achieve: to talk and behave properly. Does that make my father a snob? Beguiling in themselves, such disputes also gesture at our exemplar's one unique talent: his ability to create newspaper headlines, to reduce the small matter of government policy and its presentation to the much larger matter of himself. It is an axiom that controversial politicians attract controversy, but Mr Prescott's serial exposure at the hands of the press in the period 1997–2010 was unparalleled in modern political history. Were he to attend the Brit awards, it could be guaranteed that a radical musician would throw water over him. Campaign-trail eggs descended on his shoulders with a kind of homing instinct, and if fists had to be thrown, then he was the man to throw them. The public money used to pay the council tax on his government flat; Ms Tracey Temple, his diary secretary, adulterously entertained at his official residence; the sexual harassment claims; the two toilet seats in as many years that featured in his expenses claim . . . in the end the inexorability of the Prescott disclosures suggested that they derived not from bad luck, or snobbery, or even malicious enquiry, but from some deep-rooted psychological flaw, like those masochistic English professors whose relish at having the mistakes in their work pointed out is so acute that you wondered why they allowed them there in the first place.

All this has a figurative significance well beyond the traditional exploits of larger-than-life politicians: these are usually backbench mavericks rather than king-makers and vote-corallers who spend a decade and a half at the very highest levels of political life. More so than any politician of the modern era, Lord Prescott was a man caught between a rock and a hard place. The rock was New Labour and the hard place was the political tradition that bred him. Neither of them survived the night of 10 May 2010. Meanwhile, there is Prescott himself, whose exploits over the past twenty years might be thought to demand a kind of commemorative frieze or tapestry, its key scenes picked out by a squad of twenty-first-century needlewomen in innumerable strands of blue and red. The punch-ups! The shags! The speeding fines! The packed bags and the furious wife on the doorstep (the long-suffering Lady Prescott's part in the saga almost demands a frieze of its own)! In the end, you feel a queer kind of sympathy over the paradoxes of Lord Prescott's career. He was New Labour's conscience and its serial embarrassment, its pacifier and its pugilist, its throwback and the guarantor of its future, the guardian of its citadel and the keeper of its folly. But was he a victim of snobbery? Certainly, class prejudice had something to do with the metaphorical curtain-twitch that seemed to accompany his every move. But it could also be argued that his real enemies were the role his parliamentary masters chose him to represent and that absolutely unconquerable opponent, himself. However uncomfortable to the person who suffered them, Lord Prescott's travails are also an example of modern snobbery's complexity, its habit of revealing attitudes that are a great deal less simple than they appear on the surface, to the point where some of them may not, in the end, be snobbish at all.

3
The Great Snobographer

There are relative and positive Snobs. I mean by positive, such persons as are Snobs everywhere, in all companies, from morning to night, from youth to grave, being by Nature endowed with Snobbishness – and others who are Snobs only in certain circumstances and relations of life.

W. M. Thackeray, *The Book of Snobs* (1846–1847)

Back to first principles. Of all the major Victorian novelists, the one most exercised by petty social distinctions was William Makepeace Thackeray (1811–1863). Dickens may have made his early reputation by sending up middle-class foibles, and in *Middlemarch* George Eliot produced a wonderfully subtle account of the gradations of small-town society in the age of the Reform Bill, but for a definitive analysis of the social minutiae of the mid-nineteenth century it is necessary to turn to the author of *Vanity Fair, Pendennis* and *A Little Dinner at Timmins's* – each of which eventually reveals itself as a masterclass in the art of understanding why certain groups of people should imagine themselves superior to others. As for Thackeray's own absorption in the spectacle of social advancement, and the myth-makings of which it tends to consist, the roots of this obsession lie in his own social and economic insecurities. A rich man's son, and the heir to an East India Company fortune, he lost his patrimony in the great Indian banking crash of the 1830s and the rest of his life was a desperate struggle to accumulate the £20,000 he thought necessary for his daughters' marriage portions and the upkeep of his mad wife.

At the same time, the profession on which he reluctantly embarked was not yet respectable – early Victorian literature is top-heavy with sneers about 'hacks' and 'penny-a-liners' – and his career, consequently, comes laden with symbolic incidents primed to impress him with a sense of his own social inferiority. Hastening away from an evening party once at the Duke of Devonshire's Holland House mansion, and observing to an unknown fellow guest how free-and-easy was the atmosphere, he was straightaway informed that, yes, conditions were so lax that even that Mr Thackeray of literary celebrity had been invited. None of this was calculated to reinforce his self-esteem, and even when his novels had made him famous he could be found scheming to set up his plate outside a barrister's chambers or procure a government sinecure that would absolve him from the need of having to write at all.

Walter Bagehot once suggested, not quite approvingly, that Thackeray had a compulsion to 'amass petty detail to prove that tenth-rate people were ever striving to be ninth-rate people'. One can agree with this – there are times when his ear for pretention turns into a kind of mania – while noting that few novelists have been so astute about the myths and dreams cultivated by ordinary people with the aim of making their existences worth living. Anthony Powell once remarked that what happens to the average person in their progress through life is not important: it is what they think happens or, more significantly still, what they think other people think. What might be called the personal myth lies at the heart of snobbery: a little halo of self-belief, carefully nuanced distinction, an otherness sanctified by something as trivial as a pianoforte in your back parlour or the fact that your wife – unlike slatternly Mrs Miggins from Number 22 – is the daughter of a West Country clergyman. Nearly all of Thackeray's early work – up until *Vanity Fair* (1847–1848) and to a certain extent beyond it – follows this line, set in lodging houses, in seedy foreign *estaminets*, in shabby-genteel terrace houses in Bloomsbury squares where footmen in threadbare plush sit sunning themselves on the area steps and bailiffs lurk menacingly on the stair, and featuring characters who, whether they have seen better days or are hoping still to see them, are jockeying for position, marshalling the evidence that will demonstrate once and for all that their lives, prospects, antecedents and claims to respect are superior to those of the people next door.

First published in weekly instalments in *Punch* in 1846–1847, *The Book of Snobs*, or, to give it its proper title *The Snobs of England, By One of Themselves*, is essentially the topsoil in which *Vanity Fair* took root and prospered: certainly the chapter in which Becky Sharp and her husband Rawdon contrive to keep up a social position on an income of precisely nothing, bilking their debts and swindling their tradesmen, looks as if it was robbed wholesale from the earlier work. A prodigious hit with the magazine's middle-class readership, whose own ambitions it made no bones about satirising, the series soon took on a collaborative air: several of the instalments find Thackeray responding to readers' letters – real or imaginary – gravely considering bodies and institutions against whom he has been invited to 'pitch in', and addressing the anxieties of correspondents who fear that they themselves are snobs. Another link to the novel is that so much of it is done in narrative form: the section in which the narrator pays a visit to his 'country snob' friends, the Pontos, would make a short story in itself.

Naturally, Thackeray is keen to establish a few basic rules – he states, early on, that '*he who meanly admires mean things is a snob* – perhaps that is a safe definition of the character', and there are some illuminating remarks about 'worldliness' – but his real interest lies in straightforward illustration, in the story of Sackville Maine, the upwardly mobile coal merchant, who has his head turned by grand friends and *will* join the Sarcophagus Club to the ruin of his business, the former charity boy Crump, now president of a Cambridge college, who passes magisterially among the undergraduates with his sidekick Mr Toady crying for gentlemen to stand up, or his junior colleague Mr Hugby, who leaves a letter lying on a desk in his lecture room for a whole term beginning 'My Lord Duke' to show his students that he has the privilege of corresponding with the aristocracy.

All this – as clerical snob succeeds university snob, as City snob gives way to dining-out snob, as a coruscating paragraph or two on Irish snobs yields up to a consideration of the snob attitude to marriage – allows us a well-nigh forensic account of the characteristics that Thackeray imagines the snob to exhibit. An account, more to the point, that is always barbed by the high degree of *personal* involvement on display. Like many a satirist – Evelyn Waugh is an obvious comparison – Thackeray is half in love with the things he outwardly deplores, and there are times when his closeness to the subjects that stray under his

lens is proximate to the point of outright imbrication, something that might have been expected from a man who in later
life never saw the incongruity of writing letters complaining
that lords no longer asked him to dinner from the comfort of a
nobleman's drawing-room. Even in his assaults on the aristocracy, he is careful to distinguish between individual aristocrats
and the institution they represent: It is not out of disrespect for
the 'Peerage' that he wishes titles had been invented, he meekly
explains, 'but consider, if there were no trees, there would be no
shadows . . .' If some of the force of this assault is dissipated by
the tongue-in-cheek admission that precedes it ('have I not
said before that I should be ready to jump out of my skin if two
Dukes would walk down Pall Mall with me?') then the central
charge endures: that snobbery persists because of the titanic
forces at work in society to ensure that people are and shall
remain snobs.

If snobbery is universal then, according to *The Book of Snobs*,
this is because it is pre-determined, a consequence of the way
in which our national life operates, from the highest level to
the lowest. Having criticised a system of hereditary privilege
that values birth higher than meritocratic accomplishment, he
turns aside to enquire, 'How can we help Snobbishness, with
such a prodigious national institution erected for its worship?'
A trawl through the *Court Circular*, with its simpering reportage
from upmarket social events, inspires exactly the same kind of
outrage at the thought of the moral havoc being wreaked on its
impressionable readership: 'How can you help being the
mothers, daughters &c. of Snobs, so long as this balderdash is set
before you?' As long as such publications exist, 'how the deuce
are people whose names are chronicled in it ever to believe

themselves the equals of the cringing race which everyday reads that abominable trash?' Snobbery, in other worlds, is essentially environmental: snobs breathe it in from the air that surrounds their cradles, imbibe it with their mothers' milk, go on to live in a world where its importance is authenticated on a daily basis by the people around them and die with its leaves entwined around their coffins.

In selecting the *Court Circular* as a victim of his asperity, Thackeray was making a point that the rest of his critique repeatedly emphasises. This is that snobbery is ultimately reciprocal and collusive, a matter of give-and-take between the person who commits the snobbish act and the person, or persons, who allows him to commit it, both thereby betraying themselves as snobs by way of their complicity. To this end he devotes several paragraphs to a press report about the King-Consort of Portugal's habit, when out shooting, of declining to accept the gun loaded for him by a gamekeeper, unless it is handed over by one of the noblemen accompanying him. Each of the participants in this exchange is a snob, Thackeray insists. The keeper is perhaps the least snobbish of the three, because he is under orders, and merely carrying out a task for which he is being paid. On the other hand, 'a free Portuguese gamekeeper, who professes himself to be unworthy to communicate directly with any other person, confesses himself to be a Snob'. The nobleman in waiting is a snob, for if it degrades the prince to receive the gun from the gamekeeper then it degrades the nobleman to act as his intermediary. The King-Consort of Portugal is the worst snob of all for laying down the ordinance in the first place and insulting two of his fellow men by expecting them to carry it out.

The same complaint can be levelled at the fictitious Lord Buckram, whose melancholy and over-indulged career Thackeray follows from prep school, where he is made a pet of by the headmaster's wife, to Eton, where, although a certain amount of snobbishness is thrashed out of him ('he was birched with perfect impartiality'), bankers' sons queue up to lend him money and 'try to know him at home', and university, where, mysteriously, the Dean never notices his absences from chapel or hears any noise coming from his rooms. In these circumstances, Thackeray maintains, while deprecating the youthful aristocrat's airs and his self-satisfaction, we should acknowledge 'how difficult it is for the Snob's idol not to be a Snob'. People far less astute than Lord Buckram are prepared to accept society's valuation of them; why should he be any different? If a society is, transparently, governed by false values then is it any wonder that its citizens rush to adopt them?

Meanwhile, apart from the blanket condemnation of 'meanly admiring mean things', how do these false values work in the world of polite drawing rooms, club-land armchairs and middle-class dining tables that most of Thackeray's readers inhabit? For it is as a guide to practical, as opposed to theoretical, snobbery that *The Book of Snobs* really comes into its own. Whether you are a military snob, who by purchasing his commission displaces a Waterloo veteran, a clerical snob luxuriating in episcopal glory while the poor of the diocese go hungry, a club snob who values a well-stocked cellar above human companionship, your snobbishness, Thackeray implies, will find you out, betray itself from one moment to the next in anything from the way in which you order your dinner to the woman you decide to marry. A preoccupation with respectability, as displayed by the aristocratic families who half-starve themselves in order to keep footmen and give six dinners a year in the season, is snobbish, and so is a tendency to conceal or, alternatively, improve your social origins. Muggins, who re-christens himself de Mogyns and pays the College of Heralds to devise a sham genealogy, is a snob, and so is Mr T. Sniffles who takes holy orders and declares himself on his visiting card to be 'the Rev. T. D'Arcy Sniffles'. (Thackeray revisits this kind of imposture in *The Newcomes* (1855), all too pointedly subtitled 'Memoirs of a Most Respectable Family', in which the thoroughly *arriviste* clan of the title claim descent from Edward the Confessor's barber-surgeon and give their children Anglo-Saxon names such as Ethel and Alfred.) But so, too, is the charity boy who, like Crump the Cambridge eminence, rises in the world and brags about it, for to dwell on the privations of your early life for no other reason than to impress your auditors is quite as morally culpable as to pretend that your family came over with William the Conqueror.

Above all, the distinguishing mark of the snob is faked grandeur, false show, metaphorical diamonds which a close inspection shows to have been made of paste. And so Ireland, where Thackeray had gone to write a travel book five years before, is recollected as one of the most snobbish places on earth, a hotbed of pretentiousness and sham distinction where Mrs Mulholligan, the grocer's wife, retiring to Kingstown, calls her house 'Mulholliganville', receives her visitors at a door that won't shut and gazes at passers-by out of a window glazed with an old petticoat. No one in Ireland ever owns to so humble a trade as keeping a shop: 'A fellow whose stock in trade is a penny roll or a tumbler of lollipops, calls his cabin the

"American Flour Stores," or the "Depository for Colonial Produce," or some such name.' The point, as ever in Thackeray's assaults on faux-gentility, is as much a practical as a moral one. Surely it is better to live in a house with a door that shuts and a window that doesn't let in the breeze rather than in one with a pretentious name?

The same rule applies to people who host entertainments that they can't afford and buy in ready-made dishes from caterers rather than cooking their own ('Suppose you pretend to be richer and grander than you ought to be – you are a Dinner-giving Snob'), not only debasing themselves morally but getting a bad meal into the bargain. The chapter on 'Snobs and Marriage' rams this message home by way of the pointed little fable of Mr Goldmore, the East India director, who despises his barrister friend Gray and his wife for their poverty. Thinking to have a little fun, Gray invites Goldmore to supper at his tiny house, exaggerates his privations ('Gracious mercy!' the shocked plutocrat remarks to his fellow guest, 'how could he ask us? I really had no idea of this – this utter destitution'), cooks the food himself and at one stage pretends to despatch his wife to the public house over the way to fetch the beer. But once the meal is concluded, Gray demands of Goldmore: hasn't he had a good dinner? Croesus is forced to concede that he has, that mutton chops, roly-poly pudding and tankards of porter are far more palatable than the finest *Supreme de volaille aux truffes* concocted by a fashionable West End chef.

And snobbery, Thackeray implies, is not something you can pick up and put down as you choose, for the true snob will very soon discover that his entire existence is governed by its logic, that wife, house, career, recreations and mode of living will eventually be dictated by reasoning that is essentially snobbish. This much may be divined from the detailed description of the visit paid by the narrator, in his characteristic guise of 'Mr Snob', to his friend Major Ponto and his family in Mangelwurzelshire, where an absurdly pretentious upper-middle-class lifestyle is being dragged out on an income of £900 a year. Mr Snob arrives at 'The Evergreens', formerly known as 'Bullock's Pound', to find the Pontos in mourning for 'dear Lord Rubadub', with whom Mrs Ponto claims a remote cousinship. Instantly, indications of snobbery begin to descend on every side. Should the local baronet condescend to pay a morning call, the entire family will dash indoors to put on its best clothes to receive him. The 'game' so proudly offered at the dinner table turns out to be a shrivelled fieldfare. The governess brags about the exacting curriculum offered to her charges, but a trawl through one of Miss Ponto's manuscript books turns up five mistakes in four words of French. As for social life, the Pontos won't sit down with the doctor or the attorney, abominate the vicar as a Puseyite and confine their attentions to 'the country families', while the free-spending Wellesley Ponto, for whom a cornetcy has been purchased in the Army, is smiled upon for his friendship with young Lord Gules, 'a very short, sandy-haired and tobacco-smoking nobleman, who cannot have left the nursery very long . . .' It scarcely needs saying, by this time, that Major Ponto's desk is piled with bills or that Stripes, his manservant, confides that Mrs Ponto's penny-pinching makes him 'wonder the young ladies is alive, that I du!'

The unspoken question, lurking beneath these accounts of genteel poverty and the desperate struggle to keep up appearances at all costs, is: *why do the Pontos bother?* Why not spend the price of Wellesley Ponto's mess bills and his absurd regimental finery on something useful? Why doesn't Mrs Ponto employ the village seamstress to make her daughters' clothes rather than suffer the expense of Lady Carabas's fashionable milliner? The answer, alas, is that the Pontos have invested so much of their energies in the maintenance of their social position, their sense of who they are and what the world owes them, that to give it up would be one of the gravest humiliations they could imagine. A snob can never stop being a snob because it means denying yourself admission to the only world that is worth inhabiting. If the Pontos stopped dining with the county families and contented themselves with the society of the doctor and his lady, it would be an acknowledgement that they had failed in one of the principal tasks of their existence and that their lives, effectively, were not worth living.

But *The Book of Snobs*'s loudest tocsin is that of consanguinity. It takes one to know one. The ciphers are not interpretable to all. As for Thackeray's own credentials in this line, one might recall the celebrated 'Garrick Club Affair' of 1858 in which, infuriated by a magazine 'profile' written by a muck-raking society journalist named Edmund Yates, and believing that some of the information it contained could only have been acquired by eavesdropping, he referred the matter to the club's committee. The latter, with its six baronets, took the petitioner's side: Yates must either apologise or retire. A meeting of the entire membership subsequently voted 70–46 to uphold the decision, Yates's name was taken off the books and Dickens, his principal supporter, resigned from the committee. The final paragraph of Thackeray's letter of protest to a man who had previously regarded him as a friend is worth quoting in full:

> We meet at a Club where, before you were born I believe, I & other gentlemen have been in the habit of talking, without any idea that our conversation would supply paragraphs for professional vendors of 'Literary Talk', and I don't remember that out of that Club I ever exchanged 6 words with you. Allow me to inform you that the talk wh. you may have heard there is not intended for newspaper remark; & to beg, as I have a right to do, that you will refrain from printing comments upon my private conversation; that you will forego discussions however blundering, on my private affairs; & that you will henceforth please to consider any question of my personal truth & sincerity as quite outside the province of your criticism.

No 'Club Snob' could have put it better.

The Snob in Action I: Ralph Straus

Ralph Straus (1878–1950) is not much remembered by the literary world of the early twenty-first century, but in his day he was a considerable figure: novelist, indefatigable man-of-letters and the author of a weekly novel-review column for the *Sunday Times* so genial in tone that it brought him the nickname 'Uncle Ralph'. He was also a prodigious snob, admired by his friends not merely for the shameless delight he took in his distinguished acquaintances but for the comparatively devious manner in which he contrived to make this snobbishness public. Straus, in other words, was a subtle snob, who worked by stealth, never openly declaring himself and setting his friends the challenge of allowing them to track his social prejudices through a maze of outwardly innocuous remarks.

Part of Straus's snobbery, his memorialists attest, was focused on his ancestors. A small, stocky, bald man, with a thick black moustache and unmistakably of Jewish origin, he was fond of explaining that his family had backed the Young Pretender during the 1745 Jacobite rebellion and, after the Battle of Culloden, thought it prudent to change their name, presumably from Stuart. This led to jokes about 'the Straus tartan'. He was also keen on – unobtrusively – drawing attention to his knowledge of the *beau monde*. One of the characters in his novel *The Unseemly Adventure* is a duke. When the book was adapted for the stage the actor chosen for this role objected to a phrase that the script required him to utter, complaining that 'Dukes don't talk like that. I know dukes.' Straus's comment, in repeating the episode, was 'As though I didn't.'

Straus's way of letting his friends know, in the 1920s, that he played squash with the Prince of Wales was equally roundabout. He would begin by asking a fellow journalist, 'You know more than I do about the prices newspapers are paying now. What should I get for seven hundred words on "The Game the Prince Plays"?' The friend, flattered by this assumption of expertise, would tell him the probable fee and then, his curiosity piqued, enquire, 'What is it, by the way?' 'Squash rackets.' 'Is he any good?' 'Not bad, not bad at all,' Straus would reply, adding after a pause, 'I can give him three points but not five.' Here, albeit circuitously, yet in the space of half-a-dozen sentences, Straus would manage to convey not only the fact that he played squash with the heir to the throne but that he was also the better player.

In fact, sport seems to have been Straus's favoured medium for projecting these snobbish visions of himself. He was, for example, a devotee of court tennis – 'one of the finest hard-ball games in the world', his friend Alec Waugh conceded, while adding that he was 'sure it was not the game's intrinsic quality but its aristocratic connections that made him take it up'. When a *convive* mentioned that his game was tennis, Straus's face would brighten with friendly interest. 'Indeed. Where do you play – Lord's, Prince's, Queen's?' On discovering that the man played on grass with a soft ball, he would look faintly disappointed. 'Oh, you mean *lawn* tennis.'

4
Best Sets

'Can't you act like a gentleman and not talk to the servants?'

> Advice given to John le Carré by a member of the British Embassy staff in Bonn during an 'informal dinner' in which le Carré had complimented the housekeeper on the excellence of the food (early 1960s)

The wearer of a well-cut frock coat carries with him a certain aspect of dignified import, a kind of moral and social superiority.

> *The Gentleman's Magazine of Fashion* (1889)

The Profession of Violence, John Pearson's biography of the Kray twins, contains an illuminating episode from 1953 in which Ron and Reg, returned to the Army after deserting from National Service, found themselves incarcerated in Howe Barracks, Canterbury, awaiting court martial. The problem confronting the authorities during this three-month period was how to enforce discipline, for, as Pearson puts it, 'during the weeks at Canterbury they soon dominated the guardroom by losing all restraint when anyone attempted to control them'. Food was thrown against walls, dishes smashed and bedding burned. A colour sergeant who attempted to read Queen's Rules and Regulations to them had a latrine bucket upended over his head, and a guard who handed Ronnie a glass of water through the bars of the cell in which he was eventually confined found himself trussed up with a pair of stolen handcuffs. The corporal who entered the cell with the aim of 'teaching them a lesson' was discovered five minutes later tied to the pillar in the centre of the guardroom with the belt from his own trousers while the twins and an accomplice named Morgan spread a ring of lighted newspapers round him and performed a Red Indian war dance.

Clearly, as direct action had failed, other methods had to be brought into play. Curiously, the officer who showed himself best able to deal with the Krays was the adjutant, whom Pearson describes as 'a tall languid cavalry captain, an ex-prisoner of the Japanese'. According to Morgan, his infallible technique in countering these irruptions of temperament was simply to refuse to rise to the bait.

> He was very much the old school tie – Eton and Sandhurst and all that. And when they tried shouting at him and carrying on he just stood there and said, 'I know perfectly well what you're up to and it's all right by me. But for God's sake, do stop making such a bloody row. You'll frighten the horses.'

Where the routine enforcement of discipline had failed, semi-tolerant upper-class disdain, mysteriously, worked. Why so? Well, as Pearson hastens to explain, 'one of the East End attitudes they had inherited was an old-fashioned respect for a gentleman'. The teeming early twentieth-century world of Bethnal Green and Whitechapel turned out to be an environment that encouraged an alliance between the lower-class tearaway and the upper-class bounder. Pearson's rough-and-ready analysis of cockneydom and the Krays' place within it continues:

The true cockney tended to despise the respectable middle classes with their money and their moralizing. The twins themselves possessed an exaggerated hatred of middle-class respectability, but they also had a sort of envious respect for anyone like the adjutant who conformed to their image of what an upper-class man of action should be. It tied in with their admiration for Lawrence of Arabia and Gordon of Khartoum, and as someone who grew up with the twins explained, 'The one thing they would really have liked to be was a pair of genuine English gentleman.'

Later in his career, before his imprisonment for the murder of George Cornell, there was nothing that Ronnie liked better than hob-nobbing with peers of the realm or stalking around his Essex estate in tweeds pretending to be a country squire.

Sociological studies of the late Victorian East End tend to confirm Pearson's deduction. The socialist historian Raphael Samuel's account of the life of Arthur Harding (1885–1981), a former Barnardo boy who was imprisoned for his part in the 'Vendetta Affair' of 1911 and later did a second five-year stretch in Dartmoor, finds its subject remembering his deferential father ('He couldn't even write his name . . . but he was a Conservative') paying tribute to Sir Percy Harris, one-time Liberal MP for South-West Bethnal Green ('a gentleman . . . Percy Harris done me a lot of services') and recalling some of the class distinctions of street-level trade (of those employed in collecting old rags, 'Before 1914 you were a "totter", but not after. You was a dealer, after. It looks more posh'). The same is true of a good deal of pre-Great War rural society, where the rich man in his castle and the poor man at his gate were equally distrustful of colonisation by officious representatives of the middling sort. There is a significant moment in F. M. Mayor's novel *The Rector's Daughter* (1924), set in the moribund East Anglian hamlet of 'Dedmayne', when bright, purposeful, Labour-supporting Miss Redland succeeds in installing a properly qualified nurse. Old Susan, her uncertificated predecessor, is consoled by the sympathy of the local aristocrat, Lady Meryton, to the satisfaction of the villagers: 'Miss Redland may be what they call an educated woman, but her ladyship's real gentry.' British snobbery has always been a question of alliances, of like joining with like to exclude upstart interlopers. From the early Victorian period, on the other hand, it becomes more complicated, more likely to be a symbol of middle-class advancement, more liable to bring other social classes together to resist its progress.

British history has always been a forcing ground for snobbery. The first invading Roman to catch sight of an ancient Briton no doubt sniggered at the spectacle. To the Angevin nobleman who owed his wealth and political influence to the monarch he served, and whose prestige usually relied on kinship – most Anglo-Norman kings were distantly related to the majority of their feudal barons – pedigree was all. The officials presiding over the interrogation of the Protestant martyrs in 1555 were certainly snobs, for as Bishop Latimer succeeded Bishop Ridley into the room they made a point of removing the tablecloth on the grounds that Latimer was not a doctor of divinity. Yet snobbery, like most forms of social commentary, is a matter of a degree, its impact always likely to be ratcheted up at a time of wholesale demographic change. If, as literary critics often allege, satire always turns more pointed at a time when accepted social norms are beginning to break down and society seems to be growing more fluid, then the same can be said of snobbery. Petty social distinctions, it might be argued, are far more important to the individual's sense of his own self-esteem at a time when society itself seems to be up for grabs.

Seen in this context, no period in recent history is more snob-ridden than the mid-nineteenth century. In fact, it is not going too far to say that the distinguishing mark of Victorian life is the power of its social alliances, a battle for precedence in which the ammunition, as most contemporary chroniclers noted, derived not from what might be construed as the morally worthy but from the materially symbolic. As early as 1836, a year before Victoria came to the throne, Thomas Carlyle had declared that 'all visible things are emblems; what thou seest is not there on its own account; strictly taken, is not there at all. Matter exists only spiritually, and to represent some Idea, and *body* it forth.' The idea that social distinction was essentially arbitrary, proceeded out of what was fashionable or acceptable and could be acquired in the same way as a material possession, occurred to many a less philosophical mind than that of Carlyle. As an anonymous style-guide to etiquette, that great mid-Victorian fixation, put it three-and-a-half decades later:

> Etiquette means a code of social laws regulating the external conduct of that order of society which is emphatically styled 'good' – that is, well-bred. Now, the word 'well-bred' at once shows that 'manner' is a thing to be acquired or taught, since it depends on the 'breeding', or bringing-up; and good breeding is taught from the nursery days amongst the wealthy or aristocratic classes.

But if an aristocrat could 'teach' his children how to behave in a way in which society could approve, then so, surely, could a manufacturer of Manchester goods – provided, that is, he had access to the right teachers and the right information? A true 'gentleman', according to the old social usages, could only be born: now it seemed possible that he could be made as well, simply by conforming to the accepted codes of nineteenth-century gentlemanliness, dressing, speaking and comporting himself in the appropriate manner. In his remarks about visible things being emblems, Carlyle had noted that '*Clothes*, as despicable as we think them, are so unspeakably significant': one of the great characteristics of the Victorian age, from the social point of view, is its codification of dress styles, its solemn insistence on the correct cut of a morning coat or an evening suit and its implication that those who failed to abide by these prescriptions could expect to have the gates of Paradise slammed shut upon them forthwith. Even allowing for the lightning shifts of protocol to which fashion is subject, the standardisation of Victorian male dress styles was enforced with exceptional speed. In 1833, for example, the young Benjamin Disraeli could be observed making an entrance to a dinner party clad in 'a black velvet coat lined with satin, purple trousers with a gold band running down the outside seam, a scarlet waistcoat, long lace ruffles, white gloves with several rings outside them'. A bare twenty years later, on the other hand, such flamboyance was beginning to be frowned on: uniformity had begun to raise its head. As a fashion pundit from the 1850s put it:

> There are four kinds of coat which a well-dressed man
> must have; a morning coat, a frock-coat, a dress coat, and an

overcoat . . . The dress of an English gentleman in the present day should not cost him more than the tenth part of his income.

Not only was the number of garments prescribed by the sartorial authorities, so too was the amount of money it was permissible to spend on them. Individuality of style was everywhere subsumed into uniformity of taste. As *The Tailor and Cutter* observed in 1878, 'The dandyism of half a century back is as dead as it can be . . . at present it is the correct thing to rate a showily dressed man a snob.' To which the obvious riposte is that, on the contrary, it is the legions of soberly clad club-loungers following the standard mid-Victorian code for evening dress (black, with black silk waistcoat and a white under-waistcoat plumped up in the manner of a shawl) who are snobs, as their aim, if never quite explicitly stated, is to establish the boundaries of their own social group and exclude from it those who fail to achieve their own exacting standards. This is especially evident in the almost fanatical insistence on 'correct' sporting dress, which can be observed from about the 1870s onward, a riot of curious rules, 'colours' and covert stipulations known only to a small cognoscenti. The *Punch* cartoonist Fougasse once portrayed an athlete togged out in various sporting garments beneath the caption: 'If you are playing for the old Crundonians, you may wear a Forester scarf, an Incog blazer, an IZ sweater, a Nondescript belt, but the one thing you must not wear is anything Old Crundonian.'

All this worked its effect, and one of the fascinations of Victorian domestic history is the way in which certain items of male and female dress came to be fetishised by snobs anxious to use them as symbols of social prestige. These prescriptions took in hats, whose absence was social and professional death (a whole subplot of George Gissing's 1888 novel *A Life's Morning* takes in the tribulations of a character whose head-gear is blown out of a train window and is forced to steal the money necessary to replace it), and neckwear – Victorian style-gurus were notably sarcastic about the 'made-up tie' – but they assumed their most characteristic focus in the field of shoes and their coverings. P. G. Wodehouse remembered how, as a hard-up young man about town in the early Edwardian era, he was always careful, when calling at some grand address, to wear a new pair of spats (more accurately 'spatterdashers'). The coat, gloves and umbrella he handed to the footman might be well-worn, but the butler, announcing his arrival in the drawing room, would always be reassured by the freshness of his ankle-wear.

For Thackeray, the key snob dress fetish was boots. They turn up in all his early fiction – top boots, Blücher boots (named after the Prussian field marshal), dress boots, and a particular type of footwear known as a 'highlow' on the grounds that it was too high to be called a shoe and too low to be called a boot, whose appearance instantly damns its wearer as something less than the genuine article. Thus in *Pendennis*, Fanny Bolton cannot help admiring the 'shining boot' worn by the young man of fashion Arthur Pendennis on the grounds that it is 'so, so unlike' the highlow sported by her vulgar admirer, Sam Huxter. The same criticism is levelled at the father of a schoolboy in *The Newcomes* who comes to visit his son 'in highlows, and a shocking bad hat'. If this is an example of Thackeray's own social prejudices being given an airing, then he was also capable of using dress styles as a way of exposing the snob's moral failings. *The Fatal Boots*, for example, turns on its anti-hero Bob Stubbs's desire for a pair of top-boots. A devious and calculating Regency schoolboy, Stubbs arrays himself in a dandy's get-up – 'a thunder-and-lightning coat, a white waistcoat embroidered neatly at the pockets, a lace frill, a pair of knee-breeches and elegant white cotton or silk stockings'. All that is needed to complete this ensemble is '. . . *a pair of boots.* Three boys in the school had boots – I was mad to have them too.'

The boots cost £3. Not having this sum to hand, Stubbs procures them on credit from a German shoemaker named Stiffelkind by passing himself off as 'Lord Cornwallis'. Unfortunately, he makes the elementary mistake of leaving his shoes at the shop. The shoemaker, vowing revenge, exposes him in front of his school-mates, contrives his expulsion and tells Stubbs that he will never hear the end of his bilked debt. Sure enough, whatever scheme on which he innocently embarks is liable to be tumbled into dust by his old adversary's wiles. Should he scheme to marry an heiress, Stiffelkind will arrive to denounce him as a thief. When he ends up in the bankruptcy court after bringing down a supposedly wealthy widow who turns out to be as big a swindler as himself, the old man presents himself as a creditor for the original £3 together with sixteen years' accumulated interest. Meanwhile, through vanity and selfishness, Stubbs has managed to alienate himself from everyone who has ever loved him – the girl he might have married had her dowry not amounted to a mere £5,000, his widowed mother, off whom he diligently sponges, and the sisters who eventually see through his roguery. The story ends with him miserably confiding his tale to 'a literary man'

– presumably Thackeray himself – who 'sold my adventures for me to the booksellers: he's a strange chap; and says they're *moral*'.

The key question facing the snob-historian of the nineteenth century is: for whose benefit were these alliances contracted? The answer, by and large, is the emerging middle class. The great early Victorian obsession with social advancement, which *The Book of Snobs* both reflects and to a certain extent anticipates, is a response to the continuing transfer of power from the landed aristocracy to the commercial and professional middle class. If this was a process that most aristocrats did their best either to ignore or subtly to influence (by marrying their daughters to members of the prosperous bourgeoisie) then its forward march was quite irresistible, exemplified by everything from the Great Reform Bill of 1832 to the advent of Victoria herself, whose wholesome family life and identification with the hopes and anxieties of her middle-class subjects was a feature of the 1840s, and the foundation of the great Victorian professional associations. The British Medical Association was established in 1832, the Royal Institute of British Architects in 1837, the Institute of Chartered Accountants in England and Wales in 1880. Each represented a search for status, the drawing up of a bridge between one kind of life and another. *Punch*, founded in 1841, is in many ways the house journal of this social revolution, an emphatically middle-class periodical, contemptuous of aristocratic privilege, never so happy as when skewering *petit-bourgeois* pretension, while ever determined to celebrate the advance of middle-class mores. This skit from 1862 may be taken as representative:

HOST: Nice party, ain't it, Major le Spunger? 'Igh and low, rich and poor – *most* people are welcome to *this* 'ouse. This is 'Liberty All', *this is.* No false pride or 'umbug about *me*! I'm a self-made man *I* am.

THE MAJOR: Very nice party, indeed, Mr Shoddy! How proud your mother and father must feel! Are *they* here?

HOST: Well, no! Hang it all, you know, one *must* draw the line somewhere.

Identifying the targets of this satire is easy enough. 'Mr Shoddy' is a vainglorious *arriviste* who brags about his struggles but is embarrassed by the people who brought him up. The Major, as his name implies, is an upper-class freeloader. The audience is poised in the middle of these social opposites: respectable, reasonably well off middle-class people, we infer, who will be amused both by Mr Shoddy's dropped aitches and lack of familial loyalty and Major le Spunger's willingness to take advantage of his new friend's hospitality. Exactly the same note had been struck twenty years before in Dickens's early novels. No friend to decadent aristocrats – as Orwell observed, his portraits of noblemen and women, when taken together, amount to 'a casebook in lunacy' – Dickens was equally wary of lower-class people who might be getting above themselves. *The Pickwick Papers*, consequently, carries a loaded account of a footman's 'swarry' to which a suspicious Sam Weller ('I never heerd a biled leg o'mutton called a swarry. I wonder wot they'd call a roast one') finds himself invited. This turns out to be full of grandiloquently dressed 'gentlemen's gentlemen' aping the manners of the well-to-do, giving themselves airs, fancying that the young women whom they hand down from carriages are violently in love with them, and – Dickens gives us to understand – as much a threat to the proper workings of society as the most villainous old marquis who ever put on knee breeches and went off to snore his way through a House of Lords debate. That this kind of humour struck a chord with the middle-class audience is confirmed by the swarry's reappearance in Mrs Gaskell's *Cranford* (1853). Here it is read aloud to a group of genteel spinsters, whereupon 'Some of us laughed heartily'.

The greater part of nineteenth-century snobbery is, consequently, middle-class in origin, practised by the members of an increasingly prosperous bourgeoisie attempting to carve out space for themselves in an ever-more competitive word and guard their privileges against the social groups that exist both above and beneath them. This had a knock-on effect higher up the social scale, in that upper-class society became much keener on propagandising its own social activities in a way that emphasised their exclusiveness and the inability of less fortunately situated people to participate in them. One might note in this respect the enormous publicity allowed in late Victorian newspapers to the 'society wedding', in which dresses, guest list and presents were anatomised with a relish that to older commentators seemed vaguely indecent. Trollope, for example, describing the nuptials of an aristocrat's eldest son in *The Duke's Children* (1880), uses the event as an excuse for a brisk little homily on the artificiality of the age:

And not only were they [the bridal presents] displayed; but a list of them, with an approximating statement as to their value, appeared in one or two of the next day's newspapers; – as to which terrible sin against good taste neither was Mr or Mrs Boncassen guilty. But in these days, in which such splendid things were done on so splendid a scale, a young lady cannot herself lay out her friends' gifts so as to be properly seen by her friends. Some well-skilled, well-paid hand is needed even for that, and hence comes this public information on affairs which should surely be private.

Fifty years before, Trollope tells us, the wedding cake would be produced by the bride's mother, or at any rate the bride's mother's housekeeper. 'But we all know that terrible tower of silver which now stands niddle-noddling with its appendages of flags and spears on the modern wedding breakfast-table.' Like a morning suit or a pair of boots, a wedding has become a symbol of social status, to the detriment of the human emotions that have brought it into being. Forty years later the same kind of talismanic significance would extend to small-scale consumer artefacts such as cigarettes, with the snob-ridden campaigns to promote such brands as Abdulla (which featured a group of dandified exquisites known as 'the Bright Brigade') or de Retzke, with its posters of celebrity smokers. Naturally, this process is reflected in the culture of the day. In fact, it might be said that the animating spirit of much mid-Victorian art is its class consciousness. Thackeray's novels, for example, become less convincing as their characters grow grander. It is when he spots a social fraud or a man who is attempting to jump from one class to another without realising that some kinds of personal baggage cannot be left behind that his interest in the world laid out before him is truly aroused. By extension, the real subject of most of the fiction of the later Victorian age is social advancement, and the snobbishness that invariably lies close to its heart.

Anthony Powell's diary for late March 1985 finds him trekking across north London to lunch with friends who have recently migrated to Holloway. Although arduous for a man in his late seventies, the trip is worth it for the literary and historical associations alone. 'Their house in Penn Road . . . is authentic Pooter country,' Powell noted, 'one of those early 19th century houses in terrace, bearded helmeted classical head over front door, deity or hero.' In his memoirs, Powell confesses not to being a fan of the Grossmith brothers' *The Diary of a Nobody* (1892), although he recognises that their account of Mr Pooter's comic misadventures 'uniquely pinpoints a certain level of life in its day'. The book's background, Powell decides, is that of 'the old-fashioned middle class, when the term really had some meaning'. These reflections are prompted by the memory of 'Mr Lewis', a former colleague at the publishing house of Duckworth, where Powell worked as a young man. Although not in the least like the Grossmiths' hero, Lewis, Powell thought, shared his view of the social world in which he was compelled to operate:

> There was no one of Lewis's many cronies on the non-editorial side of publishing less prepared than he to move with the times, become assimilated with a contemporary

scene in which social differences had begun to become blurred. Lewis would have none of that. He allowed absolutely no adjustment in relations with those he considered above or below him. He knew precisely where he stood himself, desired nothing else, and neither by demeanour nor dress would alter his own stance in the smallest degree.

We first encounter the Pooters – veteran city clerk Charles and his wife Carrie – shortly after they have moved into their new rented property at 'Brickfield Terrace'. Apart from enjoying the comforts of his hearth and the society of his better half, Mr Pooter has a solitary aim in life. This is the assertion or, alternatively, the defence of his social position, a kind of eternal balancing act, which involves worshipping his employer, Mr Perkupp, respecting such 'swells' as come his way but stoutly resisting the impudence of the tradesmen and servant classes who are forever trying to get above themselves. No sooner have the Pooters established themselves in their new domicile than there is a corking row with the butter man, who declares that he will be 'hanged if he would ever serve City clerks again'. Self-esteem sorely wounded, Mr Pooter notes that 'I restrained my feelings, and quietly remarked that I thought it was possible for a City clerk to be a *gentleman*. He replied that he was very glad to hear it, and wanted to know whether I had ever come across one, for *he* hadn't.' A bit later, he conceives the original notion of painting various items of household furniture bright red. This provokes a run-in with their maid of all work ('To my mind it was an extraordinary improvement, but as an example of the ignorance of the lower classes in the matter of taste, our servant, Sarah, on seeing them, evinced no sign of pleasure, but merely said "She thought they looked very well as they was before."")

In fact, Mr Pooter's idea of 'taste' is to purchase a pair of plaster of Paris stags' heads ('They will look just the thing for our little hall, and give it style') – a decoration that would provoke shrieks of laughter in any late Victorian sophisticate, but strike a middle-class clerk as the last word in *ton*. At the same time, his snob logic is unarguable. 'Taste', to the Pooters, is not detachable from social position and therefore denied to servant girls or people who serve behind shop counters. The difficulty, alas, is that the world in which the Pooters move is changing; the old certainties are gone; Mr Pooter's prickliness about his social status is a direct response to his growing suspicion that the demarcation lines that prevailed in his youth are beginning to dissolve. Evidence of this degeneracy comes when, to his extreme gratification, he and his wife receive an invite to the Lord Mayor's Ball. All pleasure in the thought of an exclusive club to which the Pooters have been granted the admission ticket that is their due is instantly tarnished by the discovery that Mr Perkupp's head clerk is also on the guest list ('When a vulgar man like Splotch is asked I feel my invitation is considerably discounted'). Worse is to come when, attending the event, he bumps into the local ironmonger, Mr Farmerson, who when told that Mr Pooter 'never expected to see you here', replies, 'I like that – if you, why not *me*?'

Inevitably, that high Victorian contempt for 'trade' winds through *The Diary of a Nobody* like ivy through an oak forest. There is a revealing scene in which the Pooters are introduced to the rather significantly named 'Mr Murray Posh', the well-heeled purveyor of 'Posh's three shilling hats', who, once identified, replies, 'Yes, but please understand I don't try on hats myself. I take no *active* part in the business.' This Mr Pooter can thoroughly understand and sympathise with, for his own life is based on a near-identical keeping up of appearances, a concerted effort at status-brokering that allows him to maintain the fiction that he and Carrie 'don't go into Society, because we do not care for it', when the real reason is a combination of expense and social nervousness, and he suffers torments of embarrassment when Sarah proclaims the cheapness of his whisky to guests while noting that there is 'twopence returned on the bottle'.

But Mr Pooter's snobbery – innocent and traditional – is complicated and to a certain extent undermined by the return to Brickfield Terrace of his son Lupin, a terrific example of the 'masher' or 'knut' of late Victorian musical comedy, whose up-to-the-minute slang bewilders his fond parents and whose rigour in matters of dress prohibits him from walking down a seaside promenade with his father when the latter is wearing a straw hat above a frock coat. Like his father, Lupin has no doubt that he is a gentleman, and is keen on social divisions (he describes an event to which his parents are invited as a 'bounders' ball') but his social circle is far more heterodox and far less constrained, full of newer, rootless people – small businessmen and made-up, cigarette-smoking girls – whom the Pooters struggle to assimilate into their own conceptions of how the social world ought to work. If Mr Pooter's snobbery is the product of a hierarchical social structure that is now beginning to lose its sheen, then his son's is based on the vaguer but no less crucial symbolism of dress and geography. Asked whether he has any personal objection to one of his father's friends, he replies, 'Not in the least. I think Cummings looks rather an ass, but that is partly due to his patronizing "the three-and-six-one-price hat company" and wearing a reach-me-down frock coat.' No sooner does he acquire a position as a stockbroker's clerk than he decamps, at considerable expense, to a flat in Bayswater ('Lupin says one never loses by a good address, and, to use his own expression, Brickfield Terrace is a bit "off"').

As a piece of light entertainment, which, once again, first saw the light of day in *Punch*, the *Diary* runs to a fairy-tale ending in which Mr Pooter, having preserved the financial standing of his firm, is applauded by a grateful Mr Perkupp ('My faithful servant . . .You can never be sufficiently thanked') and rewarded with the title deeds to his house. On the evening of the same day comes news of Lupin's engagement. If the Pooters' apotheosis fails to convince, it is because of its failure to harmonise with some of the genuine pathos of the earlier scenes: ominously, Russian readers are supposed to have made comparisons to Chekhov. For a more realistic treatment of the late Victorian middle-class snob, it is necessary to turn to a novel like H. G. Wells's *Kipps* (1905), the impact of which derives from the fact that it not only reproduces some of the detail of Wells's own childhood but ranges through several different social levels to prove its overarching point: that snobbery, though universal, is even more important in a world that has been opened up and where the boundaries between the genteel and the non-genteel are a great deal less strictly enforced.

Orphaned and illegitimate, with a cloud of fog hanging over almost every aspect of his early life, Arthur 'Art' Kipps is brought up in the secluded Kentish town of New Romney by his shop-keeping uncle and aunt, is sent to a pretentious private school where he learns nothing and is then, like Wells himself, apprenticed to a dim-witted but exacting Folkestone draper. His salvation lies in an unexpected £26,000 – around £2 million at current values – bequeathed him by his regretful grandfather. Kipps's social rise begins from the moment in which he steps out of the lawyer's office, and before two months are up he is fearfully at large in local 'society', tremulously engaged to a 'lady', installed in his grandfather's magnificent house and nervously habituating himself to a world of servants, dressing for dinner, genteel recreation and 'the done thing' – a fish out of water, in other words, requiring only a re-encounter with an old flame to drag him back.

Essentially the moral of *Kipps* is that of *Great Expectations*, a novel written over forty years before: don't throw over the class into which you were born; don't imagine that the process of 'bettering yourself' won't involve huge amounts of compromise and self-delusion or that your dealings with the people you knew in your previous life can persist unhindered. But Wells's message is a comparatively subtle one. It is not just that social aspirations of any kind are made to seem faintly ridiculous, a matter of suborning yourself to arbitrary judgements against which every lesson of your upbringing revolts, but that the social distinctions from which they stem are unavoidable because they exist in every section of society. The old Kippses in their flyblown shop set the tone of their nephew's upbringing almost from the opening page:

> They were always very suspicious about their neighbours and other people generally; they feared the 'low' and they hated and despised the 'stuck up' and so they 'kept themselves *to* themselves', according to the English way.

Bred up in this demanding school, the eye trained by the Kippses on the circles in which they move is horribly vigilant, ever alert to the thought of people trying to rise above their rightful station. When, back on holiday in New Romney from the draper's shop, Kipps goes in search of his next-door neighbour, Ann Pornick, the object of his teenage affections, only to find that the family has moved house. 'They've cleared out all you 'ad any truck with,' his uncle triumphantly informs him. 'She's gone as help to Ashford, my boy. *Help!* Slavey is what we used to call 'em, but times are changed. Wonder they didn't say lady-'elp while they was about it. It 'ud be like them.' To the elder Kipps, a kitchen-maid not wanting to acknowledge that she is a kitchen-maid is a crime against nature.

It is the same at Kipps's dreadful private school, whose pupils are sent there not to be taught anything but to 'demonstrate the dignity of their parents and guardians', and possibly worse in Mr Shalford's drapery emporium, which is all sham gentility and slave-driven shop-girls thanking God that at least they are a cut above the skivvies of domestic service. Everyone, Wells implies, is embarked on a career of petty one-upmanship, either gazing enviously at their 'betters' or looking down their noses at inferior competition stranded beneath the salt. Curiously, or not so curiously, once Kipps's legacy is proved, the same kind of snobbery begins to declare itself, albeit at a slightly higher level. Enticing Miss Walsingham, whom Kipps courts and by whom he is accepted almost by accident, is, to him, a kind of molten goddess, as far removed from aitch-dropping Flo Bates from the cash desk as a duchess from a dairy maid, by whose conniving mother and swindling solicitor brother Kipps is completely bamboozled. And yet the world in which Miss

Walsingham moves and on which, as a representative of the genteel poor, she calmly sponges, is simply a more sophisticated version of the one Kipps has always known, in which

> There was the same subtle sense of social gradation that had moved Mrs Kipps to prohibit intercourse with labourers' children and the same dread of anything 'common' that had kept the personal quality of Mr Shalford's establishment so high.

The only thing missing from this landscape of party-going and butler-haunted vestibules is the doubt over Kipps's entrance fee. Once this has been verified, his transformation from draper's assistant to gentleman is instantly acknowledged, and possibly the funniest scene in the book comes when the news is broken to his aunt and uncle, both of whom fall over themselves to map out the contours of this spangled new world ('Y'ought to 'ave a bit o'shootin' somewheer . . . It's your duty to marry into a country family, Artie – remember that.')

And yet *Kipps* turns even more revealing when Wells pauses to examine the question of cultural, as opposed to narrowly social, snobbery – an enquiry in which, significantly enough, he ends up implicating himself. For, as Kipps is inducted into the mysteries of 'calling', introduced to the local vicar, who is, extraordinarily, both the Reverend *and* Honourable, and given an all-purpose education courtesy of his obliging new friend Chester Coote, some other judgements are moving silently into view. These, it soon becomes clear, are Wells's own. One of the most revealing passages involves an elaborate description of the study in which Mr Coote, a high-minded bachelor who lives with his 'artistic' spinster sister, occupies his leisure hours:

a little bedroom put to 'studious uses' and featuring 'an array of things he had been led to believe indicative of culture and refinement'. These include reproductions of works by Rossetti and Watts. There is also a selection of reading material – 'no worse an array of books than you find in any public library', Wells helpfully glosses – copies of the *Bookman*, a well-known middlebrow publication of the day, and much sagacious advice from Mr Coote on 'the one serious book' a cultivated man ought to read each week.

None of this, naturally, has anything to do with Kipps. Rather, it is an example of Wells, the well-read metropolitan intellectual, deciding to have a little snobbish fun with a specimen of the faded provincial culture he had doubtless had many opportunities of observing in his youth. And, as you might expect, Mr Coote ('the exemplary Coote') is quietly derided as the kind of man who picks up a copy of Ruskin's *Sesame and Lilies* in the same spirit that he pulls on a pair of lavender gloves, someone to whom the whole idea of 'culture' is at best an accessory and at worst a means to an end. At the same time there is something oddly superfluous about this demolition, the sense of a character who is not being brought into the book for his own sake, but to prove a point. There remains, too, a suspicion that it would be perfectly possible to judge Wells himself by standards even more exacting than these and find him just as wanting as Mr Chester Coote, that a real highbrow, invited to spend a few moments in Wells's own study, would think him quite as much a cultural parvenu as the Ruskin-reading worshipper of the one serious book.

None of this frenzied semaphoring from vantage points slightly above and slightly below the salt meant that upper-class snobbery had ceased to exist or become any less determined in its efforts to distance itself from an upwardly mobile and much less deferential bourgeoisie. The memoirs and autobiographies of the early twentieth century are crammed with bruised survivors of the Victorian age noting that properly to appreciate the gargantuan depths of snobbery plumbed in the era of Gladstone and Disraeli it was necessary to have been there oneself. Only personal exposure could convey the full impact of 'the correct thing' when applied to subjects as varied as where one ought to live and whom one ought to marry. The Hon. G. W. Lyttelton remembered the occasion when news came through of a female relative's engagement to a stratospherically successful public school headmaster, whereupon a 'snob aunt' declared that she thought it 'rather [pronounced *rayther*] dowdy to marry a tutor [pronounced *tooter*]'.[1] The daughters of Earl Beauchamp, on the other hand, recalled their father instructing domestics to decant champagne into jugs on the grounds that to pour it from the bottle was 'middle class'.

There is, of course, a kind of self-consciousness about this sort of snobbishness that helps to dilute its effect. Much more revealing are some of the unspoken assumptions that weave their way through the diaries and letters of the early twentieth century, in which the class divide is all the more gaping for the matter-of-fact terms in which it is expressed. The very last

---

1 The Victorians seemed particularly anxious that school-teachers should know their place. According to Matthew Arnold, the mid-nineteenth century tendency of public school staff to style themselves 'masters' rather than 'ushers' was a symbol of 'the upstart vulgarity of the age'.

entry in the million-word journal of the celebrated diarist A. C. Benson (1862–1925), a fundamentally good-natured man beloved of his servants and retainers, concerns the wife of the Master of Sidney Sussex College, Cambridge, 'a dusky, rolling-eyed hag (there is no other word for it)', Benson decides, who is over-familiar with the undergraduates. 'She is a good and active woman,' he concludes, 'but of low social origin, a hospital nurse, I believe.'

Doubtless it is significant that Benson, when he passed this judgement, was himself the head of a Cambridge college, for old-style, upper-class snobbery tended to survive in its purest and least apologetic form in institutions where the upper classes were traditionally to be found: the armed forces, the public schools and the ancient universities. Back in the 1880s, for example, Benson, after leaving Eton, had spent three years at King's College, Cambridge, a seat of learning famous for the large number of Old Etonians it admitted. A tutor, quitting a gathering of these gilded young gentlemen for a scholars' feast, was heard to refer to it as his 'bounders' dinner'. On another occasion, the father of an undergraduate anxiously enquired of his tutor what 'set' his son mixed in. 'There is only one set,' the petitioner was gravely informed. 'The best set. And your son is not in it.' If the reformers set about King's in the early twentieth century, then Christ Church, its Oxford equivalent, maintained the same air of aloofness well into the later twentieth century. In the mid-1920s, Brian Howard, the part-model for Anthony Blanche in Evelyn Waugh's *Brideshead Revisited*, is supposed to have addressed a dinner party of such blue-blooded exclusiveness that, with a meaningful look at the solitary commoner seated next to him, he was able to begin with the words 'My Lords and

Gentleman'. But according to the literary critic John Carey's recent memoir of his Oxford, this tradition persisted into the post-war era. Carey, a former grammar-school boy appointed to a temporary fellowship in the mid-1950s, once attended a college feast at which he overheard a guest asking the distinguished economist Sir Roy Harrod – responsible thirty years before for admitting the Old Etonian Howard into the college – who he was. 'Oh, he's no one,' Harrod breezily pronounced.

As to how this kind of snobbery could be enforced, the answer lies in that age-old collusion between exploiter and exploited. Carey records that the Christ Church servants were charmed by the young lordlings it was their privilege to serve and nodded approvingly over undergraduate parties where large numbers of the female guests came in fur coats. It is the same in *The Sabre Squadron* (1966), Simon Raven's novel of 1950s Army life, closely based on Raven's own experiences in the King's Own Shropshire Light Infantry, where the junior officers of 'Earl Hamilton's Light Dragoons' spend their time idling and gambling while the serious work is done by indulgent NCOs. And this unspoken alliance between rich and poor can even be glimpsed in John Prescott's account of his pre-parliamentary experiences as a steward on a Cunard liner, in which capacity he was required to ferry gins and tonic to the cabin of the recently retired Conservative Prime Minister Sir Anthony Eden – 'a real gentleman', the future Deputy Leader of the Labour Party recalled. Would Prescott have said the same of, say, a property-developer or a parvenu financier? You have a suspicion that he would have taken his cue from Reggie and Ronnie Kray.

5
Noblesse Oblige

I (V in church) watched the Cenotaph service for a few minutes. Rather impressed by appearance of Mr Major, whom I had not seen before, tall, good figure, dignified movement, distinctly aristocratic, one would have thought.

Anthony Powell, Journal (10 November 1991)

The question of where, and where not to put a coronet is a very delicate one.

Laura Talbot, *The Gentlewomen* (1952)

Almost from its opening page, *Burmese Days* (1934), George Orwell's first novel, declares itself as an immensely gloomy exercise in fatalism. Flory, its diffident and ground-down hero, is a timber merchant, his face disfigured by a hideous birthmark, who ekes out his days in the fictitious Upper Burman town of Kyauktada with visits to the bore-infested and Kipling-haunted club and frequent recourse to the gin bottle. Hope briefly stirs with the unexpected arrival of a girl named Elizabeth Lackersteen, niece of one of his fellow English expats, whom, in his solitary misery, he burns to marry. But Flory overplays his hand, makes an enemy of the local magnate U Po Kyin, is publicly humiliated by his native mistress and, in a mood of terminal depression, blows out his brains with a shotgun, here in a landscape which, with its creeping paranoia and its sense of malign exterior forces stalking a solitary defenceless victim, is uncannily prophetic of *Nineteen Eighty-Four*.

Curiously, *Burmese Days*'s most fascinating character plays only an incidental part in the working out of its comparatively simple plot. This is a fresh-faced twenty-something named Verrall, a polo-playing Military Policeman with a 'surly boyish voice' who has been posted to the district with a company of Sikh sepoys to forestall any threat of trouble from the 'local bad-mashes'. Initially the members of the English community are disposed to regard Verrall as a discourteous whipper-snapper, an ignorer of invitations and mistreater of club servants. But there is also a pro-Verrall faction, led by Elizabeth's aunt Mrs Lackersteen, who, in an idle moment, decides to look up his name in the Civil List, the directory which tells you who everyone in the colonial administration is and what they earn. All at once, her snob-ignition sparks into flame:

> When she found the name, she saw in front of it two words that startled her almost out of her wits.
>
> The words were 'The Honourable'.
>
> The *Honourable*! Lieutenants the Honourable are rare anywhere, rare as diamonds in the Indian Army, rare as dodos in Burma. And when you are the aunt of the only marriageable young woman within fifty miles, and you hear that a lieutenant the Honourable is arriving no later than tomorrow – well!

There is no chance, of course, that Verrall, the scapegrace, debt-bilking younger son of a peer, can be hoodwinked into marrying Elizabeth. An intermittent womaniser ('He was young, and women of nearly all kinds threw themselves at his head; now and again he succumbed') who thinks Elizabeth 'a peach, by Christ!', he is careful merely to toy with her affections for a month or so and then strike camp the moment it looks as if things may be turning serious. But what makes him fascinating as a character is the extraordinary admiration he evinces in certain people with whom he comes into contact – an admiration which, we infer, is shared by Orwell himself.

Like her aunt, Elizabeth is a snob of the first water, the daughter of a bankrupted tea merchant, whose childhood was irradiated by the very brief period of prosperity in which her father was able to send her to an expensive boarding school: like her future boyfriend, 'four of the girls at the school were the Honourable'. Two terms spent 'rubbing shoulders with the rich' work their inevitable effect. Thereafter, Orwell explains, her whole code of living is summed up in one belief: 'It was that the Good ("lovely" was her name for it) is synonymous with the expensive, the elegant, the aristocratic; and the Bad ("beastly") is the cheap, the low, the shabby, the laborious.' Reduced to living in shabby-genteel poverty with her improvident artist mother in post-war Paris, she spends her spare time poring nostalgically over society magazines such as the *Sketch* and the *Tatler*, and decides that 'real people ... decent people – people who shot grouse, went to Ascot, yachted at Cowes – were not brainy'. Naturally, Lieutenant Verrall is just her kind of young man. Less foreseeable, perhaps, is that – up to a point – he should turn out to be Orwell's kind of young man as well.

We first see Verrall through Flory's eyes, riding his pony out on the maidan:

He was a youth of about twenty-five, lank but very straight, and manifestly a cavalry officer. He had one of those rabbit-like faces common among English soldiers, with pale blue eyes and a little triangle of fore-teeth visible between the lips; yet hard, fearless and even brutal in a careless fashion – a rabbit, perhaps, but a tough and martial rabbit. He sat on his horse as though he were part of it, and he looked offensively young and fit. His fresh face was tanned to the exact shade that went with his light-coloured eyes, and he was as elegant as a picture with his white buckskin topi and his polo-boots that gleamed like an old meerschaum pipe.

Matched against this cynosure of looks, dress sense and deportment, the desiccated timber-merchant feels 'uncomfortable in his presence from the start'. The discomfort is, of course, Flory's. Yet the more we learn about Verrall, his habits and inclinations, the more the suspicion grows that many of the judgements being filed about him are Orwell's own. A subsequent chapter, for example, offers more information about the eye – 'a disconcerting eye, pale blue and a little protuberant, but exceedingly clear' – which Verrall turns to the world. If you were the right kind of man, Orwell tells us – that is, a cavalry officer and a polo-player – Verrall took you for granted and even treated you with a surly respect. If you were any other type, 'he despised you so utterly that he could not have hidden it even if he would'. And Verrall's opinion of his fellow men has, we learn, nothing to do with whether they happen to be rich or poor, 'for in the social sense he was not more than normally a snob'. Realising that this kind of statement needs an explanatory gloss, Orwell continues:

Of course, like all sons of rich families, he thought poverty disgusting and that poor people are poor because they prefer disgusting habits. But he despised soft living. Spending, or rather owing, fabulous sums on clothes, he yet lived almost as ascetically as a monk. He exercised himself ceaselessly and brutally, rationed his drink and his cigarettes, slept on a camp bed (in silk pyjamas) and bathed in cold water in the bitterest winter. Horsemanship and physical fitness were the only gods he knew. The stamp of hoofs on the maidan, the strong, poised feeling of his body, wedded centaur-like to the saddle, the polo-stick springy in his hand – these were his religion, the breath of his life.

It should be noted that Orwell, when he came to write this, was a thirty-year-old private school-teacher with his health already in ruins. Clearly, during the five years he had spent in Burma (1922–1927) on the staff of the Imperial police force, he had, in the course of his duties, come across someone like Verrall. Equally clearly, despite his progressive views about wealth, privilege and hereditary titles, he could not stop himself from admiring him. For there is a wistfulness, a luxuriance almost, about his description of the 'tough and martial rabbit' with his Spartan code sufficient to hint that Lieutenant Verrall – Lieutenant *The Honourable* Verrall – is, in some degree, the kind of person that Orwell would have liked to be, rather than the son of a minor colonial administrator, born into what he described as 'the lower-upper-middle classes' and compelled to endure a domestic life in which there was never quite enough money to go round.

Outwardly, aristocrat worship, the respect accorded to certain men and women because they happen to bear a title, is the most peculiar kind of snobbery available, a kind of voodoo variation whose fundamental illogicality defies any rational analysis. To admire a man solely because he earns £5 million a year and to excuse any human failings he may have picked up along the way on the basis of his accumulated wealth may be snobbish, but it is not quite so absurd as to admire a man because his remote ancestor was appointed First Lord of the Powder Closet by George IV and he is thereby entitled to wear an ermine cape. *The Book of Snobs* has a pointed little chapter entitled 'The Influence of the Aristocracy on Snobs' in which Thackeray laments the process of posthumous exaltation that attends any early Victorian whose talents induce a grateful country to reward him with 'a gold coronet . . . and a title, and a rank as legislator'.

'Your merits are so great,' says the nation, 'that your children shall be allowed to reign over us, in a manner. It does not in the least matter that your eldest son be a fool: we think your services so remarkable, that he shall have the reversion of your honours when death vacates your noble shoes. If you are poor, we will give you such a sum of money as shall enable you and the eldest-born of your race for ever to live in fat and splendour. It is our wish that there should be a race set apart in this happy country who shall hold the first rank, have the first prizes and chances in all government jobs and patronages. We cannot make all your dear children Peers – that would make Peerage common and crowd the House of Lords uncomfortably – but the young ones shall everything a Government can give . . .'

If the force of these remarks is somewhat dissipated by Thackeray's later fondness for highly born company, then the point remains, for the respect granted to members of the peerage is one of the great elementals of the national fabric, capable of surviving Labour governments and alleged social revolution and colonising huge areas of our cultural life in what are sometimes rather startling ways. According to Anthony Powell, the most popular individual part of his twelve-volume sequence *A Dance to the Music of Time* (1951–1975) was always the fourth, *At Lady Molly's* (1957) – an accomplished novel, certainly, but would it have sold better than the other eleven were it not for the fact that the character who supplies the title is a marchioness? Naturally, aristocrat worship cuts across class and political boundaries. The propensity of Labour MPs to enjoy titles and grand company quite as much as their Conservative opponents is a satirist's byword, and Richard Ingrams, when editor of *Private Eye*, noted the habit of the left-wing MP Tom Driberg, later ennobled as Lord Bradwell, of filing such reproofs as 'My dear Richard, I'm astonished that you don't appear to know the correct way of referring to the younger daughter of a Marquess' when invited to one of the magazine's lunches.

Equally significant, perhaps, are the mythologising tendencies that can regularly be detected in these conceptions of upper-class life, that Mitford-esque absorption in Hons Cupboards and courtesy titles which had such a devastating effect on the library subscribers of the immediate post-war era. *Modern Types* (1955), a collection of representative 1950s figures by the anthropologist Geoffrey Gorer with drawings by Ronald Searle, contains a sketch of a woman called 'The Hon. Mrs Peddy-Green', younger daughter of 'a very obscure peer', whose exceedingly dull life is transformed by the quirk of fate that places Nancy Mitford's novel *The Pursuit of Love* in her influenza-stricken hand. Affecting to recognise herself in the bright, enticing and aristocratic world of Radlett, Mrs Peddy-Green starts to reconstruct her childhood and early life accordingly, remembering 'quite distinctly that there had been an airing cupboard in her old home', and convincing herself that 'surely she had spent at least an hour in it with a noble cousin during a game of hide-and-seek; she had a Hon Cupboard in her background.'

Nowhere, perhaps, is this habit of finding merit, virtue and moral salubriousness in the aristocracy more pronounced than when it comes to dukes and duchesses. Honourables have their fans (see, for example, the wonderful scene in *Dad's Army* in which Sergeant Wilson, suddenly finding himself styled 'The Honourable Arthur Wilson', is instantly invited to join the exclusive local golf club, much to Captain Mainwaring's fury); earldoms are much coveted (in extreme old age, Anthony Powell once confessed that he would like to have been an earl); but for some reason it is the scent of strawberry leaves, that time-honoured ornament of a ducal coronet, which nearly always sets the non-aristocratic nose a-twitch. The absolute awe and veneration in which the average duke was held in the Victorian age is one of Trollope's special subjects; several sections of his Palliser novels puzzle themselves over the question of why the Duke of Omnium, uncle to Plantagenet Palliser, should be quite so respected for doing quite so little with his wealth. The Duke has never taken any legislative role; he is not a philanthropist; he has never interested himself in any branch of the arts. In fact, Trollope more or less explicitly states, he is merely a selfish old rogue who has devoted his four-score years on the planet to pleasing himself. And yet with the old man's passing there is a widespread belief that a notable figure has gone, that the world has been diminished by his passing, and that Palliser, who somewhat reluctantly succeeds to the dukedom, is a shadow of his predecessor whose earnest desire to serve his fellow man is somehow demeaning to his title. It is left to Madame Max Goesler, hastening away from the deathbed where she has informed her old friend 'that he had ever lived as a great nobleman ought to live', to reflect that 'no man should dare to live as idly as the Duke had lived'.

None of this, though, can deflect the general belief that the Duke, with his divinely sanctioned pre-eminence, his precedence over smaller aristocratic fry, is a paragon, someone whose opinion carries weight merely because of his social position. How curious then that this quaint assumption, which novelists had begun to question from the mid-nineteenth century onwards, should still be going strong 150 years later. For one of the abiding tendencies of the great gentleman diarists of the 1980s and 1990s is their readiness to use the higher aristocracy as yardsticks, walking paradigms against which variant forms of human behaviour can be matched. Invited to dine with Mrs Thatcher, for example, by whom he is greatly impressed, Anthony Powell immediately pauses to wonder whether she would have been different if 'well born'. In the end he decides that good birth 'would diminish her attack. She says things like: "When I sent the Task Force [to the Falklands]", which would sound no less egotistical from an aristocrat ... Then Mrs Thatcher's voice would jar in a duchess.' No doubt this an astute piece of observation, but the middle-class reader will be tempted to wonder why exactly a duchess is the benchmark against which the UK's first woman prime minister should be rated. On the other hand, Powell clearly hails from a world whose non-aristocratic members know exactly where real evaluative power resides. Writing about his friend Evelyn Waugh's early career, for example, he decides that Waugh, once he felt he had 'arrived', assumed for daily use 'what he imagined to be the persona of a duke'. Creative success, you see, is simply the means to a social end.

Increasingly this fascination is concentrated on one particular duke and duchess. Two of the great heroes of Anthony Powell's three volumes of journals, which cover the years 1982–1992, and James Lees-Milne's voluminous diaries, which peter to a close in 1997, turn out to be Andrew Cavendish, Duke of Devonshire, and his wife Deborah ('Debo'), formerly Mitford. 'I was pleased at this,' Powell writes when he learns that the Duke thinks his contribution to a television programme about the writers of the Second World War 'marvellous', the novelist 'regarding Andrew as a most desirable member of the non-professional public to have liked my own appearance in a programme with which I felt decidedly fed up…' Again, the middle-class reader will wonder what exactly gives the Duke's commendation its value. Is he an expert on the literature of the period? Does he know anything about TV interviewing? Do his credentials, in fact, extend to anything other than his being the Duke of Devonshire? It is the same with James Lees-Milne's obsession with 'Debo', the chatelaine of Chatsworth – her spirit, her enthusiasm, her ability to talk to 'ordinary people' – an enduring fixation which, to do him justice, he spends quite a lot of time in interrogating. 'I consider Debo the most remarkable woman I know,' he writes on 18 April 1989. Is this because she is a duchess? Largely yes, Lees–Milne decides, 'because this status has brought out her astonishing Mitford qualities'. And what are these? 'I feel that, in any crisis, she would come out top, organise, keep her head, show her innate courage and self-assurance. As it is, her charm, her "unbending" (for she does have to unbend from her Olympian height), and her dignity never fail to captivate.'

The four tantalising abstract nouns which Lees–Milne selects for this piece of propagandising are those classic aristocratic values of 'courage', 'self-assurance', 'charm' and 'dignity'. The implication is that only long years spent marinating in a potent genetic sauce can produce this extraordinary effect on the personality in whom these virtues are concentrated, that poise – an indefinable conviction of one's personal status – of the kind the duchess displays in her dealings with anyone from a member of the royal family to an employee of the Chatsworth gift shop can neither be bought or worked at. They are merely *there*, and the non-aristocrat, whether it is James Lees–Milne or Orwell's envious timber merchant sulking at the maidan's edge, can either envy or admire. As it happens I once exchanged a few words with Debo, then in her eightieth year, at a lunch at Simpson's in the Strand. Although indisputably friendly, she struck me as the most terrifying woman I had ever met, with the possible exception of Mrs E. F. Macquire, my headmaster's secretary, and Miss Barbara Harvey, a Somerville don who shook her head over my inability to master the Latin documents required for the Oxford History School's Norman Conquest special subject. So perhaps James Lees–Milne – and Orwell – had a point.

But if aristocrats are, historically, a focus for snobbery then they are occasionally able to play a valuable role in exposing some of snobbery's excesses. A relatively common sight in English social history, consequently, is the well-bred renegade, the escapee from several centuries' worth of stifling upper-society protocol who uses the insider information thereby acquired to draw attention to some of its shortcomings. Consider, for example, the career – literary and otherwise – of 'Laura Talbot', or, to give this lady her full name, Lady Ursula Chetwynd-Talbot (1908–1966), eldest daughter of Viscount Ingestre, heir to the twenty first Earldom of Shrewsbury, whose father died on the eve of the Great War, leaving her brother to inherit the title. First married to Hector Stewart, who died in 1935, and subsequently to his cousin, Lieutenant Commander Michael Stewart, 'La', as she was known to her intimates, was, by the late 1940s, consorting with the novelist and playwright Patrick Hamilton, whose second wife she became in 1954. A keen Marxist, never so happy as when predicting the immediate fall of capitalism, Hamilton was far from insensible to what one of his biographers calls 'the intricacies of aristocratic nomenclature'. When he came to reveal his new girlfriend's name to his brother, the explanation took two paragraphs:

> She is the sister of an Earl (Shrewsbury) and this means that it is one of those titles you carry about with you whoever you marry. (Thus, she was Lady Ursula Stewart when I first met her.) The *names* this woman has had! She was born *Miss* Ursula *Talbot* (Talbot being the Shrewsbury family name), 'Miss' because the grandfather was still alive. Then she became

Lady Ursula Talbot. Then (3) Lady Ursula Stewart. Then (4) Lady U. Stewart again! Then (5) Laura Talbot – the struggling writer. And then (6!) at Hove Street, Lady Ursula *Hamilton*! You may think this rather weird (I mean why not Mrs Patrick Hamilton?) but the complications were such that it was necessary to employ this device in order not to be exposed as *flagrantly* living in sin.

And now she is hovering between Laura Talbot, Lady U.S., and Lady U.*H*! Absolutely fantastic – you should see the variations in names when she gets a large post.

It was as 'Laura Talbot', on the other hand, that Lady Ursula penned the five novels that she published between 1950 and 1961. Each of them has sharp things to say about the snob world in which 'La' had passed her formative years, but in *The Gentlewomen* (1952), she produced a book whose message is that virtually the whole of mid-century British society is infected by the snob virus, from the aristocracy in their country houses to the retainers who support them in their roles and the respectful middle-classes who look on enviously from afar. Talbot's heroine is the elderly Miss Bolby who quits the boarding house pied-à-terre in which she has taken refuge in the early months of the Second World War for a governess's job at the home of 'Lord and Lady Rushford'. We first glimpse her offering a forwarding address to her landlady's daughter ('Rush*ford*, Milly. C/o Lord Rushford. The Lord Rushford') before attending to a conversation between her fellow lodgers, each of them genteelly touching up their aitches in the presence of a servant-girl who has none. Miss Bolby's path through life, it turns out, has been sustained by a highly consoling personal myth, the memory of her Indian childhood, all aglow with the iridescent sheen of the saris bestowed on her mother by maharajahs and the glamour of a marriage contracted by her sister to a subaltern who rises through the Army's ranks to become a general. There is an arresting flashback in which her parents, learning of the engagement but knowing nothing of the young man's status and emoluments, telegraph the message, 'Your father cannot give his consent without full details whose son cable immediately.' Happily, the reply ('Son of the Dean of Waterbury and Lady Alice Atherton-Broadleigh') removes any doubt as to the advantages of the marriage.

But if Miss Bolby is a fanatical middle-class snob, then her punctiliousness is more than matched by her employer, Lady Rushford or, to be scrupulously correct about these matters, Elizabeth, Lady Rushford. 'Lisbeth', a stickler for protocol, is introduced to us on the telephone to her stepdaughter Jessy, whose complaints about her train journey from New Street Station, Birmingham, to the family home ('I absolutely can't travel with a coronet suitcase again . . . It makes me feel silly') are briskly dismissed ('I don't see anything silly about it'), as are the Americanisms of her speech ('And don't say O.K., darling, it's awful'). As the clan and its newly hired contingent of retainers assemble at a Rushford laid low by rationing, shortages, bad news on the wireless and the nightly hum of the departing bombers overhead, her first instructions to Reenie the parlour maid are naturally to do with correct forms of address ('And by the way, you should call me m'lady, not Lady Rushford'). There is also the pressing matter of whether a visiting friend should be called 'Lady Archie' or 'Lady Meredith'. The latter is as fixated on the symbols of aristocratic life as her hostess and can at one point be found enquiring whether it is acceptable for a coronet to be emblazoned on a shirt cuff.

To Miss Bolby, alas, Rushford is, in the end, a serious disappointment. Although she eventually contrives a lodgement in the room in which Edward VII once stayed, with Lord Rushford away on active service, laxity is in the air. The five children – two each from their parents' previous marriages and a fifth, younger girl – are unruly and self-willed and call their parents 'Larry' and 'Lisbeth'. Even worse, perhaps, is their indulgence of members of the household whom the exasperated governess judges to be below the salt. 'Why should such a fuss be made of a common girl like Reenie, who was not at all the type of girl one would expect to find in such a house?' Miss Bolby wonders. Even Lady Archie, with her propensity for slang ('It seems to ring a bell . . . Same here'), looks as if she might not be quite out of the top drawer. But worse is to come. Lady Archie, we deduce, has some mysterious connection to the Atherton-Broadleigh family in the rays of whose lustre Miss Bolby so happily luxuriates. It is left to Lord Rushford, home on leave and dropping a few incautious remarks about Lady Archie's bygone adventures, to blow his employee's mythological world apart.

If *The Gentlewomen* has a message, it is that Miss Bolby lacks her employers' resilience. Whatever the pressures of a hostile world, whatever the indignities to which they may be subject when carrying a monogrammed suitcase on a crowded train, the Rushfords and their ilk will survive. It is the governess who finds the countless little vanities and assurances of social position that she needs to sustain her image of herself no longer available and whose identity begins to crumble into dust. One of the novel's most significant moments comes shortly after Miss Bolby has called time on Lord Rushford's recitation of what the young Lady Archie got up to with the governess's brother-in-law ('I regret to say that I cannot sit here listening to scandal, nothing more than vile and malicious gossip'). Wandering into the morning room, Larry comes across the friendly, respectful but distinctly unsnobbish parlour-maid. After Miss Bolby, this is like a sea breeze, Larry thinks. 'Thank God there is still someone sane and whole in the house. Thank God for Reenie.'

An even more significant moment comes when Miss Bolby is confronted by Lady Rushford's scatter-brained but well-meaning secretary, after the governess, taking offence at a piece of badinage, has accused Miss Pickford of stealing some valuable bracelets which she herself has concealed in her colleague's room. 'Oh you're wicked, Miss Bolby!' Miss Pickford informs her. 'Yes, wicked. I looked for good and I found evil, and you're not even a lady – Reenie is more of a lady. You're a snob, Miss Bolby.' Shortly afterwards, leaving the house at break-neck speed, Miss Pickford is killed in a road accident. But it is not that Miss Bolby, the sister-in-law of General Atherton Broadleigh, and a bona-fide gentlewoman, is evil. It is merely that she has lived her life according to a set of false values derived from an outdated conception of 'good society' – values that long-term exposure to that society have twisted into misery, ill-will and, ultimately, tragedy.

The Snob in Action II:
Mrs Thatcher and Her Critics

Everything She Wants, the second volume of Charles Moore's gargantuan biography of Mrs Thatcher, contains a chapter entitled 'What They Saw in Her'. 'They' turn out to be interested parties who watched her in action – members of her private staff and party administrators brought into her orbit on a day-to-day basis, but also cartoonists, journalists, dramatists and novelists regarding her from afar. With a few prominent exceptions the latter were usually vociferous opponents of the entire Thatcherite project and the personality of the person carrying it out.

But how was this criticism expressed? Here is the playwright Dennis Potter, quoted in the *Daily Telegraph* shortly before the general election of June 1987: 'The most obviously repellent manifestation of the most obviously arrogant, dishonest, divisive and dangerous government since the war.' And this, you might think, is fair enough. Potter was not a Conservative, and the failings he attributed to this embodiment of Conservatism were all at least arguable; most Labour-supporting voters would have said the same. As for 'repellent', a socialist may very well be 'repelled' by his political opponents. Similar insults were directed by the right at the veteran Labour leader Michael Foot in the contest of four years before.

At the same time, much of the disparagement of Mrs Thatcher that burned through the newspaper comment columns of the late 1980s had its roots in a prejudice that was as much social or intellectual as narrowly political. The distinguished academic Dame Mary Warnock, for example, once took it upon herself to criticise the Tory government's attitude to higher education. Mrs Thatcher, she declared, 'had a total lack of understanding of what universities are about'. Curiously, Dame Mary then went on to remark that, even if the Prime Minister's views changed, she would still not be acceptable, because 'watching her choose clothes at Marks and Spencer, there was something really quite obscene about it'.

Dame Mary, it should be remembered, was an exceptionally clever woman, and here she is basing her estimate of a politician's competence to govern the country on the way in which she selects clothing in a department store, the implication being that in matters of personal adornment the custodian of Number 10 lacks taste. On the other hand, some well-nigh identical insults were thrown in Mrs Thatcher's path by the novelist Angela Carter, who described her as part nanny, part Elizabeth I as Gloriana and part vampire, while adding, for good measure, that she 'coos like a dove, hisses like a serpent, bays like a hound'. In both cases, an argument that ought to be about politics is being blown off course into straightforward social and intellectual contempt.

That so much of the left-inclined hostility to Mrs Thatcher should be founded on snobbery no doubt says something about the force of her assault on some of the vested interests of the time. Rather than attacking her policies, it was sometimes much easier to concentrate on her skirts, her hats or her vocal tone (David Hare talked about her 'funny accent'), or to complain about her on class or cultural grounds. One might note, in this context, the very common use of the insult 'suburban' – as if 25 per cent of the UK's population don't live in the suburbs! – and the references to the 'grocer's daughter', as if there were something vaguely disreputable about your father running a small shop in a Midlands town. Or there was the habit, very common among the literary left in the mid-1980s, of tagging her as a 'philistine' – this of a woman who convened intellectual dinner parties at which she could discuss the issues of the day with Oxbridge dons, read Dostoevsky in the hope that it might help her to understand the Russian psyche, and went so far as to appoint a practising poet – Lord Gowrie – as her arts minister.

The writers and artists who derided Mrs Thatcher were perfectly entitled to dislike her politics. But when it came to it, a great deal of the criticism she attracted in the 1980s was simple belittlement of an aesthetic taste, a social background and a series of cultural assumptions which sophisticated observers tended not to share. As the historian John Vincent once put it, she became

> the point at which all snobberies meet: intellectual snobbery, social snobbery . . . the snobbery about scientists among those educated in the arts, the snobbery of the metropolis about the provincial, the snobbery of the South about the North, and the snobbery of men about career women.

And also, one might say, the snobbery of other women outraged by the presence of opinions that for some unaccountable reason happen not to agree with their own.

Pockthorpe Manners

6
The Pockthorpe Factor

Flip's face always beamed with innocent snobbishness when she spoke of Scotland. Occasionally she even attempted a trace of Scottish accent. Scotland was a private paradise which a few initiates could talk about and make outsiders feel small.

George Orwell, remembering the wife of his prep-school headmaster, *Such, Such Were the Joys* (1952)

A nthony Powell was always greatly exercised – obsessed is not too strong a word – by the question of his Welshness. Although, outwardly, no one could have been more English than this Eton-educated, lieutenant-colonel's son, who lived most of his life either in London or the West Country, the author of *A Dance to the Music of Time* liked to believe that his spiritual home was somewhere in the Wye Valley. There were happy hours spent on the premises of the Society of Genealogists investigating the exploits and progeny of a certain 'Rhys the Hoarse', a twelfth-century Radnorshire despot from whom the clan apparently derived, not to mention legions of medieval ap-hywels who supposedly gave the Powells their name. The day in January 1992 on which a letter arrived conveying the offer of an Honorary Doctorate of Letters from the University of Wales was, one suspects, one of the proudest of his career.

Powell was not in the least snobbish about his Cambrian forebears – rather the reverse, as he feared the lack of visible signs might disqualify him from serious consideration as a Welshman. When, in the wake of the University of Wales's press release, a reporter rang up from the *Western Mail* to probe his authenticity, Powell records himself rather despairingly 'trying to convince her' of his Welshness. On the other hand, he was keenly alert to manifestations of Welsh snobbishness. There is, for example, an earlier entry in his journals where he recounts a story told to him by his cousin, the much more Welsh-sounding Trevor Powell. The latter 'had been in North Wales not long ago, one of the locals referred to him as a "bloody Englishman", or something of that sort'. Piqued by this insult, Trevor Powell countered that as a matter of fact he had Welsh blood. Of what kind? 'I'm directly descended from Howel Dda.' The North Walesian, Powell notes, altogether flattened by a snobbery infinitely greater than his own, 'absolutely crawled'.

Nationalism, as defined by George Orwell in his essay 'Notes on Nationalism', falls into two categories. On the one hand, the habit of assuming that human beings can be classified like insects and that millions of people can be unhesitatingly labelled 'good' or 'bad'; on the other, the habit of identifying oneself with a single national or other unit, placing it beyond good or evil and recognising no other duty than that of advancing its interests, however illogical or self-defeating the task may ultimately become. The idea that the nationalist stance is essentially an extreme form of snobbery is a staple of early Victorian travel writing. The American chapters of *Martin Chuzzlewit*, with

their digs at the *New York Rowdy Journal* and its war correspondent Mr Jefferson Brick, not to mention the character who
declares that 'the libation of freedom must sometimes be
quaffed in blood', are a testimony to Dickens's delighted realisation that the average New Yorker was as keen on arbitrary
distinctions as any inhabitant of a Mayfair drawing room. But it
was Thackeray, in an extended essay from the 1840s entitled
'Memorials of Gourmandising', who first put his finger on the
sheer absurdity of imagining that national characteristics – if
indeed they are national characteristics – are capable of proving
a moral point. Here, addressing a notional English reader, keen
on the pleasures on the table, he remarks:

> I say to you that you are better than a Frenchman. I would
> lay even money that you who are reading this are more than
> five feet seven in height, and weigh eleven stone; while a
> Frenchman is five feet four, and does not weigh nine. The
> Frenchman has after his soup a dish of vegetables, while you
> have one of meat. You are a different and superior animal – a
> French-beating animal (the history of hundreds of years has
> shown you to be so) . . .

The critical consensus is that this is meant ironically, that a
writer so manifestly sane and sensible as Thackeray could not
possibly have believed that a three-inch difference in height
and a leguminous diet were enough to separate one race from
another. This may well be true, but it should be pointed out
that several of his musings on the subject of Anglo-French relations, a quarter of a century after Waterloo, are a great deal
more equivocal. His famous essay 'The Second Funeral of

Napoleon', for example, is a series of assaults on Gallic pretensions, swagger and bombast. 'Real feelings they have,' he
observes of the Parisian crowds, 'but they distort them by exaggeration; real courage, which they render ludicrous by
intolerable braggadocio.' There is a very similar passage in the
Paris Sketch Book, when he goes to see a French dramatisation
of *Nicholas Nickleby* and is deeply unimpressed by the meagre
dimensions of the actor playing Wackford Squeers junior: 'Such
a poor, shrivelled creature I never saw; it is like a French pig, as
lanky as a greyhound. Both animals give one a thorough contempt for the nation.' What Thackeray really thought of the
French is further complicated by his keenness in settling in
France with his wife in the later 1830s and thereafter referring
to Paris as 'home': 'Memorials of Gourmandising', too, just
happens to be a paean of praise to French cookery. Perhaps, like
his father-in-law Major Carmichael-Smyth, another long-term
resident of the French capital, who named his dog 'Waterloo' so
he could have the pleasure of annoying the locals by loudly
calling for it in the street, he simply wanted to have his cake
and eat it too.

If nationalism thrives on the idea of the stereotype – the
undersized Frenchman who smells of garlic in greasy pursuit of
les mademoiselles, beef-eating John Bull 'taking off' his foaming
tankard in the tap-room – then these caricatures of nationhood
are, inevitably, founded on snobbery. One might note, in this
regard, a diptych found in one of Thackeray's early sketchbooks
on the theme of 'England versus France'. In the top frame a
stout, frock-coated, red-faced Englishman is accepting a tray,
held out to him by a demure and thoroughly respectable-
looking serving maid, on which rests a glass and what looks like

a bottle of claret. In the bottom frame, a side-whiskered Frenchman in a cockaded hat and a military jacket with an enormous nose and an eagerly extended wine glass is going through the same procedure. The nuances involved in this piece of portraiture are relatively subtle, and not wholly one-sided, but if John Bull looks pompous and faintly overbearing then his French equivalent, with his leer and his gleaming eye, seems positively sinister and certainly more of a figure of fun − not a thousand miles from the representations of Scotsmen (kilt, flaming red hair, usually drunk) or Welshmen (carrying giant leeks and calling everyone 'boyo') that until fairly recently could be found on comic postcards.

As to where these stereotypes came from − for no caricature is simply self-generating − then they are as collusive as any other form of snobbery (see Chapter 1). Just as no duke can ever patronise his less than aristocratic neighbour without the victim conniving in the patronage, so national stereotypes rarely come into being without the consent − sometimes reluctantly granted, but consent nonetheless − of the entity undergoing the stereotyping. The first wave of travel books written by early Victorian visitors to southern Ireland, for example, are full of picturesque, carroty-haired peasants with names like Seamus and Padraig creeping forward from the village green to enquire, 'Wad yer honour loike to see a big pig?' and generally playing up their rustic servility. Modern social historians tend to conclude that such behaviour was not authentic but stage-managed and self-conscious, that Seamus and Padraig, all too aware that the free-spending tourists had come in search of local colour, were determined to supply it, even if the necessity to send themselves up became part of the bargain. The same point could be made of Great War-era West Country agricultural labourers who, as somebody once remarked, in the wake of Hardy's novels 'acquired the vanity of the artist's model'. Kingsley Amis noticed a variant of this tendency on his first trip to the United States in the late 1950s, when, while dining à *deux* in New York with the Georgia-born novelist Carson McCullers, a black maid came into the room, warmly embraced her employer and announced in the accent of the Deep South 'Why, Miss Carson, dear, and just how lovely it is to see you.' McCullers instantly tuned up her own barely discernible southern tones and replied, 'Just fine, Bessie, darling, and my, you looking well youself, and how you-all down back home?' Amis had 'the illusion, or delusion, that a scene had been staged for my benefit'.

Here the usual laws of snobbery have been reversed, or rather cleverly extended, allowing two people who might normally be regarded as superior and inferior, snob and sub-snob, to gang up and discomfort a third party, in this case their wide-eyed British visitor. Neither is the snobbery on display a form of nationalism. Rather, it is – unless you still regard the US states below the Mason–Dixon Line as a nation in themselves – regional snobbery of the many-spangled southern American variety, erected on a foundation of mint juleps, tobacco plantations, *Gone with the Wind* and, more recently, Lynyrd Skynyrd's 'Sweet Home Alabama'. The same kind of regionalist idealism could be found in certain parts of mid-twentieth-century France. The propagandist historian J. de La Varende, for example, was so determined to proclaim the advantages of living in Normandy that he managed to sing the praises of its rain – preferable, he declared, to the 'stupid and stupefying sun' of the south – and even defended its high rates of illegitimacy on the grounds that bastardy, the product of vigorous blood rather than marriages of convenience, was a valuable element in Norman society.

Naturally, what might be called the snobbery of place is capable of almost infinite dilution, capable of setting confederated state against confederated state, county against county, town against town (think of Springfield's eternal hostility to nearby Shelbyville in *The Simpsons*) and, down at localised bedrock level, one street against the road that runs parallel to it. At the same time, snobbery being snobbery – that is, arbitrary and illogical – and prey to the most ungovernable whims and changes of perspective, these attitudes are rarely set in stone. Regional snobbery in Britain, for example, has undergone extraordinary transformations in the last couple of centuries, most of them attributable to shifts in economic power. If the south now tends to feel that it has the edge on brutish, benighted northerners, then a century and a half ago, in the wake of the Industrial Revolution, when mill-owners and coal barons built palaces for themselves on the Yorkshire moors, the north was much likelier to incubate snobbish feelings about the areas south of the Trent, much of which was seen as terminally backward and whose local magnates seemed to lack polish and sophistication. Becky Sharp in *Vanity Fair*, arriving at the Hampshire home of her new employer Sir Pitt Crawley Bt, finds 'an old, stumpy, short, vulgar, and very dirty man, in old clothes and shabby old gaiters', who cooks his own supper in a saucepan and speaks with 'a country accent'.

But if nineteenth-century regional snobbery had a particular point of focus it could be found in the curious cult of Scottishness that began to pervade middle-class English life at about this time. Whatever its original stimulus – and likely explanations include the widespread popularity of Walter Scott's novels and a lurking sense of guilt over Culloden and the Highland clearances – by the 1860s the bandwagon had rolled south into many a suburban drawing room. Queen Victoria was known for her 'Jacobite moods', her delight in her northern retreat at Balmoral, her fondness for Scotch whisky and the company of her Scottish servant John Brown and the long periods of Deeside sequestration that led to the publication of her bestselling book, *Leaves from the Journal of Our Life in the Highlands, from 1848 to 1861* (1868). And unlike many Victorian fads the phenomenon was genuinely popular, observable in everything from the 'Scotch songs' that began to be sung on music hall stages – these reached their apogee in the career of Sir Harry Lauder, who typically appeared in caricature get-up of kilt, sporran and feathered Highland bonnet – to the sentimental and morally earnest school of 'kailyard' (i.e. 'cabbage patch') fiction pioneered by such luminaries as J. M. Barrie and Ian Maclaren. That 'Scottishness' was, in some degree, a condition to be coveted and aspired to is evident from its use as a device in comic novels. One of the subplots in Patrick Hamilton's *Craven House* (1926) hangs on a woman called Mrs Nixon, who talks airily of 'taking care of our bairns up there' (i.e. north of the border), and boasts a son named 'Jock' and a daughter made to wear tartan skirts, only to be exposed as a native of Bootle.

From the angle of the upper classes, Scottishness quickly became important as a mark of social status. *Such, Such Were the Joys*, Orwell's bitter memento of the years he spent at a south coast preparatory school, contains a horribly shrewd account of the psychological forces that propelled this fixation on banks, braes, grouse moors and blue heather. The headmaster's wife, Mrs Wilkes, known to her charges as 'Flip', claimed Scottish ancestry, an ancestral grounding that encouraged her to favour the Scottish boys, and allow them to wear kilts instead of the school uniform. Yet, as Orwell notes, the Scottish cult 'brought out the fundamental contradiction in our standard of values'. Officially the boys were invited to admire the Scots on what were largely moral grounds, their 'grimness', 'dourness' and prowess on the field of battle being continually invoked. The picture of Scotland canvassed to them was, consequently, made up of 'burns, braes, kilts, sporrans, claymores, bagpipes and the like, all somehow mixed up with the invigorating effects of porridge, Protestantism and a cold climate'. Underlying this, though, Orwell suspected, was a quite different motive. Not only was the cult of Scotland a cover for the bad conscience of the English occupiers, it was also an advertisement for wealth and social position: 'only very rich people could spend their summers there'. A specimen conversation about the summer holidays might run:

'You going to Scotland this hols?'

'Rather! We go every year.'

'My pater's got three miles of river.'

'My pater's giving me a new gun for the twelfth. There's jolly good black game where we go. Get out, Smith! What are you listening for? You've never been to Scotland. I bet you don't know what a blackcock looks like.'

Following on this, imitations of the cry of a blackcock, or the roaring of a stag, of the accent of 'our ghillies', etc. etc.

All this was, incidentally, enough to give Orwell a life-long dislike of Scotland, the Scots and most emanations of Scottishness. A letter to Anthony Powell from 1936, thanking him for a copy of *Caledonia*, a mock-epic poem sending up Scotland's penetration of the inter-war era arts world, notes that 'It is so rare nowadays to find anyone hitting back at the Scots cult. I am glad to see you make a point of calling them "Scotchmen", not "Scotsmen" as they like to be called. I find this a good easy way of annoying them.' Presumably the attraction of the inner Hebridean island of Jura, where he spent the last years of his life, was the tiny size of its native population.

There were, of course, Scottish snobs who were themselves Scottish, but the Scottish cult increasingly looks like a piece of cultural expropriation, the snob searching for a weapon and finding it in Burns, *Ivanhoe*, the Sutherland Highlanders and the Glorious Twelfth. The same point could be made of the even more fashionable cult of 'northerness', which kicked into gear at about the same time as the Scottish revival and is still going strong 150 years later, and the attribution to those living north of the Trent of collective moral qualities that they could not possibly possess. Orwell, again, in *The Road to Wigan Pier* (1937), his tour of the industrial areas laid low by the Depression, records his experience of driving through Suffolk with a friend, brought up in the south of England but now living in the north. They were passing through a picturesque village, when the friend glanced disapprovingly at the row of cottages and remarked:

Of course, most of the villages in Yorkshire are hideous, but the Yorkshiremen are splendid chaps. Down here it's just the other way about – beautiful villages and rotten people. All the people in those cottages there are worthless, absolutely worthless.

Did he happen to know any of the people in the village? Orwell enquired. No, he did not know them; but because this was East Anglia, they were obviously worthless.

Seeking an explanation for this astonishing piece of bigotry, Orwell thought he detected it in the early English nationalists' awareness that their island lay very high in the northern hemisphere: this prompted the evolution of the pleasing theory that the further north you lived the more virtuous you became. 'Better it is for us,' claimed a *Quarterly Review* writer in 1827, 'to be condemned to labour for our country's good than to luxuriate amid olives, vines and vices'. It seems much more likely that northern bumptiousness and northern self-satisfaction, what Orwell calls 'the North-South antithesis which has been rubbed into us for so long', took root in the half century that followed the Industrial Revolution. Mr Bounderby in *Hard Times* (1854) is an early example of a character type which becomes increasingly common in English fiction as the Victorian era progresses: the self-made northern ogre, forever bragging about his early struggles, contrasting his grit, honesty and determination with the idleness of the soft, delinquent south.

Mr Bounderby is, of course, a wealthy man, but the really significant aspect of the northern cult is how far it penetrated into less socially elevated parts of the demographic. The reader who sets foot in J. B. Priestley's fictitious town of 'Bruddersford' – an amalgam of Huddersfield and Bradford – will instantly be aware of the kind of moral glow that hangs above its inhabit-ants, the overwhelming feeling that this, despite its ravaged landscape, its poverty and the hulking inequalities that lurk on every street corner, is God's Own Country. The same feeling rises, thirty years later, from the Monty Python sketch 'The Four Yorkshiremen', in which each speaker tries zealously to outdo the others over the matter of his impoverished upbringing, and it can be glimpsed a quarter of a century after that in the south-baiting lyrics of the Fall's Mark E. Smith ('I hate the countryside so much') with their assumption that human worth resides not amid rolling acres that are 'stuffed to the gills with crusty brown bread' but in tough, grimy northern cities — no doubt awash with car fumes and coal dust but displaying a type of authenticity of which southern population centres can only dream.

What partly undermined the northern cult was the steady post-war retreat of the north's industrial base and the unignorable shift of prosperity to the south — a transfer whose consequences are apparent throughout the popular culture of the 1970s and 1980s. The comedian Harry Enfield once revealed that he got the idea for 'Loadsamoney', the loudmouthed chancer inviting envious onlookers to inspect his 'wad', after reading reports of football games in the north where Chelsea fans, seeking to annoy rival supporters in cities like Liverpool and Newcastle, brandished handfuls of £5 notes at them. Modern-day northern snobbery is, consequently, much more likely to be based on defiance rather than triumphalism, a heightening of temperamental characteristics or accent born of defensive solidarity. Linguistic experts, to particularise, have noted the 'coarsening' of the Merseyside accent over the past forty years, with the inevitable stereotyping that accompanies it, to the horror of famous Liverpudlians used to more genteel locutions (as the novelist Beryl Bainbridge, a native of Formby, once noted when asked to contribute to a radio programme about modern varieties of 'Scouse', 'My aunts never spoke like that'). Music historians, on the other hand, sometimes put the blame on John, Paul, George and Ringo who, in the early days of Beatlemania, were encouraged to play up their Liverpool accents to the annoyance of their middle-class relatives. Street-level 'Scottishness' can be seen, similarly somewhat overplayed, in the novels of Irvine Welsh and James Kelman, of whose novels a critic once remarked that if you knew the meaning of the word 'fuck' you had read 10 per cent of his work already.

All this might give the impression that regional snobbery in the United Kingdom is a matter of the north jockeying for position against the south and vice versa. In fact, these historic oppositions have always disguised a large amount of inter-regional snobbery, in which particular counties or larger geographical areas have lined up to throw snob insults at each other. As with any other form of snobbery, the materials change over time, but a survey of the following half-dozen English counties would probably produce the following snob assumptions:

> *Essex.* Until late Victorian times, Essex was regarded as one of the last haunts of the pagan survival (see Arthur Morrison's novel, *Cunning Murrell*, 1900). Now increasingly seen as a centre for organised crime, owing to its popularity among migrating East Enders, and the home of bottle blondes, 'ETs' (Essex Tarts) and, in recent years, supporters of UKIP, whose solitary MP sits for Clacton. The television series *The Only Way is Essex* has done further, incalculable harm.

Norfolk. Apart from offering a handful of watering holes for the vacationing well-to-do or upwardly mobile second-homers (Burnham Market, Holt, etc.), country estates on which pheasants can be shot and broads on which to sail, pretty much the end of the geographical line. Inhabitants variously stigmatised as 'swede-bashers', 'carrot crunchers' or 'NFN' (i.e. 'Normal for Norfolk', an acronym allegedly used by local doctors to denote levels of intellectual waywardness whose impact is lessened by their being standard for the area).

Suffolk. 'Silly Suffolk' (the traditional Norfolk insult, dating from the medieval period). Inhabitants of Ipswich known colloquially as 'scum', as in the Norwich City supporters' chant: 'We beat the scum 1–0'. Also stigmatised for its lack of a cathedral city, back-wardness, rural sequestration, etc. My father, when crossing the Norfolk–Suffolk border just outside the town of Beccles, would ostentatiously inflate his lungs for 'the last clean breath of air'.

Gloucestershire/Dorset/Wiltshire/Somerset. Cider swilling yokels, conversing in Mummerset accents where 'I am certain' is repro-duced as 'I be zartin' (Interestingly, such is the current metropolitan confusion about English regional accents that a radio actor asked to come up with 'broad Norfolk' will very often produce something located in about the Barnstaple area.) Prone to intermarriage, incest (see the *Viz* strip 'Farmer Palmer') and bestiality, especially 'sheep-shagging': 'Wessex Fusiliers means country boys, see, and country boys means shepherds, and shepherds means fun and games with sheep,' remarks the Corporal-Major in Simon Raven's *The Sabre Squadron.*

That the parts of England about which it is still possible to make snobbish jokes seem to come exclusively from the margins is no doubt a mark of the uniformity that now characterises most of the southern English counties and the thought that there is now very little to differentiate, say, Sussex from Hampshire. But what about if you live in one of these extremities yourself? What do you do to satisfy your snobbish instincts? All of which takes us to a place long since vanished from the maps, an almost mythical domicile well-nigh displaced from memory by the march of time, the hamlet of Pockthorpe.

Like many working-class men of his generation, sprung from one milieu into another where he sometimes felt slightly less at home, my father was both a victim of snobbery and a snob himself. Sent by the eleven-plus to a minor public school, where he was mercilessly patronised by some of the other young gentlemen for preferring football to rugby and living on a council estate, and procuring a white-collar job by virtue of his superior education, he became, as he grew older, increasingly conscious of the distance he had travelled. He was, for example, furious when in the 1980s a plumber moved into the house next door and left his van in the drive, on the grounds that 'The man is an *artisan*.' This, no doubt, was snobbish. On the other hand, it grew out of something that manifestly wasn't – the desperate working-class struggle in the early years of the twentieth century to 'keep yourself respectable', which Richard Hoggart writes about so convincingly in *The Uses of Literacy* (1957), where what is at stake is your own integrity and room for manoeuvre rather than your superiority to the people next door.

Having preserved and extended his respectability, my father was also keen to exaggerate the difference between his own upbringing and that of his wife. 'Silver spoons', he would remark of the social atmosphere of my mother's childhood, while my maternal grandfather's younger days were summed up by the seven-word slogan 'Young Master Tom in the governor's cart.' In fact, my grandfather was the son of the smallest of small shopkeepers in a Suffolk market town, but it suited his son-in-law to pretend that his marriage involved leaping over a vast array of outsize obstacles to claim his bride – which, judging from some of his recollections of the courtship, it may well have done. Despite, or perhaps because of, his relatively humble origins my father was a stickler for social protocol. 'Bikes in the living room,' he would sometimes say when the name of a family friend he had known for forty years strayed into the conversation, just in case anyone had forgotten that the parents of Miss Maureen Artiss, as she then was, had not enjoyed the luxury of a garden shed. But lapses from the kind of standards that had prevailed in his mother's parlour at 5 Hodgson Road, Norwich, in the 1930s, were usually registered by a piece of one-word shorthand – the technical term, I suppose, is a synecdoche – 'Pockthorpe'.

A half-full bottle of milk left on the dining-room table rather than being decanted into a jug; appearance at a social function minus a collar and tie; forgetting to shave; hair that fell over the ears: teenage intransigence; front-room curtains still gaping at twilight: all this was denounced as 'Pockthorpe' or, very occasionally, 'Pockthorpe manners'. But where was Pockthorpe? How did you get to it? And what went on there that had the effect of turning the word into a behavioural slur?

A little research among the local history books revealed that Pockthorpe was, or rather had been, a tiny district on the northern side of Norwich near the site of the former Pockthorpe Gate, built into the now mostly demolished city wall, and lending its name to the church of St James's Pockthorpe, currently home to the Norwich Puppet Theatre. A mid-Victorian directory lists something over 2,000 inhabitants, living in a maze of tenement houses and cottages and largely employed as silk and hand-loom weavers. If anything distinguished this shabby enclave, dominated by Steward & Patteson's brewery and the horse barracks that gave its name to nearby Barrack Street, it was a combination of poverty and unruliness sometimes extending to outright criminality. An inspector sent to investigate poor housing conditions in 1850 found it 'the residence of the worst characters in the city'. An early twentieth-century history noted that 'to a Londoner, accustomed to what Norwich people no doubt refer to as East End slums, it is still something of an adventure to go through the unlighted nooks and corners of Ber Street or Pockthorpe after dark'. The poor housing endured, and as late as 1900, when permission was given for new houses to be built, the sanitation arrangements consisted of earth closets at the bottom of the garden.

The Pockthorpe trail led in other directions. I once came across it in a late Victorian copy of the *Norvicensian*, Norwich School's termly magazine, which contained an item entitled 'The Schoolboy: Or, the duty of the baths', a class-conscious Gilbertian spoof featuring a teenage rower who falls for the ferryman's daughter and at one point is invited to visit her home in 'sunny Pockthorpe'. But one of the curious aspects of

Pockthorpe is how my father even knew of its existence. He was born in 1921, several miles away from this slough of despond, in rented rooms in Sandringham Road. The clearance of the Norwich slums began in the wake of the Artizans' and Labourers' Dwelling Improvement Act of 1875 and continued apace through the late Victorian and Edwardian eras. Pockthorpe had vanished long before my father could have walked down its dusty streets. So how had he found out about it? Clearly, someone – probably my paternal grandfather – had now and again invoked its name: my father's memory of Barrack Street as the toughest thoroughfare in Norwich, where the police only dared venture in twos, probably comes from the same source. As such, although in the end obliquely, it became part of the complex mythology that governed his attitude to the social distinctions of the city in which he spent his life.

The Taylors, once decamped from Sandringham Road, fetched up on the newly built Earlham Estate. This was important to them and to the other inhabitants of Hodgson Road, for Earlham was 'respectable' in a way that certain of the other estates then going up all over the post-Great War city were not. The least respectable of all – West Earlham – lay close at hand, its boundaries marked by the Earlham Road, one of the main thoroughfares out of west Norwich, and the frontier territory of the Five Ways roundabout. It was here, sometime in the mid-1930s, that my father was involved in a symbolic confrontation between respectable and unrespectable working-class Norwich, when the St Thomas's church choir of which he was a member, pitching their harmonium at the roadside in preparation for an open-air service, were chased away by a stone-throwing mob. The Five Ways, too, abutted Cadge Road, reliably disparaged throughout my childhood as the worst street in Norwich and, as such, regularly featured in the *Eastern Evening News* court reports ('The accused, of Cadge Road, claimed that he had not thrown the brick . . . The accused's common-law wife, also of Cadge Road, said that . . .', etc.). For West Earlham, in other words, a watchful trip to which in my teens was known as going 'up the Bowthorpe' (Road) or 'up the Larkman' (Lane), read Pockthorpe.

Inevitably, these fault-lines persist. Eighty years after the harmonium was hastily packed away and my father and his fellow-choristers fled back along the Earlham Road, West Earlham is still unrespectable, still a poverty trap, still featured in the newspaper court cases and still a byword for rather snobbish jokes. All that has changed is the terminology, which is that the West Earlhamites tend to be logged by way of their postcode and referred to collectively as 'NR5'. Dad, who died some years before this usage became current, would perfectly have understood.

7
Two Snob Portraits:
J. L.-M. and 'The Beast'

Billa [Harrod], to whom I said I could no longer accept meals from local friends here since I could not return their hospitality, gave a snort down the telephone. 'How can you be so middle-class? Of course, accept every one you want to go to, and don't give it a thought. After all, you are very old.'

James Lees-Milne, Diary (8 June 1994)

On Thursday, 20 October 1994, James Lees-Milne, then in his eighty-sixth year, spent the day at leisure in London. The visit was typical of the routines and affiliations that characterised the last half decade of the veteran diarist's life: a trip to the National Portrait Gallery to view an exhibition about the Sitwells; lunch with a woman researching a three-part television series about Winston Churchill ('I think I was able to help her with memories of Randolph and Johnnie, though I declined to be interviewed on film'), followed by a deferential interview conducted by Naim Attallah, proprietor of the *Oldie* magazine. Unhappily, a nasty shock awaited him on the train home to Gloucestershire: 'read disobliging review of *A Mingled Measure* in *Private Eye*, accusing me of being a crashing snob and bore, accompanied by cartoon of me looking like an old queen'. The younger Lees-Milne would doubtless have lost his temper over this assault on his *amour propre*; the world-weary octogenarian was less ready to take offence. 'Am not unduly wounded,' he declared, when he came to write the incident up in his journal, 'but can't say I like it.' *A Mingled Measure: Diaries 1953–1972*, published three weeks before, had received an almost universally favourable reception, with Candia McWilliam, to name only one respectful critic, writing in the *Independent on Sunday* that 'it is hard to imagine a better reporter from this particular world and generation than James Lees-Milne'.

Coming across this lament a decade or so later in the posthumous *The Milk of Paradise: Diaries 1993–1997* (2004), I confess to having experienced a nasty shock myself, for I was the anonymous *Private Eye* reviewer who, together with the cartoonist Willie Rushton, had thrust this steely dart into Lees-Milne's plump and patrician hide. A brief moment of unease at the thought of having caused unnecessary pain to a blameless old gentleman in the twilight of his days was countered by the certainty that Lees-Milne, even in his eighties, was a tough cookie, a sharp operator, well able to look after himself, and that people who write books in which the lead role is played by themselves shouldn't be discountenanced if reviewers make their own valuation of the personality on display. Moreover, the accusation itself is unarguable. Lees-Milne may not have been a bore, but he was unquestionably a snob of a deep-dyed and manifestly unrepentant kind, a peddler of false values to rank with Beau Brummell, Marie Antoinette and Mapp and Lucia. At the same time, his snobbery was of a rather unusual cast: nuanced, layered, endlessly reflective and built on a view of the world that, however much it might be deplored by egalitarians, was ominously consistent. One of the great things about Lees-Milne's position, in fact, is how regularly he turns out to despise the people whom a sociologist unversed in the subtleties of English social life would assume to be his natural allies.

To Lees-Milne, as to the collection of immensely well-connected gentlefolk with whom he spent the majority of his time, moral salubriousness was, at heart, a matter of ancestral voices – which just happens to be the title of one of his diaries. There is a significant moment towards the end of his life in which he schemes to write a letter to the Prime Minister, John Major, whose policies he otherwise endorses, warning him that the two planks of mid-1990s Conservative policy – to go 'back to basics' and encourage 'a classless society' – are incompatible: 'For basic politeness and civilised behaviour are the attributes of a gentleman, nurtured in country houses and on the playing fields of Eton.'

Equally significant is a literary luncheon held at Pratt's Club when the Bloomsbury diarist Frances Partridge enquires of the establishment's owner, the Duke of Devonshire, how one becomes a member. 'Well, the Brigade of Guards, a respectable public school, and a passable family used to be *de rigueur*; this is sometimes now relaxed, but whenever it is we are apt to get cads,' His Grace replies. It is meant as a joke, but practically every occasion on which Lees-Milne and the Duke sit in a room together offers a testimony to how highly they value these qualifications. No late twentieth-century British writer is quite so keen on where people had come from and who they 'were'. Forced to endure a couple of hours in the company of the legendarily discourteous Sir Edward Heath ('utterly without charm or grace'), he can only conclude that Heath's

inadequacies stem from a lack of 'breeding', that the circumstances of his ascent through life have spoiled him and made
him 'arrogant'.

The importance of 'breeding', naturally, is the spiritual caste-
mark it mysteriously bestows. A 'gentleman' not only knows
instinctively how to behave, but how to talk and how to
respond; the assumptions on which the upper-class life in which
he is expected to participate are based will never have to be
explained to him, for he will have cracked their code in
childhood. When Lees-Milne's step-granddaughter Oenone
arrives for the weekend sometime in 1988 with an Old Etonian
boyfriend named Guy Lubbock in tow, this exigent critic of
socially indeterminate young men is, for once, impressed: 'a
gent for a nice change . . . knows lots of our friends' children
and speaks our language'. There is no danger, with Lubbock on
the premises, of any of his hosts' remarks being lost in translation.
The England that Lees-Milne and his friends inhabit may, as
they constantly remind each other, be going to hell in a hand-
cart but if there is a consolation it lies in the thought of solidarity,
class collectivism, stray gleams of seemly bygone usages glimpsed
periodically through the murk, and some of the most revealing
passages from his *oeuvre* date from the mid-1970s when the
trades unions are holding the country to ransom, Russian tanks
are hourly expected and letters to the *Daily Telegraph* are being
written by candlelight.

But what were Lees-Milne's own qualifications for entry
into this glittering palisade of lustre and éclat? How many of
the Pratt's Club desiderata obligingly set down by the Duke
of Devonshire did he fulfil himself? Certainly he had been to
Eton, spent three years at one of the great upper-class Oxford

colleges (Magdalen) and – briefly – served in the Irish Guards in the early months of the Second World War before being invalided out with what look like the symptoms of a nervous breakdown. Beyond this, though, a fair amount of obliquity begins to declare itself. His semi-autobiographical novel *Another Self* (1970) conveys the impression that he hailed from an old country family, with an ancestral seat at Wickhamford in Worcestershire, but the reality is rather less straightforward. In fact, Lees-Milne senior had got his money from a Lancashire cotton mill and moved to Worcestershire only a year or so before his son's birth; stealing over a landscape of rolling acres and squirearchichal prerogatives is the unmistakable taint of 'trade'. On the other hand, the family had been small landowners for several centuries and Lees-Milne's description of himself as 'lower upper class' accurately reflects the view he took of himself as a social being: neither born into the purple, nor outstandingly rich, but – unless the company turned horribly exalted – able to move with ease through nearly any situation in which he found himself.

If Jim – who, naturally, hated to be called Jim by non-intimates – was a snob by birth, training and temperament then two supplementary factors conspired to refine his extraordinarily hierarchical conception of the world. The first was his Catholicism – traditional and romantic in the manner of Evelyn Waugh – although he eventually fell out with the Church over its attitude to birth control. The second was his long-term employment by the National Trust, in which capacity he was directly responsible for the salvage of many an English country house that would otherwise have gone to ruin. All this encouraged a view of society that was not so much old-fashioned as essentially feudal, a souped-up version of Mrs Alexander's famous hymn 'All Things Bright and Beautiful' with its long-since superannuated line about 'the rich man in his castle/the poor man at his gate', controlled at its upper level by a collection of aesthetically minded and public-spirited aristocrats animated, above all, by their sense of duty. There is a characteristic eulogy for the Earl of Crawford, a former National Trust chairman, in December 1975. 'His obituary in today's *Times* must indicate even to the most prejudiced Leftist that men such as he are unique not just to England but to the world. Such sense of duty, such dedication to the arts and civilised being, such utter selflessness.'

Clearly there was a substantial niche in this world for the working classes, of whom Lees-Milne thoroughly approves provided they know their place and acquiesce in their betters' whims. Living on the Badminton estate in the 1970s he is charmed by the subservience of the resident labour force: 'All the cottages are inhabited by people working on the estate. They are all friendly, contented and respectful. All the men say, "Good morning, Good night, sir", as of old.' Peggy, the Lees-Milnes' daily 'help', is everything he requires in a retainer: respectful, discreet, never likely to overstep the mark that separates deference and over-familiarity. 'I like to hear her bustling about,' he writes in 1994. 'She never interrupts me, whereas I talk to her when it suits me. I almost miss her when she is not about. She has the tact of the true lady she is.' What he really hates, on the other hand, are the upstart middle classes, moneyed entrepreneurs busy despoiling ancient town centres with their development plans or selfish nouveau riche who aspire to settle themselves in the country without taking on any of the obligations that such a lifestyle traditionally enjoins. A tour of the Cotswolds in the 1980s produces some withering remarks about the new breed of weekly commuters: 'The village people don't like these fly by night, new rich, suburban-minded, non-country folk, who bring their middle-class friends and cocktail bars for a few days and are of no use to the community.'

It would take several paragraphs to deconstruct the assumptions on which this sentence is based but, broadly speaking, the inference is that a) country life is best left to people who live in the country, for only they are fitted to sample its delights; b) 'new money' is hopelessly vulgar; and c) the bourgeoisie have no taste. Useless to maintain, as an upwardly mobile incomer to the Cotswolds would probably wish to do, that rural homes are better tenanted by *arrivistes* than remaining vacant, that people are entitled to choose their own entertainments, and that Lees-Milne, on the evidence of his published work, was not averse to the occasional cocktail himself; the charge-sheet is non-negotiable. And yet the curious thing about Lees-Milne's perpetual journey through the by ways of the mob ruined civilisation he has the misfortune to inhabit is quite how many distinctions have to be drawn. A natural defender of dukes, marquises, earls and hereditary privilege generally, he is uncomfortably aware that the great local aristocrat, the Duke of Beaufort, is merely an evil old man interested in nothing but slaughtering foxes (the Duke reciprocated this distrust, once enquiring 'What is the *point* of those Lees-Milnes? They don't hunt, they don't shoot, they don't fish'). On the other hand, a duke is a duke and such rebellions as Jim and his wife Alvilde allow themselves are timorous in the extreme. There is a rather dreadful episode in May 1979 in which the Lees-Milnes' whippets stray onto ducal land, to the fury of its owner ('He was almost apoplectic . . . Bloody this and bloody that. He would get his gun and shoot them'). Having made an abusive appearance on the Lees-Milnes' doorstep and followed it up with a ranting telephone call, the Duke then sends his keeper to inform them that the dogs will be destroyed if they are ever again seen loose.

A middle-class person would by this stage have told Henry Somerset, 10th Duke of Beaufort, that he was a preposterous old idiot, or perhaps simply have laughed at him. But the Lees-Milnes, you suspect, have invested too much in the myths of the world they inhabit to desert the ship to whose barnacled hull they continue to cling, and Lees-Milne can only relieve his feelings with a diary entry about 'ghastly values' and 'ghastly people'. It is the same, up to a point, with the royal family, an institution that every ancestral prompting urges him to respect only for a series of wanton personal failings to call the merits of its individual representatives seriously into question. The Queen is beyond reproach, and the Prince of Wales admired for his interest in conservation, but the Queen Mother, though indefatigable in her engagements, betrays herself with 'sugary insincerity', and the Duke of Gloucester turns out to be 'an undistinguished youth, badly dressed in a sloppy City suit'.

Lees-Milne died in 1998, his disdain for the middle classes kept up until the end. Even in his last illness he could be found excusing the 'utterly disgusting' food at the Royal United Hospital in Bath as 'in a way less ghastly' than that on offer at the Bath Clinic 'which is sheer middle-class pretentious Trust House style'. It is the authentic, antediluvian, patrician note, always more hospitable to plebeian obtuseness than bourgeois airs, utterly opposed to the spirit of the time and, unlike most varieties of snobbery, sharply aware of its animating spirit. One might note, for example, the reflections prompted by his refusal of the offer of a CBE. 'Another reason for refusing this absurd decoration is that many regard me as a snob,' he informs his diary. 'Yet I am not their sort of snob, and content to be an ordinary esquire, to which I am entitled by virtue of being armigerous. An ounce of heredity . . . is worth a pound of merit.' Yet pride in his origins, his upbringing, his lifelong mission to preserve a few chipped fragments of the glorious past for a debased modern age to admire is always compromised by a sneaking suspicion that many of these values may be false, and that real virtue rests elsewhere. When his sister Audrey dies he is mortified by memories of his unkindness to her. 'She was as good as gold, and never harboured an ungenerous thought or did a mean thing, which cannot be said of me. And let's face it, goodness is greatness; nothing else counts for much in the sight of God.' On the other hand, the very next sentence straightaway returns us to the dense, romantic visions in which he specialises. 'I am now the last of the Wickhamford family, and feel like a plant torn out of the earth.'

There are no references anywhere in the twelve volumes of James Lees-Milne's diaries to Dennis Skinner, a former coal-miner and Labour MP for the Bolsover constituency since 1970. Nonetheless, it is possible to tease out one or two points of indirect contact between the Squire of Wickhamford and this scion of what Anthony Powell would doubtless have called the 'Bolsover Skinners'. One of them is an incident from December 1973, when the Lees-Milnes are lunching with their great friend Diana, Countess of Westmorland. The Countess, blazing with fury against Joe Gormley, President of the National Union of Mineworkers (NUM), announces that she wishes to send him a letter complaining about the current round of strikes and the inconvenience caused to the general public. What should she write? Lees-Milne suggests: 'The Dowager Countess of Westmorland presents her compliments to Mr Gormley and begs to inform him that he is a shit.' Another comes in 1975, when in a parliamentary debate convened to hinder the Chatsworth Estates' plan to develop Eastbourne harbour, Dennis Skinner cheerfully refers to the Duke of Devonshire as a 'benevolent despot' while His Grace looks on from the gallery.

But what really unites the 'Beast of Bolsover', to borrow the nickname bestowed by an exasperated fellow Labour MP, and Gentleman Jim in his Gloucestershire library is the unrepentant snobbishness of their respective attitudes to life: each, with varying degrees of asperity, nurtures a view of the world built on class prejudice, undisguised sectarianism, highly simplistic views of societal divisions, and the conviction that virtue resides in social and geographical provenance. The son of a Derbyshire pitman blacklisted during the General Strike, bolshie, self-conscious and determined to return any slight offered him with interest, Skinner regards the 'good working-class mining stock' from which he hails with approximately the same fervour as a dowager duchess combing through her pedigree. Even when it comes to sport, he inclines to whichever northern club is matched against a bunch of soft, degenerate southerners ('It's a natural preference. I can't shake it'). The snubs and put-downs that attended his early career are naturally a source of pride to him, as is the terrific cleverness that he and other members of the Skinner family display in frustrating a 'system' that is avid to grind them down.

A limited world, perhaps, but one whose limitations Skinner seems to have been anxious to keep firmly in place. The overriding impression left by his no-nonsense autobiography *Sailing Close to the Wind*, in fact, is of a man determined to frustrate the exercise of his own abilities to prove some wider sectarian point. Winning a scholarship to the local grammar school, where he excels at Latin and mathematics, passes the School Certificate and wins the cross-country championship, he gives up the chance of a university education to go down the pit ('Mam and Dad were devastated'). Told by a succession of coal board supervisors and technical college tutors that a dazzling career in management awaits him if he can pass the necessary exams, he dismisses any thought of advancement or promotion as 'middle-class rubbish'. His sole ambition at this point in his life is 'to work with my mates and stay with the NUM', and his father's flat cap is the spiritual equivalent of the landowner's top-hat worn to the Ascot Enclosure.

None of this is to disguise the fact that Skinner, once he gets into his stride, is a man of talent, industry and moral force – the doughtiest champion that the working people of this particular quadrant of the East Midlands will ever have: a Robert Smillie Scholar of Ruskin College, Oxford, a non-chain-of-office-wearing chair of the local Urban District Council, and elected to Parliament against the Tory surge of 1970 with a majority of 20,000 and 77 per cent of the vote. Meanwhile, there is a broader question beginning to rumble through his horribly partisan accounts of three-day weeks, secondary pickets and the celebrated Clay Cross Council dispute, which is the nature of the national fabric that the newly elected MP has so zealously begun to unpick. How does he imagine the world he has fetched up in, and of what aspects does it socio-economically consist? Oddly enough, and even allowing for the 180-degree political separation, Skinner's view of the world is remarkably like that of James Lees-Milne, made up of vast, undifferentiated blocks of people and sectional interests – 'the rich', 'the poor', 'toffs', 'big business', 'the workers' and so on, in which individual quiddity is always liable to be subsumed into a collective tag. As with Lees-Milne, the bourgeoisie are of no interest, other than as something to be sneered at, and the gradations of middle-class life (working-class life, too, if it comes to that) entirely escape him. It is Orwell's point about the Marxist bent on dissecting the carcass of the English class system who approaches that subtle and impervious an organism with a chopper.

Not, of course, that the similarities end here. Like many inverted snobs, habituated to wearing the materials of arbitrary superiority next to his skin, Skinner has a habit of seeing snobbery where none is intended. Quite the funniest paragraph in *Sailing Close to the Wind*, for example, comes when the young Labour MP is invited to fill in the form sent him by *Who's Who* and supply details of the clubs of which he happens to be a member. Naturally, Skinner suspects an Establishment plot – 'I realised this section was the place to list the Pall Mall boltholes of a ruling class, the posh centres of power where a tiny, wealthy, privileged elite endured, over gin-and-tonics served to them by liveried flunkies as they luxuriated in deep leather armchairs' – and is first disposed to throw the form away. Later, he relents sufficiently to admit to membership of Bestwood Working Men's Club in Clay Cross and various Derbyshire miners' welfare institutes, but by this time even the well-disposed reader will begin to suspect that quite a lot of cake is being had and eaten too. *Who's Who* may very well be an Establishment aide memoire, designed to make a proletarian upstart quake in his galoshes, but its chief function is simply to record information; why should Skinner be 'surprised' that the details of his social life are set down without demur? And what, from the other side of the social coin, could be more elitist, more sectarian or − another characteristic to link it to White's or Brooks's, where the wicked old factory-owners wallow in gin − more hostile to the idea of admitting women than an East Midlands working-men's club of the early 1970s?

But then what justifies a snob other than his snobbery? Skinner, we divine, needs these symbols, these simplifications, these substitutes for serious thought in the same way that Lees-Milne needs his country houses, his deferential 'dailies' and the Duke of Devonshire's welcoming handshake, for without them he would hardly be able to make sense of the world. And so the inconsistencies of the Skinner position flutter to the ground like parliamentary order papers. Edward Heath, as a Conservative politician, is damned for taking the United Kingdom into Europe in the early 1970s without a referendum, but the NUM, as the fount of all collectivist virtue, is excused for not holding strike ballots ten years later on the grounds of its federal structure. Dennis is opposed to fox-hunting − not on class grounds, he explains, but in consequence of its cruelty − while remaining mysteriously silent about the pain inflicted on fish by hundreds of thousands of predominantly working-class anglers. Even his election to Parliament turns out to be a sectarian stitch-up, when, after a TV personality is rumoured to be pursuing the Bolsover nomination, the NUM realises that 'another seat could slip from our union's grasp' and hastily drafts in him as the local candidate. Imagine the fuss that would have been made if the Institute of Directors, having failed to shoehorn its secretary-general into a safe Conservative constituency on the south coast, had talked about a seat 'slipping from our grasp'!

Skinner, to do him justice, would probably maintain that the odds are so stacked against working people achieving any sort of status or meaningful existence in a society run on neo-liberal principles that this kind of subterfuge is entirely justified – a throwback to the 'ducking and diving' of his own childhood that, however narrowly, 'made life bearable'. You can never beat the Conservatives at their own game so you might as well play your own. Inevitably, he declines office when the offer is dangled before him by James Callaghan and Tony Blair ('if you accept a ministerial job you're swallowing patronage . . . I wasn't tempted. I suspect he wanted to buy me off'), and equally inevitably he refuses to be presented to the Queen and an invitation – conveyed by the Tory MP Nicholas Soames – to meet Prince Charles. The non-encounter with HRH is almost, but not quite, as funny as the *Pravda*-style account of the gentlemen's clubs of St James's: 'It was unbelievable, really. Soames thought I would fall into Charlie's lap.' The Prince, for the record, had expressed a wish to talk to him 'as a working-class Labour man and an ex-miner'. Once again we are whisked away to a highly reductive fantasy land stalked by bloated capitalists and conniving royalty where left-wing politicians are enticed to royal palaces and relieved of their principles in an orgy of five-course meals, damask tablecloths and powdered footmen. Dennis Skinner might think that Britain was, as he puts it, 'a happier place in the 1970s'; James Lees-Milne might reckon it a sink of greed, duplicity and disorganised labour. Mysteriously, the mental outlook they brought to these contending panoramas was exactly the same.

The Snob in Action III:
W. G. Grace

The celebrated English cricketer W. G. Grace (1848–1915) operated in an area where several varieties of Victorian snobbery collided head-on. On the one hand, he was an amateur sportsman in an age increasingly dominated by professionals. On the other, his comparatively humble birth placed him at a social disadvantage with many of the sport's most influential patrons. At the same time, the livelihood he practised when not at the cricket square – medicine – was only narrowly respectable. Doctors in early Victorian novels have names like 'Filgrave' and 'Sawyer'; it is only towards the end of the century that fictional medical men are seen wearing frock coats and paying their calls in carriages.

Grace's ability to transcend these barriers is both a tribute to his sporting skill – a distinction that cancelled out all other failings – and a mark of the flexibility of the social compartments through which he clambered, testimony to the snob's perpetual ability, when the chips are down, to recruit among non-snobs and to recreate them in his own image. Grace's last years come crammed with eyewitness accounts of the airs he gave, or was allowed to give himself, when on public display. He was once seen grandly getting out of a cab 'as though no cabby in his senses could expect payment from one who had been Emperor of the Cricket World for thirty years'. It was left to the former Australian test captain Billy Murdoch to pick up the fare.

All this was doubly unfortunate, what with the symbolic value to cricket which Grace was later thought to possess. The cricketing historian C. L. R. James – a Marxist, but the same claim was made by the right – once described him as 'the single figure who established cricket in the life of the nation'. As a deep-dyed Conservative, Grace himself would have been horrified by the idea that he was a social revolutionary whose personal progress had proved some wider point. In fact, he was a social climber who traded on his talent, a butler's grandson from provincial Gloucestershire who might in other circumstances have been ostracised by the ex-public schoolboys whom he encountered on his first overseas tour to North America in 1872, only to be feted by them for the size of his batting average.

The Marylebone Cricket Club, meanwhile, was prepared to overlook his West Country accent, his doubtful origins and the fact that he played for a minor county in the knowledge that he was keen to retain his amateur status. Henceforth the MCC's continued dominance of the game was guaranteed by the expedient of what one cricketing pundit called 'hanging onto W. G's shirt-tails'. Not, of course, that the great man was prepared to forsake the pecuniary advantages of being the country's best-known bat, and for the next thirty years, by way of stealthy subsidies and what would now be known as the sale of his image rights, he continued to make more money out of the game than most of the sportsmen who played it professionally.

Neither was he prepared to give up the social exclusiveness that went with being a 'gentleman' – he was 'W. G. Grace Esq.' on the match-programme rather than plain 'Smith' or 'Jones' – and the apartheid of separate entrances and accommodation. As a journalist witheringly remarked during the tour of Australia in 1873–1874, 'Mr Grace and the other gentlemen cricketers take good care to secure the lion's share of the profits of the expedition, but they object to share the hospitality of the people of Warrnambool if the professional cricketers are permitted to "come between the wind and their nobility anywhere but on the cricket ground".' Grace issued an indignant rebuttal claiming that amateurs and professionals stayed at different hotels because they wanted to, that like was merely clinging to like, yet when the professionals complained that they were forced to travel steerage on the boat home he was loudly critical of what he called their 'pretensions to equality'.

It was the same at the bread-and-butter county level, where less socially exalted performers trifled with Grace at their peril. On one occasion a visiting team happened to contain a groundsman who complained at having to play on a pitch that had already been used and exhibited signs of wear-and-tear. Grace simply informed the opposing captain that unless an apology was received 'There'll be no match today.' A royal prince subscribed to his testimonial and, even in the depths of the Great War, his obituary tributes dominated the newspapers – no mean achievement for a man who, at the height of his sporting career, was thought to resemble 'a prosperous farmer'.

8
Snob Lingo

'Posh?' said Templer. 'Sweetie, what an awful word. Please
never use it in my presence again.'

Anthony Powell, *The Acceptance World* (1955)

Phone for the fish-knives, Norman,
As Cook is a little unnerved;
You kiddies have crumpled the serviettes
And I must have things daintily served. . .

John Betjeman, 'How to Get On in Society' (1958)

Although dress, gesture, deportment, consumer goods,
houses and motorised transport each have their place in the
cultivation of snobbery, nothing, in the end, is more important
to the snob than language. Practised exponents of the art can
impose their personality and scale of values on a group of
onlookers with a single sentence – in some cases a solitary word.
A husband and wife team, for example, forced to make
conversation at a social event with another couple whose
pretensions they disdain can wreak havoc merely by having one
of them ask of the other, in a tone slightly louder than that
demanded by the occasion, 'Isn't that the Palamountains?',
semaphoring wildly across the room to an additional couple now

entering it and then remarking, confidentially, 'I'm surprised he can find the time to be here, what with the market in the state it's in.' Mr Palamountain may be only the dowdiest of small stockbrokers, and his wife an aspirate-free cockney with dyed hair, but the damage is done, the myth created, a snob alliance formed and, more important, a third party excluded from it.

Naturally, the codes of snob language have been weakened, or perhaps only extended by time. In the days when 'Society' was much more tightly regulated than it has since become – that 'Upper Ten Thousand' of whom Victorian novelists so confidently speak – everyone knew their cue. A guest invited to inspect a newly refurbished Mayfair townhouse in the early Victorian era would be careful to pronounce it 'chaste' – an immensely specialised cult usage of the adjective, unknown even to the *Shorter Oxford Dictionary*, conveying the sense of decorousness and restraint. The keenness of the great snob primers – Nancy Mitford's *Noblesse Oblige*, say, or the *Official Sloane Ranger Handbook* – on linguistic short-hand stems, consequently, from the greater fluidity of twentieth-century social arrangements. Rules that were once tacitly understood now need to be formally set down as there is a danger that even insiders may now begin to forget them.

Noblesse Oblige is famous for its discussion of the 'U' and 'non-U' controversy (i.e. 'Upper Class' and 'non-Upper Class'). This (mostly) humorous topic, which enflamed the broadsheet newspapers of the mid-1950s, began life in a scholarly essay in sociological linguistics – the original title was 'Linguistic class-indicators in present-day English' – contributed by Professor Alan S. C. Ross of the University of Birmingham to a Finnish philological periodical named *Neuphilologische Mitteilungen*.

Many of the distinctions drawn by Professor Ross between U and non-U speech – lavatory/toilet, writing-paper/note-paper, lunch/dinner – are still in evidence sixty years later. Mitford's compendium also contains her own essay on 'The English Aristocracy', Evelyn Waugh's chiding response, John Betjeman's immortal poem 'How to Get On in Society' (a treasure-trove of non-U language) and an amusing piece by Waugh's first biographer, Christopher Sykes, on 'What U-Future?' In many ways, though, its highlight is an expanded *Spectator* article by 'Strix' on the subject of 'Posh Lingo'.

Strix was the pseudonym of the writer Peter Fleming, brother of Ian, and celebrated for his mastery of ironic understatement. An acquaintance who met him in the street wearing a white tie and a tailcoat with miniature decorations was tersely informed that he was going 'to help a friend give a hot meal to the Queen'. While illuminating on such topics as the post-war decline into parody of RAF slang expressions (smashing, wizard, etc.), 'Posh Lingo' is also memorable for its restatement of the very common mid-twentieth-century belief that upper-class linguistic codes are essentially unsnobbish. As Strix puts it:

> It cannot be too strongly emphasized that U-speech is not
> – as many believe – an arrogant and 'snooty' institution, used
> mainly, like lorgnettes, for outfacing non-U speakers. It is the
> natural idiom of a relatively small class and exists to further
> the purposes of communication within that class.

And so, according to Strix – writing, let us remember, in 1956 – U-speakers in conversation with a non-U speaker will go out of their way to avoid usages that may appear obscure or ostentatious. Thus a U-speaker invited to stay at Shinwell Hall, Shropshire, will only say 'I'm going to Shinwell' to someone who knows of the existence of this particular country house and the identity of its owners. Similarly, a U-speaker giving directions to a gardener will very often replace a U-word with a non-U one in order not to appear snobbish, as in 'You'd better finish that job after you've had your dinner' rather than 'after you've had your lunch'. The implication is that U-speech is only employed snobbishly by the parvenu who, to return to Betjeman's poem, wants to get on in society only to betray him- or herself by talking about 'kiddies' (U-word *children*), 'lounge' (U-word *sitting room*) and 'sweet' (U-word *pudding*).

All this, of course, was sixty years ago, a world in which there was, arguably, still such a thing as a distinctive and self-contained upper-class. The number of people included in this social category might have been put at as little as 2 per cent, yet its frontiers were kept firmly in place by inter-marriage and close association. According to the Mass Observation Survey conducted by Professor Margaret Stace between 1948 and 1951 in the Oxfordshire market town of Banbury, 'it was impossible to ignore the existence of upper-class people'. Also 'in so far as this class sets the standards and aspirations of traditional class attitudes . . . it is important out of all proportion to its size'. On the other hand, the message of many a supposedly 'upper-class' novel of the period – Powell's *Dance to the Music of Time*, for example – is quite how frail these hurdles were becoming and the ease with which the socially adventurous could jump over them or in some cases crawl underneath. Although today the upper-classes still have their chosen redoubts, their exclusive territory on which an interloper trespasses at his peril, by and large Strix's 'Posh Lingo' has turned into 'Snob Lingo', the highly occluded cipher by which a supposedly superior class impresses its status on an allegedly inferior one. Unlike many forms of snobbery, this is seldom reciprocal or collusive, but simply a matter of *distancing*, the snob and his ally − who understands snob code − ganging up to exclude third parties.

Modern snob lingo may be divided into perhaps eight broad categories:

U and non-U. Many of these traditional distinctions endure, for example 'Sorry?' or 'What?' (U) and 'Pardon?' (non-U, although 'I beg your pardon?' remains U) and 'They have a lovely home' (non-U) and 'They have a lovely house' (U). Elderly snobs very occasionally refer to a married couple going on their wedding tour rather than the more bourgeois honeymoon. Several new separations have emerged, post-Ross, for example 'We're away' (U) and 'We're on holiday' (non-U) or the even less acceptable 'We're on vacation' (non-U). At the same time, in an age where social class is much less susceptible to precise demarcation, they have been to some extent confused and complicated by gradual extension into a third category, what might be termed sub-U. See, for example, the tripartite 'television' (U), 'TV' or 'the box' (non-U) and 'telly' (sub-U). This process is sometimes noticeable in pronunciation, as in 'gar*age*' (U), '*gar*age' (non-U) and 'garridge' (sub-U). Uniquely among U-speakers, the late James Lees-Milne used to refer to the place where he kept his car as a 'motor-house'.

The area of higher and further education provides an example of U and non-U confusion. An undergraduate returning to Oxford or Cambridge after the vacation would probably say they were 'going back to college', in tribute to its collegiate status. Equally a student at an FE institute would probably talk of being 'at college'. All this is complicated by the habit of 90 per cent of undergraduates of referring to 'uni', a truncation loathed by most snobs. A few very elderly snobs still cling to the by now almost obsolete formulation 'the university' (i.e. Oxford and Cambridge).

Foreign words. Formerly a staple of the snob vocabulary, now somewhat diminished. The old colonial importations, e.g. 'tiffin' (a light meal), 'wallah' (anyone working in a subordinate capacity, i.e. box-wallah), 'nabobs' (the rich), 'bwana' (boss) are now almost obsolete. 'Pukka' has, inevitably, been devalued by its association with celebrity chefs and 'Pukka Pies'. Snobs are, naturally, fond of Latin tags with their hint of exclusive private educations, but the decline of the classical languages, even in public schools, has sharply reduced their use. The days when a Greats-reading educated gentleman lounging in the billiard room of a country house could utter the words '*Timeo Danaos . . .*' in the certainty that the man next to him would respond '. . . *et dona ferentes*' are long gone. On the other hand, such well-worn quotations as '*Ex Africa, semper aliquid novi*', '*Nil est desperandum*' and '*De mortuis nil nisi bonum*' (invaluable at funerals) still have their advocates. The only Greek phrase in current snob usage is '*hoi polloi*' (= 'the people', i.e. 'the communality'). Use of the superfluous definite article – 'the hoi polloi' – instantly betrays the speaker as non-U.

Among modern languages, the ancient snob prejudice against pronouncing French words correctly endures. See, for example, F. M. Mayor's *The Rector's Daughter*: 'If any English person, particularly any English *man*, tried to pronounce French correctly, Canon

Jocelyn would say afterwards, "There is a little affectation about him; I cannot tell precisely what it is."' Stock Gallic phrases such as '*Après moi le deluge*' are, consequently, nearly always uttered mock-humorously. The influence of 'Franglais', the French–English combination devised by the late Miles Kington, persists – '*Vous êtes staying pour le weekend?*' snobs will demand of each other across a crowded pub – along with the memory of bygone television comedy. '*Ou est maman?*' '*Maman est departe avec un matelot?*', etc.

The same air of quiet ridicule applies to pieces of American vernacular that have crossed the Atlantic in the past twenty years: 'I think she's gone to the *rest-room*'; 'We'll have to take a *raincheck* on that'.

Archaisms. In mythological terms, snobs see themselves as the equivalent of Old Believers, crouched over a dying fire as, in the street outside, the Protestant mob goes stamping by. Outdated clichés are, consequently, central to the snob view of language, reinforcing the sense of a minority culture with very few entry routes, full of esoterica needing to be decoded by those in the know. If some of the really antiquated expressions of bygone upper-class life have now disappeared – although the present writer has heard the phrase 'to take a dish of tea' used unironically within the last ten years – then snobs happily admit to 'putting up a black' (making a serious mistake) and 'being torn off a strip' (reprimanded by a superior). Similarly, the diehard snob doesn't have a bath, he 'takes his tub'. This habit extends to the use of slang involving historical personalities. The snob will commend a notably tidy room as 'All Sir Garnett' after Sir Garnett Wolseley, the martinet Victorian general, or when remarking 'Bob's your uncle', expect his listener to have heard of the nepotistic Robert Gascoyne-Cecil, 3rd Marquess of Salisbury, from whom the phrase derives.

Much of this kind of snob usage can be traced back to the language of P. G. Wodehouse, itself largely constructed out of 'smart' Edwardian-era upper-class argot. The snob does not walk, proceed or travel, he toddles, scoots, buzzes, nips, beetles, pootles, saunters or, in dire extremity, whizzes or even whooshes. He is also fond of spots, as in a spot of tea, a spot of lunch, though not, it goes without saying, a spot of bother. The snob usage can also have its roots in preparatory school demotic. Snobs in late middle-age still talk artlessly of having 'made a bish' (i.e. a mistake), an expression popularised over half a century ago by the 'Jennings' books of Anthony Buckeridge. This is particularly noticeable in the realm of sanitation. A snob may pay a visit to the bogs, the jakes or the rears, or in the case of elderly snobs with naval experience take the opportunity to pump ship. Old-style girls' boarding schools offer an even more exotic vocabulary – the aunt, the potting shed, etc. The old upper-class formulation 'to spend a penny' is now practically obsolete and in any case conflicted, the pleasant sense of using a phrase that lost its original meaning half a century ago balanced by the memory that it involved the use of a public lavatory.

Military or civil authority also allows for a wide range of anachronistic reference. It is still possible to come across snobs who talk about 'the Andrew' when they mean the Navy, the 'boys in blue', 'rozzers' or 'titheads' (Mod slang from the 1960s, deriving from the shape of a policeman's helmet).

Acronyms. Snobs love the challenge of an acronym. Part of the fun of serving in the armed forces, to the military snob, is the recondite shorthand – DAAG, say, A&Q or OCTU – that springs up on all sides, and the chance to tell friends that you intend to put the SOPT in his place. In civilian life, the snob will invariably want an ETA (estimated time of arrival). Let down a snob and you can expect him to be SHAH ('so hurt and humiliated', generally used of very minor personal inconvenience). There are still one or two snob parents capable of murmuring 'NQOCD' to their children – 'Not quite our class, darling', and intended to see off unsuitable playmates.

Acronyms are also an excellent way of expressing encrypted disapproval. See, for example, NBG (no bloody good) or BF (bloody fool). 'I always thought he was a CAUC' ('complete and utter cunt'). Squeamish female snobs will sometimes complain that a particular man of their acquaintance is an 'SH one T'.

Pronunciation. Non-snobs frequently assume that snobs are obsessed by 'correct' pronunciation. This is not the case. The snobs, in articulating a word or sentence, aim to distinguish themselves from the vast majority of other people employing it, a process that can involve anything from absurd truncations and stiffened aspirates to dangerously over-flattened vowels. Snobs will talk about staying in 'an h'tel', or, when in search of shared rental accommodation, will 'ring up Fletcher' – that is, the well-known London letting agency Flatshare. On the other hand, linguistic experts have detected several long-term developments in the cadences of snob talk. Just as the old, stylised drawl of the Edwardian society lady, as in 'What djer mean?', had largely perished by the 1930s, so the exaggeration that characterised pre- and post-war vocal embellishment ('absolutely mahvellous', 'I was rahly pleased', etc.) is now only used for comic effect. Two enduring snob markers, alternatively, are the trick of laying undue stress on the definite article ('Will you please open *thee* door?') and the habit of precisely articulating individual syllables ('I ab-so-lute-ly a-gree'). Snobs are also fond of mangling or truncating personal pronouns. Half-a-dozen Old Etonians gathered together will invariably return to the subject of 'M'tutor', but note also the occasional deliberate mockery of lower-class speech, as in 'Me mum' or sometimes even 'Me old mum'.

Needless to say, snobs have a field day with tricky-sounding place names. At least half the relish of visiting such population centres in rural Norfolk as Hunstanton ('Hunston'), Wymondham ('Windham'), 'Great Hautbois' ('Hubbis'), Stiffkey ('Stukey') and 'Happisburgh' ('Hazeborough') is that you know how to pronounce their names. The same goes for Hawick ('Hoick'), Hertfordshire ('Harfordshire') and Cirencester ('Sissister'). A similar snobbism applies to surnames (see 'A Note on Names and Titles').

The 180-degree turn. This is a classic snob ploy, which involves imputing meanings to words that are vastly different from their dictionary definitions. One might note the snob's historic dislike of the adjective 'expensive'. In Orwell's *Burmese Days* (1934), Mrs Lackersteen, instructing her unmarried niece in the correct way to pick up a suitor, assures her that a girl 'should *never* make herself too cheap with a man; she should make herself – but the opposite of "cheap" seemed to be "expensive", and that did not sound at all right . . .' This rule still applies. 'He was wearing a very expensive suit' or 'He's bought a very expensive house' implies ostentation, even – that great snob bugbear – 'showing off'. Much more approving is 'presentable', 'stylish' or 'civilised' ('I thought Hermione's boyfriend was very presentable'/'Your mother and I had a very civilised holiday on Lake Como').

Yet more incomprehensible to the outsider is use of the adjective 'clever'. Commendatory when applied to inanimate objects ('That's a very clever car/ring-bound folder', etc.), its role in appraisals of actual brain-power is nearly always disparaging. 'He's very clever', essentially means 'too clever for his own good'. A non-snob in conversation with a snob who mints some particularly original remark will be greeted with a shout of 'Oh I say, that's very clever.' Other snob expressions used to disparage intellectual ability are 'highbrow' ('That's a bit highbrow') and 'solid' ('Charles made me read a very solid article in the *Spectator*'). The old snob insult 'inty', meaning 'intellectual', is now obsolete.

Although there are still snobs – see 'The snob pedant', below – who prefer to use 'nice' in its original sense of 'fine' ('That's a nice distinction'), general use encompasses wildly oscillating variations. Thus:

'I daresay he's quite a nice man' (*not a nice man*).

'She's very nice' (*she's very nice*).

'Very nice if you like that kind of thing' (*fine for the non-snob*).

'He was nice enough' (*rude*).

Understatement. This lies at the heart of the snob approach to language, not only because it involves the continual use of irony, but owing to its hint of stoicism and disinclination to make a fuss, all qualities valued for their ability to set the snob apart from the non-snob. As Peter Fleming's biographer notes, the most effective retort to anyone setting off across a grouse moor who ineptly discharges his weapon into the undergrowth next to three fellow-shooters (the correct snob word is, of course, 'guns') before the birds have taken flight is a laconic, 'I wouldn't do that again if I were you.' In much the same way, the 'Old Boys' Notes' section of the Summerfields school magazine in 1942 is supposed to have contained the news that 'Wavell mi has done well in North Africa.'

Amateur snobs generally concentrate on talking up their achievements as a way of claiming status. The true snob, alternatively, is keener to play down his success in business or his state of health, as they know that in this lies the path to greater caste solidarity and the approbation of their fellow-snobs. Thus the true snob will talk of someone being 'a bit under the weather' or 'not terribly well at the moment' when he is, in fact, gravely ill, or 'not quite hitting it off' with someone with whom he may very nearly have come to blows, or of a friend 'doing rather well at his job', when the man in question has just been appointed Chairman of Lloyds. Other standard snob expressions in this line are:

'Not bad looking/a bit of a looker' (on seeing a picture of Kate Winslet, Gemma Arterton, etc. in Sunday supplement).

'He'll cut up for a few bob, I dare say' (of a multi-millionaire).

'Gavin's really quite bright' (of a child who has just achieved a starred first at Cambridge).

'They've got a nice little place' (of someone's fifty-acre country estate).

Closely allied to the above is the snob fondness for euphemism. Thus a business acquaintance in danger of being declared bankrupt may be 'sailing close to the wind' or even about to 'come a cropper'. By the same token, the number of snob expressions for sexual intercourse is practically limitless – 'getting the lady to the sticking point', 'doing the dirty deed', 'making the beast with two backs', 'the horizontal Charleston', etc. This generalisation ignores the substantial minority of snobs who, in sexual matters, prefer to call a spade a spade, dislike the use of the word 'partner', especially in the cases where the couple are not living in the same house ('she's his mistress'), and, above all, 'gay' ('he's homosexual, isn't he?').

The snob pedant. Grammar might have been expressly devised for the snob – an abstruse system of linguistic rules, tyrannised over by various self-appointed authorities ('I think we'll have to refer that one to Fowler,' snobs murmur, in tribute to the legendary H. W. Fowler, author of *Modern English Usage* (1926), offering countless opportunities for one-upmanship and the display of caste solidarity. 'Thank God I went to a school where they taught you to parse sentences,' veterans will declare. No grammar snob, consequently, ever picks up a piece of printed paper without itching to correct the half-dozen grammatical mistakes and vagrant apostrophes that will doubtless be lurking in it. The snob can often be found in front of office notice boards thoughtfully correcting the split infinitives or non-agreeing verbs with a righteously wielded marker-pen. The grammar snob is, naturally, keen on prepositions being in their right place, i.e. not dumped at the end of sentences ('That is language up with which I will not put,' snobs sometimes chant) and given to despairing over the fact that nobody, but nobody, seems to know what a gerund is any more (a phrase such as 'It was a shame about him making a fuss' will always have a grammar snob shaking his head – it's 'It was a shame about *his* making a fuss', as the verb turns into a noun, you see). Taxed with nit-picking, the snob will piously remark that language is governed by laws, just like everything else, and without them 'we'd all just be grunting at each other'.

Closely associated with the grammar snob is the snob pedant, a Canute-like figure proudly resisting the unstoppable tide of early twenty-first century demotic, bewailing the confusion of 'disinterested' (i.e. neutral) with 'uninterested' and the use of 'impact' as a verb, lamenting the fact that nobody now appreciates the distinction between 'may' and 'might', as in 'Manchester United may have lost last Saturday', and complaining that it is surely incorrect for a village in the Balkans to be described as 'decimated' by an earthquake if more than 10 per cent of the population has died. The snob pedant also enjoys explaining the 'real' meaning of words – that 'chaos', for example, is actually a Greek term meaning 'gas' and that 'effete' is not a synonym for 'camp' but in its original form (*e-fetus*) Latin for a woman exhausted by the pangs of childbirth. They are particularly annoyed by television newscasters and pundits known for their syntactical laxity. One of the great snob media hate-figures, for example, is ITV's Robert Peston ('They really ought to give him elocution lessons'). His political equivalent is Lord Prescott. Craig Brown's *Private Eye* parodies of international celebrities appearing on chat shows, in which their conversation is reproduced with near-phonetic precision ('Wowcum Baby Spice', etc.) have language snobs *in fits*. Praiseworthy as these interventions are, they frequently allow individual trees to obscure the woods that lie around them. The literary critic Raymond Mortimer, asked what he thought of the typescript of Michael Holroyd's ground-breaking life of Lytton Strachey, observed that it was wrong for Holroyd to write about certain members of the Bloomsbury Group being gathered around a 'small card-table' as all card-tables were the same size, and that he himself would have put 'different than' rather than 'different to'.

All this might suggest that 'talking snob' is relatively straight-forward. In fact, the accumulation of nuance, inference and carefully seeded detail can take a lifetime to master:

SCENE:	*A crowded railway carriage, somewhere in the north of England, on a Saturday morning in October. Two elderly men, one on each side of a table, nod to each other.*
FIRST SNOB:	There seems to be rather a lot of people about this morning.
SECOND SNOB:	I think there must be a football match on or something.*
FIRST SNOB:	Not really my kind of game,** I'm afraid.
SECOND SNOB:	Nor*** mine. Not that one*** gets to see much rugger*** these days. Although my grandson turns out*** for Thirsk Colts now and again.
FIRST SNOB:	Thirsk? You must know James Mainwaring?
SECOND SNOB:	Jimmy? He's rather grand for us these days,**** since he got the Lord Lieutenancy.
FIRST SNOB:	Oh, Jimmy's not so bad when you get to know him. A great one for the ladies, one always hears.
SECOND SNOB:	Calmed down a lot, they say, since he took up with Marcia . . . I say, there seems to be rather a lot of noise coming from the next carriage.
FIRST SNOB:	*Civis Romanum sum. Odi profanum vulgus.*****
SECOND SNOB:	Yes, indeed.

* Feigning ignorance of a major public or sporting event – in this case the Manchester United–Manchester City derby – is a classic snob gambit.

** It is unnecessary to say which other sport you prefer. In this context, 'my kind of game' means rugby.

*** All well-known snob signifiers. The non-snob would say 'or', 'my', 'rugby' and 'plays for'.

**** A cunning piece of snob positioning which conveys insider knowledge ('Jimmy') while maintaining the pose of self-deprecation.

***** 'I am a Roman citizen. I hate vulgar, profane people.' A somewhat bold stroke, which relies on the assumption that the vis-à-vis knows Latin, in this case justified.

This is one kind of snob–parlay, its objective to seek out a fellow snob, console, humour him and establish some sort of consanguinity. But there is another kind, whose aim is the straightforward pursuit of status and in which the other person is there merely to be intimidated. The objective in this type of conversation is to reach 50 points – 10 points being awarded for each successive piece of exclusion.

SCENE: The refectory of a boys' private school somewhere in rural Suffolk on the day in early September when new pupils are being welcomed aboard.

FEMALE NON-SNOB: Is your son starting here this term?

MALE SNOB: Tobes? [*10 points for use of slightly abstruse nickname*] Yes, I'm pleased to say he's finally joining the ranks of the limpets.

FEMALE NON-SNOB: I don't think I know what a limpet is, I'm afraid.

MALE SNOB: Oh, I'm sorry. It's what they call the boys halfway between the lower and the upper school – 'in limbo', you see. [*10 points*]

FEMALE NON-SNOB: You must have been here yourself?

MALE SNOB: Not a very distinguished career, I'm afraid. The head man [*10 points – non-snobs would say 'headmaster'*] was so surprised I got into Oxford that he thought my father had re-endowed the college library. [*10 points plus an extra 10 points for having a father of whom this could plausibly be said*]

FEMALE NON-SNOB: And where did Toby go to school before St Cakes?

MALE SNOB: God knows how, but he managed to get into Colet Court. [*10 points*] But to be perfectly honest, the City was becoming a bit much [*10 points*] and we decided to come back here . . . Where was your son?

FEMALE NON-SNOB: Oh, there was a rather good primary school in the village.

Seventy points, is of course, wholly unnecessary. Superiority will have been established long before mention of the college library. The real art of snobbery, it may be said, is knowing where to stop.

Map of Snobs

9

'These people ought to be shot':
The Future of Snobbery

'Lot o' snobbery still about in this country. It pops up all the time.'

Mr Golspie in J. B. Priestley, *Angel Pavement* (1930)

Although *Nineteen Eighty-Four* (1949) was always intended as a warning rather than a forecast, George Orwell is quite a prophet in his way. Professor Peter Davison, who laboured over the magisterial twenty-volume edition of his collected works, once produced a fascinating essay about the number of things he adjudged Orwell to have 'got right' in his vision of the autocratic, oligarchical, surveillance-hungry late twentieth century, where Big Brother's portrait stares from every street corner and newspaper archives are continually updated to expunge disagreeable truths about the past. They included the parcelling up of the world into eternally belligerent and ever-contending spheres of influence, the corruption of language and by extension any kind of objective moral standard, government's ability to monitor the day-to-day activities of its citizens, deforestation and the mass distribution of pornography to the politically disengaged working classes.

One thing that Orwell seems much less able to predict, on the other hand, is the future of snobbery.

Coming to the end of *Such, Such Were the Joys*, in which the false values of an early twentieth-century upper-class preparatory school education are so witheringly set down that you begin to speculate whether the author's psyche really survived exposure to them, Orwell wonders whether school-children go through the same kind of experiences thirty years later. Impossible to tell, he decides, while adding that 'The snobbishness that was an integral part of my own education would be unthinkable, because the society that nourished it is dead.' This aperçu is backed up by the memory of a conversation with a Russian pupil that must have taken place in about 1915. 'How much a year has your father got?' the boy demands. Orwell tells him what he thinks it is ('adding a few hundreds to make it sound better'), whereupon his interrogator produces pencil and note-book, makes a calculation and announces, 'with a sort of amused contempt', that his father 'has over two hundred times as much money as yours'.

What happened to that money a couple of years later, Orwell wonders, while concluding that 'clearly there has been a vast change of outlook, a general growth of "enlightenment", even among ordinary, unthinking middle-class people'. The date at which *Such, Such Were the Joys*, which was published posthumously in 1952, was written has never been definitely established, but most scholars assume that it was conceived shortly after the end of the Second World War, a time when social and political change was in the air, a reforming Labour government was shaking up the country's institutions and class distinctions were presumed to be in sharp retreat. As such,

Orwell's remarks about the 'general growth of enlightenment' can be read as a codicil to the final paragraph of his 1941 essay *The Lion and the Unicorn*, in which he imagines the probable shape of post-war social arrangements: 'It is goodbye to the *Tatler* and the *Bystander*, and farewell to the lady in the Rolls-Royce car.'

In fact, had he lived, Orwell would doubtless have been horrified by the post-war era's tendency to confound his expectations of it. For the 1950s, once the Attlee government had been dispensed with, was an unrepentantly snobbish decade, in which most of the manifestations of class privilege that Orwell had railed against ten years before, from the House of Lords to the public schools, not only survived unscathed but in some cases even enhanced their position. Fifteen years after *Brideshead Revisited* (1945) Evelyn Waugh found himself admitting that this lament for the passing of aristocratic privilege had been pronounced over an empty coffin: 'It seemed then that the ancestral seats which were our chief national artistic achievement were doomed to decay and spoliation like the monasteries in the sixteenth century ... And the English aristocracy has maintained its identity to a degree that then seemed impossible.' His own wartime novels *Men at Arms* (1952), *Officers and Gentlemen* (1955) and *Unconditional Surrender* (1961), like those of his friend Anthony Powell, are what might be called exercises in retrospective teleology, written to prove a political point that, they believed, had only become apparent after hostilities had ceased. The thing that they are attacking is the idea of a 'people's war', fought, as Orwell puts it, with the aim of 'bringing the real England to the surface'. And yet the 'real England' that stole into view in the age of Eden and

Macmillan seemed quite as class-bound and inherently snobbish as the one it was thought to have replaced.

How had this happened? Why should the snob appurtenances of the 1950s – debutante balls, Royal Ascot, the Eton–Harrow match (in which, it should be pointed out, Orwell himself always took a lively interest) – have survived to ornament an age that many commentators of the right had assumed to be awash in egalitarianism? The answer lies in the ability of so many ancient British institutions to preserve their moral focus deep into the post-war age, and the regularity with which newer institutions brought into being alongside them contrived to administer themselves on more or less the same lines. For an example of the former, one might take the Army, the subject of a scarifying essay contributed by Simon Raven to Hugh Thomas's 1959 volume *The Establishment*. Raven had spent two years in uniform immediately after the war as a National Service conscript. Re-joining in 1953 he expected, he tells us, to find 'a new kind of Army . . . no longer an established club for established people, or a useful repository for the slow-witted or superfluous members of Establishment families, but a new Army freed from the grip of social prejudice, in which only the meritorious could aspire to success or even to place'.

What did he find in the four years spent in the King's Own Shropshire Light Infantry (KSLI), before an accumulation of gambling debts and the experience of being warned off the turf obliged him to resign his commission? One obvious deduction is that, as far as the infantry is concerned, 'the correspondence between regiment and certain educational scales is almost mathematically exact'. To join a regiment of Foot Guards it was preferable to have been at Eton, Winchester or Harrow, though a recruit would have been tolerated had he attended one of the other 'big six' public schools (Charterhouse, Shrewsbury, Rugby, etc.) or a Catholic establishment such as Ampleforth or Downside. Going down the scale, to be commissioned into a Rifle regiment required an almost similar educational status, while, descending to the regiments of Light Infantry and Fusiliers, though 'it is almost essential to have been to a public school, it does not matter if it is a pretty shoddy public school: equally it is exceptional for grammar school boys to be accepted'. These outcasts found a place in 'middle-class regiments of the line', for while it was 'unthinkable that a grammar school boy should hold a Regular Commission in the Grenadier Guards', there is no doubt that such a candidate 'will easily be received into the dingier corners of the Establishment . . . provided that he is of suitable material to be stamped with the imprimatur of that particular branch'.

But in many ways, as Raven acknowledges, social and educational provenance was much less important than mystique. Joining the KSLI, he anticipated that he might find some officers who 'would be snobbish in a conventional, *Daily Mirror* baiting, way', yet, above all things, he expected to find that everything would be ultimately dependent on what he calls 'a purely *professional* attitude', that the officers' claim to authority would rest on a professional sense of professional status attained as a result of professional qualifications and professional training. What emerged was something altogether different, a relationship between those in command and those subservient to them that was practically feudal in nature. There follows a catalogue of bad manners and misplaced superiority – officers who refuse to use troops' lavatories or undertake menial tasks, complain that the NCO who invites them into his quarters to have tea with his wife is 'getting familiar' or regard their men as 'rather like pet animals' – whose origin, Raven insists, is more or less detached from social background. For none of these exemplars are Old Etonians expressing a caste solidarity.

> My four examples were all middle class boys of desperately respectable, decent and dutiful families. There was no question of their having absorbed patrician ideas at their mothers' knee. Their families were not even military, so that neither was there any question of their having been reared in an atmosphere of cantonments and command. And yet here they were, plainly conscious that it was their absolute right to exercise unquestioned personal authority of this essentially feudal nature.

The mental landscape that the Army had managed to nurture in its officer recruits, Raven concluded, was peopled by a naturally born moral elite, buttressed by pride and segregation – in other words, an institution driven by snobbery. This might perhaps have been expected of a body centuries old and, at any rate at its upper level, traditionally the resort of the highly born. Rather more surprising is the penetration of these attitudes into newer institutions, some of which had only come of age in the post-war era, where more egalitarian attitudes might have been expected. But even such new-fangled branches of commerce as advertising can sometimes look thoroughly patrician in their make-up. The world of Roger Longrigg's novel *A High-Pitched Buzz* (1956), for example, is one of discreetly worn regimental ties and prospective employers complaining

about 'the kind of people one has to work with', in which it is
the sheer matter-of-factness of the social assumptions on display that gives the comedy its edge. Henry Fenwick, its
twenty-something narrator who works for the firm of Johnson
& Jol, inhabits what is essentially a snob-world populated by
young men with whom he went to school and university, and
girls met at deb dances, full of complaints about brown suits
and howling cads, and in its lovingly reproduced West End pub
chat offering a distinctive class element. The pub bores, on
whose conversation he eavesdrops, represent what Henry calls
'Corduroy Cap Conservatism'. They have been 'commissioned
during the war into obscure and inglorious branches of the
non-fighting corps of the army and the non-flying depart-
ments of the Air Force', whereas Henry and his chums went to
public schools and did their National Service in 'smart' regiments. One of *A High-Pitched Buzz*'s most telling subtexts, it
turns out, is its interest in 'smartness', as when Henry's pal
Hugo remarks of advertising that 'It's smart in the wrong way.
That's the most awful thing there is.'

   The discovery that snobbery was alive and well in the
immediate post-war era and would continue to flourish
beyond it begs several questions. One of them, naturally, is
political. In his essay on the Army Raven notes the habit of
'smart' regiments to insist that their young officers should
possess small private incomes – 'despite the objections of
Socialist Ministers for War'. How was it, the observer of sixty
years later will enquire, that this kind of snootiness could
endure, given the size of the 'progressive' and egalitarian
forces ranged against it? After all, even the post-war
Conservative Party had felt the need to democratise itself, to

rely less on landed privilege and more on the self-made entrepreneur. To browse through the lists of Tory MPs from the 1950 intake, for example, is to find the usual catalogue of knights of the shires, but also a new breed of lower-middle-class types, such as the future Prime Minister Edward Heath, the son of a builder, while the roster of defeated candidates includes Miss M. H. Roberts, the grocer's daughter from Grantham. It is not, of course, that meritocrats aren't sometimes snobs – a glance at Mr Bounderby in *Hard Times* is enough to dispel that illusion – merely that the whole post-war tendency in politics and beyond it is so anti-elitist, or rather *officially* anti-elitist, that the modern commentator is entitled to wonder why so few of the social distinctions the 'progressives' spent so much of their time attacking were swept away.

The answer, inevitably enough, is that the progressive political movement of the 1950s and 1960s was itself riven by snobbery, and that the social baggage that most of the 'intellectuals' who penetrated the heart of the Labour Party of Hugh Gaitskell and Harold Wilson brought with them was horribly difficult to wish away. The Highgate School and Trinity College Oxford-educated Anthony Crosland, author of *The Future of Socialism* (1956), Secretary of State for the Environment in the second Wilson administration and later Foreign Secretary until his untimely death, seems to have walked a kind of class tightrope, forever bemoaning his 'la-di-dah' accent of his radio appearances yet all too patrician in his treatment of underlings and prone, however mischievously, to detect the glimmerings of 'officer material' in the Labour backbenchers with whom he dealt. The same point could be made of the Stonyhurst and Magdalen College Oxford-educated *New Statesman* editor

Paul Johnson, an enthusiastic supporter of Wilson's proposals for trades union reform, who, as his friend Alan Watkins once remarked, 'believed in an elite . . . thought he knew what was good for people and . . . had no faith in the working classes'. There was a memorable evening in 1967 when, turning up at the magazine's printing works in High Wycombe to discover that production had come virtually to a halt owing to a televised European Cup final between Celtic and Inter Milan, Johnson uttered the immortal condemnation 'These people ought to be shot.'

The point could also be made of much of the left-leaning fiction of the period, whose surface egalitarianism is nearly always undermined by the unreconstructed social attitudes that course beneath. From one angle Margaret Drabble's *The Millstone* (1965) is a classic 'issue' novel from the Age of Aquarius, the story of a single woman who, becoming pregnant at a time when illegitimacy was frowned upon, determines not to tell the father and keep the baby. Rosamund Stacey, Drabble's heroine, comes from an impeccably left-wing, upper-bourgeois background (an 'extraordinary blend of socialist principle and middle-class scruple'), which has impressed upon her the importance of laissez-faire, tolerance and the need for persons of her own class to make amends to those less fortunately situated for the privilege to which they were born. Choosing teaching as a career, 'because of my social conscience', her personal life is governed by guilt, unwillingness to offend and a thoroughgoing attention to other people's feelings. It is also characterised by a habit of passing immensely complex social and moral judgements on people with whose political opinions she happens to disagree.

Here, for example, is her boyfriend Roger, 'a wealthy, well-descended Tory accountant person, clearly set for a career that would be aided more by personality than ability'. Then there is her brother, who has the misfortune to be married to a 'ghastly girl' whose father was a colonel and who now lives in Dorking where he apparently spends his time 'having absolutely worthless people to dinner'. Her sister Beatrice, on the other hand, gets bad marks for forbidding her children to play with a working-class child named Sandra. Surely this kind of exclusion ought to be against her principles, Rosamund informs her, adding that she is sure that 'upper-class children are just as silly and vulgar and horrid, aren't they?' Yes, they probably are, Beatrice thinks, but in a way she can do something about. 'I can't do anything with that child but shout at her . . . I really don't see what else I could do.' Later Rosamund will brood over the 'square and yelling' Sandra and think 'what a pity it was that resentments should breed so near the cradle, that people should so have had it from birth.'

Yet if anything frustrates Rosamund's own efforts to 'connect' it is the upbringing that enabled her to recognise and disapprove of social inequality in the first place. Attending the ante-natal clinic on the Marylebone Road, where she is addressed as 'Mrs Stacey', she realises that the only thing she has in common with the other, predominantly working-class mothers is her physical condition, and that 'I disliked the look of them, that I felt a stranger and a foreigner there.' While many of the contradictions of her view of life have previously escaped her, the irony of her pregnancy is soon made plain. As it is, her ability to give birth unmarried and alone is a direct result of her social status. 'If I had not been who I am . . . I would probably never have done it,' she sternly concludes. She assumes that 'she got away with' this monstrous infringement of a moral code because the ambulance came to collect her from a good address 'and not from a bedsitter or a basement in ever-weeping Paddington'. And so Rosamund survives the prospect of embarrassment and humiliation by virtue of her social position. In the end she has taken advantage of some of the administrative arrangements of a society that she has always distrusted: 'by pretending to be above its structures, I was merely turning its anomalies to my own use'. The message of *The Millstone*, in other words, is that middle-class privilege – and the snobbery that goes with it – is quite indestructible, however much individual members of the middle classes may dislike the fact.

The dilemma that Drabble sets out – how do you move outside your class without bringing all your social prejudices with you? – is essentially that of the polemical second half of *The Road to Wigan Pier*, in which Orwell notes the well-meaning socialist intellectual's habit of returning from his first encounter with a member of the class with whom he is trying to connect minus £5 and muttering 'But dash it, the follow's not a gentleman.' 'We have nothing to lose but our aitches,' Orwell concludes, but the fact remains that there are many people, eighty years later, for whom the dropping of an aitch is still a step too far and whose conception of themselves as social beings is dependent on differentiation rather than mass solidarity.

Not, of course, that there is anything surprising in this. For the message of practically any cultural artefact designed to reflect the arrangements of British social life at any given point in its history is that, by and large, people prefer their own kind, even if the precise nature of that kind is sometimes rather difficult to establish. Thus the great eighteenth-century diarist Parson Woodforde, though hugely respectful of his well-bred Norfolk neighbours the Custances, and appreciating their habit of asking him to dinner when great people came to stay, found that the great people were not much to his liking. 'One must confess,' he observed, 'that being with our equals is much more agreeable.' However straitened the shabby-genteel circumstances in which they are compelled to live, the ladies of Mrs Gaskell's *Cranford* are consoled by what they conceive to be the advantages of their social position. Nervous of the company of the really grand, eternally disdainful of 'trade', approving of, and generally well-disposed to deferential members of the servant class who 'know their place', their entire existence is predicated on a series of fussy social judgements involving criteria at which outsiders can only marvel. The merit of the value system that underlies them derives from the fact that they are indisputably 'gentlewomen', the daughters of country rectors, Army captains and medium-grade commercial men. Crucially, the system is upheld even by the less socially exalted among their number.

There is, for example, a wonderful scene in *Cranford* in which Miss Betty Barker, a former ladies' maid and proprietress of a milliner's shop, decides to host a tea-party. Planning the guest list involves the most minute social discriminations, in which Miss Barker constantly advertises her own humble origins, while displaying her own keen eye for social *placement*. Thus a Mrs Forrester is invited on the grounds that 'she was born a Tyrrell, and we can never forget her alliance to the Biggs of Bigelow Hall'. On the other hand, there is no place for Mrs Fitz-Adam ('No, madam, I must draw a line somewhere'). Snobs all the participants in this transaction may be, according to strict definition, but their snobbishness is understandable, in some cases even desirable, a vital part of the face they prepare for the other faces that they meet. 'If you took poetry away from Edith she mightn't die, but she'd be bloody sick', Dylan Thomas is once supposed to have remarked of Dame Edith Sitwell. The same could be said of the Misses Deborah and Matilda Jenkyns living in their Cranford cottage and glorying in the memory of their distant kinship with the local baronet. In some ways bankruptcy would be preferable to, say, having to consort with the wives of shopkeepers.

If snobbery, whatever its variant forms and preoccupations, is always with us then this doesn't quite explain the terrific early twenty-first century preoccupation with snobs and the periodic rush of newspaper commentators to identify and expose them. Part of the explanation, it might be said, is straightforwardly taxonomic, a matter of onlookers failing to define terms, of diagnosing snobbishness when the subject under discussion is something quite different, or – worse – of making snobbery a scapegoat for their own inability to formulate or accept a judgement. Culturally, we live in a highly relativist age in which the idea of 'taste' has all but disappeared, in which the notion that there might be such a thing as generally accepted aesthetic standards – or indeed any other standards – tends to be deeply resented and in which the opinion of the Amazon reviewer is arguably just as valid as the 'expert' in the *London Review of Books*. Quite half the complaints about snobbery that well up in newspaper comment columns or letters pages, consequently, come from people who are simply cross about a judgement with which they happen to disagree. To return to some of the material quoted in Chapter 1, it may be invidious to separate one child from another on grounds of academic ability; it may not even be educationally or politically desirable; but it is not snobbish in the Thackerayan sense of the word.

It is the same with the by now almost ritual complaints about snobbery in the arts world that tend to surface whenever a slightly abstruse novel or book of poems wins a literary prize. Some years ago, for example, the *Independent* columnist Janet Street-Porter wrote a piece entitled 'Booker Prize snobs have lost the plot' in which she identified the British publishing industry as 'the last bastion of true snobbishness' and excoriated literary festivals as the resort of 'middle-class luvvies' come to 'pat each other on the back'. Worse even than this, apparently, was 'the massive disparity ... between books people actually buy and read ... and the stuff that gets reviewed favourably in newspapers.' Although the items chosen by the Richard and Judy Book Club will sell more copies than any Man Booker winner, Street-Porter concludes, 'booksellers still regard the words mass-market as really meaning of second-rate value'.

And what, you might enquire, is Ms Street-Porter's definition of snobbishness? On this evidence, it seems to mean the filing of any judgement whatsoever, especially one with which she happens to disagree. The world of books, as she conceptualises it, is a kind of highbrow conspiracy kept up by a gang of middle-class elitists bent on excluding anything 'popular' from serious consideration. Doubtless the average literary festival audience *is* made up of people who shop at Waitrose and wouldn't know a Tinie Tempah CD if it fell on their heads from a great height. On the other hand, why shouldn't members of the bourgeoisie be allowed to pursue their innocent cultural recreation, given the catchpenny feebleness of alternatives like television and cinema? And why should it be automatically assumed that five literary editors, English dons and media types – the sort of people customarily recruited to judge the Man Booker – will be governed by snobbery? As my old Oxford tutor once somewhat loftily observed when I suggested that a particular comment of his was a value judgement, 'We're here to make them' – a snobbish remark, perhaps, on the Street-Porter scale of values but conveying rather well the now rather old-fashioned idea that judgements are probably best made by the people best qualified to make them.

It is worth asking, too, in this context, exactly what a bookshop or a prize shortlist filled with 'non-snobbish' books would look like? Judging by the enraged yelps of people who seem personally affronted by the idea that there are some books that refuse to yield up their import in half an hour and whose subtleties are worth persevering with, it would be a world of bright, primary colours, in which the person who shouts the loudest scoops the pot, devoid of nuance and with not a half-tone in sight. Meanwhile, there are any number of reasons why *genuine* snobbery looks set to occupy an even more prominent role in the social and political arrangements of the twenty-first century. One of them, inevitably, is the triumph of free market economics and the emergence of a landscape in which worldly success is not only paramount but rated by way of its visible symbols – the size of your house, the make and number of your cars and so forth. But another is the increasing specialisation of modern life and the subdivision of its financial and administrative side into an ever-more proliferating number of separate compartments, each of them allowing maximum scope for pulling rank on those without the technical knowledge to compete. Seventy years ago anyone introduced to a stockbroker or a loss-adjuster at a party would probably have a reasonable idea of how he earned his living. The working life of a modern-day hedge-fund manager or a derivatives trader is incomprehensible by comparison, a closed and esoteric world, only penetrable by members of the cult.

Even more important, perhaps, to the future of snobbery is technology. Generally speaking, the technological fixations of the modern world present the snob with an enviable dilemma. Either they can ignore them altogether, frowning upon mobile phone use, eschewing social media and defiantly ringing up the bank every twenty-four hours to see whether payments have gone through, or share them so wholeheartedly that averagely proficient users of apps and assorted computer software feel embarrassed by their perceived lack of nous. The elderly lady who, rather proudly, announces that she is afraid she doesn't 'do' email is just as much a snob as the hectic twenty-five-year-old who bores his fellow-commuters senseless by loudly discussing gigabytes and Spotify subscriptions with the person sitting next to him, or, to reverse the clock a couple of hundred years, Beau Brummell ostentatiously discarding one cravat after another to the edification of his valet. Which is perhaps only a way of saying that snobbery will always find fresh materials, new tricks, better food to feed on, ever more up-to-date techniques for disguising a style preference as a moral template.

And in a world where four-fifths of the population would probably place themselves in the same social category, these materials are everywhere to hand. The description 'middle class', as sociologists never cease to remind us, has very little meaning here in the second decade of the twenty-first century, for the demographic it represents is so capacious, taking in the family on £30,000 a year and the family on £300,000, the doctor's receptionist and the barrister, the novelist and the bank clerk, the salesman and the estate agent. Strictly speaking the modern middle class probably runs to a dozen different layers, each with their own protocols, their own conceptions of how things ought to be done and how life ought to be lived. Its snobbery, consequently, has none of the exactness that prevailed a century and a half ago. Rather it is variegated, community-specific, defying any attempt to establish general rules and proscriptions.

But this doesn't mean that its impact is any way diluted or dispersed. In fact, it could be argued that snobbery becomes yet more virulent in periods of social flux, these being the times when a need to distinguish yourself from the people around you, to carve out personal space in a crowded and unsettling world, becomes that much more important. It is worth pointing out, in this context, that snobbery has very little to do with inequality as traditionally framed by left-wing politicians. A society run on genuinely egalitarian lines, in which incomes were broadly similar and individual success judged by its contribution to the common good, would still have a substantial cargo of snobs, canvassing their superiority not through material goods or social position but by the depth of their commitment to the cause. It is recorded, for example, that the woman who looked after Lenin in his final illness read aloud to him from the stories of Jack London, until such time as Lenin dismissed the work as 'saturated with bourgeois morals'. This has always struck me as an intensely snobbish remark.

The Snob in Action IV:
Beau Brummell

As a snob exemplar, George Bryan 'Beau' Brummell (1788–1840) reposes in the very highest class. Although no one could have been more practical when it came to the optimum width of a shoe-buckle or the best way of tying of a cravat – the Prince of Wales is supposed to have spent hours staring raptly from an armchair as Brummell went about this exacting task – there is something almost abstract about his lifetime's quest for behavioural superiority, the sense of a race in which inferior rivals were overhauled almost from the moment the starting gun went off, and the only real competition was between Brummell and the man he stared at so lovingly each morning in the looking glass.

How was it that Brummell fashioned such a career for himself in the demanding landscapes of early nineteenth-century Mayfair, where an incautious remark could mean ostracism and a nobleman's snub social death? He had no hereditary advantages – his grandfather had let rooms in St James's. He had no great fortune – his father, while upwardly mobile and a prime minister's secretary, had left him capital of no more than £30,000, although he took the adroit step of sending his son to Eton. He was not good-looking – his profile was disfigured by a broken nose. He had no profession, having left the Army when the regiment was ordered north ('I really could not go – think, your Royal Highness, Manchester!') and yet noblewomen encountering him in Knightsbridge drawing rooms warned their daughters to be on their best behaviour 'for that is the celebrated Mr Brummell'.

But what exactly was Mr Brummell celebrated *for*? What had he done that made dowagers quake on their sofas at the prospect of being introduced to him and marriageable young women freeze into silence? Byron talks about 'a certain exquisite propriety' that he bore around with him in the way that another man might carry a cloak. His dress was the acme of perfection – it was said that a chair was brought to his dressing room to transport him out into the Mayfair pavements for fear of disarrangement – so meticulously yet chastely assembled that every other man in the room seemed a ragamuffin. He had none of the dandy's traditional flamboyancy – he was neither loud nor self-advertising – yet every eye fell on him when he entered a room. And then there was his conversation: elegant and sparing, ironical and allusive, quizzical and amused, yet at all times quietly outrageous and concentrated on the minutest points of social detail. He is once supposed to have remarked that he could not keep up his association with a certain Lady Mary after discovering that she ate cabbage.

Doubtless the particular nature of the environment in which he moved had something to do with it. A snob, after all, is only as good as his milieu, but Brummell had the advantage of operating in that fantastic hothouse world of the Regency, excited yet profoundly scared by the events taking place across the Channel and, as a consequence, even more obsessed by its own social advantages, in which *ton* was everything and its arbiters as celebrated as the country's naval and military chieftains. Here Brummell scored very high. Not only had he set a sartorial standard that every other club-lounger schemed to emulate, with his template for daywear (plain Hessian boots, new-fangled pantaloons, blue coat, buff waistcoat to advertise a notional allegiance to the Whigs), but the pre-eminence that this and other innovations brought him enabled him to criticise those who were markedly his social superiors. 'Bedford, do you call this thing a coat?' he once demanded of a duke, while even the Prince, with whom he had fallen out, and who had made the grievous error of trying to cut him in the street, was pulled up sharp when Brummell demanded of the man with whom His Royal Highness was walking, 'Who's your fat friend?'

Inevitably, it could not last. If Brummell had the snob's innate confidence in his own judgement, that precise understanding of what does and doesn't matter, of the persons one can be seen talking to and the persons whom one cannot, then he also had the snob's time-honoured habit of going too far. It was a mistake to nickname the Prince 'Ben' after an overweight porter at the Carlton Club and it was a mistake to make jokes about his mistress, Mrs Fitzherbert. The immediately post-Waterloo period, when veterans swarmed back from France and the gaming table stakes grew higher, badly flustered him. He was accustomed to a small, tightly regulated world that was susceptible to his control, and now here he was losing money to men he scarcely knew. His final £10,000 came and went, and then there was a day in July 1816 when he dined alone off a cold fowl and a bottle of claret, attended the opera, had himself driven to Dover and took ship for France.

Even in his long continental exile, first at Calais and then at Caen, he remained a snob. The French countesses with whom he dined might not have been very genteel but they were still noblewomen and the Calais labourers christened him 'George, ring the bell'. His old life haunted him through the destitution and insanity that finally overwhelmed him. He had visions of the Duchess of Devonshire climbing the dusty staircase as he sat in his rickety armchair waiting to receive her. But the Duchess was long dead, together with the Prince, and Lord Alvaney and Lady Mary and all the others who had sustained him in his prime, and having lived like a snob, one day in 1840, with his head shaved on the doctor's orders and his wardrobe reduced to a single pair of trousers, he died like a snob as well.

10
In Defence of the Snob

Erridge was a recognised eccentric. In taking Mona abroad he had even, in a sense, improved his reputation for normality by showing himself capable of such an act. George, on the other hand, was fond of drawing attention — especially in contrasting himself with Erridge — to the exemplary, even, as he insisted, deliberately snobbish lines upon which his own life was run. 'I can never see the objection to being a snob,' George used to say. 'It seems far the most sensible thing to be.' Apparent simplicity of outlook is always suspicious. This remark should have put everyone on their guard.

Anthony Powell, *Casanova's Chinese Restaurant* (1960)

> The doctor Is a fool
> He's just a callous snob
> He spent sixteen years in the Jesuit school
> And now he's not fit for any job
> He just sneers and he drives a big car . . .

Microdisney, 'Rack' (1987)

Most of the material about snobs assembled in the preceding chapters may have tended to suggest, if only by implication, that snobbery is a bad thing, and that to want to separate yourself from your fellow men and women by way of imagined social distinction or presumed technical expertise is injurious both to you and to the people thereby detached. On the other hand, much of the evidence offered by art, literature, domestic politics and indeed everyday life insists that the world would be a poorer place without it, and that the cultivation of an arbitrary superiority is a vital part of the curious behavioural compound that makes us who we are. Thackeray certainly thought this. His characters would not be properly themselves without snobbery. In the majority of cases it is snobbery that drives them, that governs their view both of themselves and the world they inhabit, that hangs over the cradle into which they are born and decorates the catafalque that carries them away to their graves. They are its victims, but also its exponents, zealously colluding with its protocols, endlessly succumbing to its blandishments, permanently engrossed, always keen to demonstrate that a landscape free of social one-upmanship would be a very tedious place in which to linger.

Inevitably, much of this has to do with snobbery's intimate relation to the personal myth. It is Anthony Powell's point that people can put up with practically any setback or humiliation provided the mythical vision that they have of themselves is untarnished. Naturally, this vision is nearly always connected to thinking yourself 'better' than, or at least not inferior to, the people around you. One of Orwell's most symbolic analyses of the class struggle dates from a period at the end of the 1920s when he occupied lodgings in the Portobello Road, Notting Hill. His landlady had previously worked for a lady of title, a position which, rather than inspiring in her feelings of resentment against a social system governed by birth and wealth, made her, if anything, even more determined to maintain class distinctions than the aristocrats for whom she had laboured. These beliefs took on a practical focus on the day when she, her husband and

Orwell found themselves locked out of the house. The neighbouring property was owned by a jobbing plumber, from whom, Orwell suggested, it would surely be possible to borrow a ladder and break in through the upstairs window. No, his landlady explained, they had never spoken to the people next door and, even in dire extremity, were not about to break the habit. In the end Orwell and her husband had to trek nearly a mile through the west London backstreets to borrow a ladder from a relative.

Clearly, the years spent drudging for some well-descended honourable or dowager duchess had provided Orwell's landlady with her personal myth, the private assurance that, set down in the somewhat dingy purlieus of inter-war era W11, she was the equivalent of a flamingo becalmed on a lawn full of starlings. A left-wing politician invited to comment on this story would doubtless argue that the exceptionalism it exposes is horribly futile, that the woman's interests would have been best served by making a friend of her next-door neighbour, of expressing solidarity rather than attempting to differentiate herself, that the existence of the great majority of British citizens would be a far more enjoyable and worthwhile affair if we could put aside our inbred social instincts and operate communally rather than individually, bring ourselves nearer together rather than driving ourselves further apart. All this, though, ignores the fact that this is not how most people want to live, and the inhabitant of a mid-terrace house in a socially 'mixed' area would, in most cases, sooner die than pursue a relationship with the people in the housing association maisonette two doors down. We are back to the spectacle of my grandmother, in her stucco council house in Hodgson Road, Norwich, voting Conservative, pining for her 'double bay front', urging her husband to quit his electrical work for the superior job of meter reading (which, in a deeply ironical reverse, turned out to pay less money) and her son to secure a white-collar job, and commending the lease of the private house into which she and my father moved after my grandfather's death on the grounds that it forbade the airing of washing on a Sunday.

Should we laugh at this? I don't think so, and not only because the woman in question was my grandmother. It is the same with my father's disparagement of his own jobbing plumber who lived next door – poor, innocuous Mr Temple with his neatly parked van that lay like a giant blot across my father's spiritual horizons. Orwell might have sniffed, but I can see my dad's point entirely, for to him it was the equivalent of climbing the upper slopes of Mount Everest only to find a burger bar newly opened on the summit. What, after all, is the point of a pay-rise, or an A* at GCSE, or a first-class degree if everyone gets them? Perhaps this is simply a way of saying that not all social aspiration is snobbish and that to want to succeed and to delight in your success is not necessarily to betray a moral failing. In *Culture and Anarchy* (1869), for example, Matthew Arnold has a great deal of fun with the figure of Sir Daniel Gooch, the Victorian railway engineer, who regaled his assembled workmen at Swindon with the sentence his mother had repeated to him every morning as he set out to work: 'Ever remember, my dear Dan, that you should look forward to being someday manager of that concern!' Doubtless this kind of thing was excruciating to listen to, but as the critic John Gross reminds us there was another Gooch, 'the boy whom Brunel appointed locomotive superintendent on the Great Western Railway at the age of twenty-one, and who took advantage of the G.W.R.'s broad gauge to design locomotives on strikingly original lines'.

Set against these profoundly important achievements, little jokes about 'Mrs Gooch's Golden Rule' seem faintly churlish, and one might think that the real snob here is Arnold.

And if it is occasionally difficult to disentangle snobbery from straightforward social aspiration, then it is equally difficult to detach it from some of the protocols that necessarily attend the living of any kind of life, whether in the state rooms at Chatsworth or a semi-detached house in the Old Kent Road. Any kind of social existence has its rules, its shibboleths, its unspoken ordnances and prohibitions, and at one level their enforcement is not so much an adherence to a snob-ideal as an understanding of how life works, an acknowledgement that most people prefer to associate with their peers and are either amused or fretful when taken out of their customary social milieu. It is, for example, possible to be a member of the Labour Party and still travel in a first-class railway carriage (on the grounds that it is quieter, less crowded, the extra space enables you to get more work done, and presumably free citizens of a free country can spend their money any way they like). Like inclines to like, however great our desire for universalism and common good-fellowship, and the middle-class people who don't believe that Lord Prescott, say, is a great comic figure are not really being true to their own identity.

In many ways all these arguments are merely equivocation. Perhaps the greatest plank in snobbery's defence is to ask what things would be like if it were taken away. Here the consequences would extend far beyond the boundaries of the individual personal myth. To name only the most obvious branches of our cultural life, without snobbery the English novel would more or less cease to exist, as would British humour, with visual art not far behind. Popular music has been snob-ridden almost from the moment that the Beatles intellectualised it by recording *Sgt. Pepper's Lonely Hearts Club Band* (1967). Without snobbery, in fact, we should have no art, but merely reportage, a form largely devoid of a content. To read a novel like *Dombey and Son* or *Vanity Fair* – each, it should be noted, pitched at a slightly different level of the early Victorian social scale – is to observe a world whose motivating forces can be largely defined in socio-aspirational terms and in which snobbery is the glue that holds the fabric of the milieu together. Like bores, skinflints or narcissists, snobs are, in most cases, great comic figures, fools whose foolishness is enhanced by their lack of self-awareness, their innate belief in their own rectitude.

They are also likely to be a relativist, comfortably aware that the snob-house of twenty-first century Britain has many mansions, and that snobbery, given that so many people consciously or unconsciously practise it, is a unifying as much as a divisive force. Certainly there are snobs who are cruel and heartless, whose pursuit of advantage is merely vindictive and whose jokes about 'chavs' are primed by spite rather than innocent amusement. But to look at nearly all forms of snobbish behaviour is, however obscurely, to see yourself reflected in them. I, for example, become a snob whenever I hear Adele on the radio, walk onto the top deck of a bus to find a teenager with a can of lager or listen to one of the Channel 4 youth presenters tumbling over her glottal stops. There is nothing anyone can do about this, and one might as well complain about a Labrador chasing a rabbit.

Meanwhile, we have much to thank snobbery for. If we have never had a revolution in these isles, and there has never really been such a thing as working-class solidarity, it is because so many ordinary people are, at heart, snobs who prefer day-dreaming about their individual superiority to any kind of communal action. From the outside my electricity-meter reading grandfather might seem to be exactly the kind of voter to whom the Labour Party of the inter-war era should have appealed: a veteran of two conflicts (Boer War and Great War) who lived in a council house, earned a pittance and disparaged the Conservatives with the question 'What have they ever done for the working man?' In fact, he regarded the party of Ramsay MacDonald, Philip Snowden and George Lansbury as 'a lot of riff-raff'. It is the true snob attitude, here bred up on a Norwich council estate, and, eighty years later, something I rather admire. For however much we may deplore them, however great the nuisance they may make of themselves, however intolerable the airs they may give themselves, it seems safe to say that there will always be snobs. And if we live in an age where snobbery is not only becoming more pronounced, and yet at the same time both stealthier and more subtle, it is because the tense, variegated and socially complex atmosphere of the early twenty-first century demands it. To be a snob, after all, is to take the first steps in establishing your identity – well-nigh existential act that the paraphernalia of the modern age seems almost expressly designed to inhibit.

The Snob in Action V:
Tom Driberg

Thomas Edward Neil Driberg (1905–1976) was, successively, at school with Evelyn Waugh, at Oxford with W. H. Auden, compiler of the 'William Hickey' gossip-column for the *Daily Express*, an Independent – later Labour – MP for the remote Essex constituency of Maldon (1942–1955), Chairman of the Labour Party, Labour MP for the east London seat of Barking (1959–1974) and, at the very end of his life, ennobled as Baron Bradwell of Bradwell juxta Mare. He was also a high-churchman, a socialite, an associate of the Kray twins, a friend of Mick Jagger – whom he encouraged to stand for Parliament – a promiscuous homosexual and a snob, who after surveying the guests at the party given to celebrate his seventieth birthday remarked to a friend, 'One duke, two dukes' daughters, sundry lords, a bishop, a poet laureate – not bad for an old left-wing MP, eh?'

The poet laureate was John Betjeman, part of whose fond verse tribute ran 'who would guess/That you would ever write for the *Express*/A Presbyterian journal with a tone/More puritan and moral than your own?' As to where this tone came from, it could hardly have been prompted by Driberg's early life, which was lived out in an atmosphere of stultifying upper-middle-class respectability in the Sussex town of Crowborough. Possibly it had something to do with the exalted social atmosphere of Christ Church College, Oxford, to which he proceeded with a classical scholarship in 1924 and where he recalled a wealthy undergraduate putting his head round the door of his tutor's room to announce that 'I shan't be coming to any tutorials or lectures this term, because I've managed to get four days' hunting a week.' This Driberg found 'irresistibly exhilarating'.

Driberg never hunted foxes. His principal quarry was men, usually of the working class, often run to ground in public lavatories. These, as his posthumously published autobiography makes plain, were a source of life-long fascination. He was at this point a member of the Communist Party. Thereafter his taste for well-bred friends, low-life sexual escapades and left-wing politics developed simultaneously, although these compartments existed in comparative isolation from each other. But there were occasional points of overlap. One of these came in 1935, when, charged with sexually assaulting two unemployed Scottish miners whom he had invited to spend the night in his flat, he produced as his character witnesses Colonel the Hon. Wilfred Egerton and Lord Sysonby, who gave his address as St James's Palace. The case was dropped.

A cynic might suppose that Driberg's political stance was merely a form of teasing. Nothing could be further from the case. He sincerely believed in such left-wing causes as the redistribution of wealth, the dismantling of the 'Establishment', greater opportunities for the underprivileged and independence for British colonies. Many of these opinions were a source of disquiet to Lord Beaverbrook, proprietor of the *Express*. On the other hand, his disdain for ordinary people frequently got the better of him. He was famous for his bad manners to waiters and domestic servants, when not bent on seducing them, and his social antennae extended even to right-wing trades union nominees on the Labour Party's National Executive. 'I can't bear the *vulgarity* of those people,' he would complain to his fellow Executive member Ian Mikardo.

It was even worse when, in the late 1950s, he was elected to Parliament for Barking. Here, as his biographer observes, 'he often gave the impression that every moment spent in the constituency was an excruciating ordeal for him'. On the rare occasions when he was persuaded to attend a social function he stood about the room with a scowl on his face, complaining if he were brought any other drink than Bell's whisky with ice. After half-an-hour he would announce 'I've had enough' and demand to be driven back to London. In the end he reached an agreement with John Parker, member for the neighbouring seat of Dagenham, that when both of them were asked to an official function locally they would 'both go or neither go – and on the whole go to as few as possible'. 'He was a very, very bad constituency MP,' Mikardo remembered. 'He despised his constituency party. It was an absolute *mésalliance*, the Barking Labour Party and Tom – it was like Zsa Zsa Gabor marrying Freddie Ayer.'

Part of Driberg's snobbery had to do with his rigid observance of social protocol. Well before the opening day of the Labour Party's conference at Scarborough in 1958, where he would officiate as chairman, he wrote to the manager of the conference hotel, the Grand, demanding an assurance that there would be no sauce bottles or other condiments on the dining tables during his stay. But his snobbery was also connected to his keen sense of pedantry. Sent to Rome in the early part of 1939 to report on the funeral of Pope Pius XI and the Coronation of Pius XII a month later, he enjoyed himself correcting some of the 'strange errors' of other English newspapers that had covered these events. *The Times*, for instance, had said that the lying-in-state was in a chapel on the south side of St Peter's, whereas it was actually on the north, although, Driberg could not prevent himself from adding, 'in a less learned journal the mistake might have been overlooked, for St Peter's "faces" west rather than east'. What the readers of the *Daily Express* made of these learned corrigenda is anyone's guess.

It was the same with his interventions in the field of Labour Party policy. After the Scarborough conference of 1958 he was invited to contribute to the production of a pamphlet intended to set out the party's position in simple language that could be understood by the ordinary voter. Richard Crossman, who had been put in charge of the project by the party leader, Hugh Gaitskell, recorded that 'Peter Shore came in at three o'clock and so did Tom Driberg, who had insisted, against my will, on studying the draft. He's the greatest verbal snob in the world and I knew we were in for trouble.' After Gaitskell had read for an hour he announced that the revisions ought not to take him long as he had only three or four points to make. Crossman then made what he called 'the fatal mistake' of suggesting that they went over them with the party chairman. Forty minutes later, as he grimly recalled, 'we were still drooling over the first page, of which practically every sentence had been almost rewritten, including Driberg's semi-colons and Gaitskell's policy haverings, which always recur when he has time to rethink.'

Part Two
Among the Snobs – Sketches

Some Country Snobs

It is three years now since the Sargents – early fortysomething Nigel, his wife Annalise, thirteen-year-old Tom and eleven-year-old Bella – quit their four-bedroomed mid-terrace in Putney for a fantastically remote part of south-west Norfolk. The reasons given for this eighty-mile migration varied, according to which friend or relative was being addressed, from the profoundly important (the poor quality of state education in Wandsworth) to the relatively trivial (Nigel being fed up with having to listen to next door's children's flute practice coming through the wall). Yet underlying them ran a fervently expressed desire to pursue 'a healthier style of life' and 'not to keep the children cooped up in this depressing city', buttressed by Nigel's discovery that the train ride between Diss and Liverpool Street could at a pinch be done in an hour and twenty minutes. That was it. The children were taken out of their shabby Church of England primary school, the house, put on the market for £900,000, sold for its asking price within a week, Annalise took out a subscription to *Country Life*, and a giant pantechnicon arrived to carry the four of them off to the rented barn conversion on the Suffolk border from which Nigel proposed, as he put it, 'to spy out the land'.

No one could say that, having arrived in rural East Anglia, the Sargents didn't throw themselves into the life of the place. They joined the Campaign for the Preservation of Rural England within a fortnight, enrolled the children in the local pony club, attended the county fair and kitted themselves out with a variety of waxed jackets, shooting sticks, Swiss Army knives, Wellington boots, Inverness capes and whatnot at the Stowmarket branch of Gallyons. The emails and Facebook postings despatched to metropolitan acquaintances from The Old Rectory, Appleton, Norfolk (in fact, the correct address is The Old Rectory, Low Road, Appleton, Near Diss, Norfolk NR-- ---, which means that a fair amount of their post goes astray, but bless you, Nigel and Annalise don't mind) struck an almost messianic note. The view from their extensive back garden adorned the first family Christmas card sent out from this new domicile, and though, to be sure, one flat field in winter looks pretty much like another, their friends were suitably impressed. 'Do come and see us in our rural nook,' wrote Annalise in their round-robin Christmas letter (she worked in the PR department at Laura Ashley before her marriage and has a pretty turn of phrase). Nigel, meanwhile, offered glowing accounts of the convenience of his commute and the amount of work he was getting done on the train.

Made curious by these incessant volleys of propaganda ('I don't think I could *bear* to live in London ever again,' Annalise fervently remarks whenever the subject of their old life is raised.'I don't know how people stand it.') one or two of their friends have indeed made the long and laborious trip up to Appleton for the weekend. The house, by general agreement, is commodious, if rather remote and smelling faintly of damp, but there is a feeling that Nigel looks rather tired. As for Annalise, did ever a woman spend so much time in her car? The local state establishments turned out to be quite as bad as in Wandsworth, so Tom and Bella go to private schools in Norwich, which means a daily round-trip of fifty miles plus extra journeys on Saturdays to collect Tom from rugby. The nearest supermarket is ten miles away and the local game shop, which supplies the pheasants and partridges with which the Sargents regale their weekend guests, is only open three days in the week. When not fetching and carrying, Annalise occupies herself in worrying about the Old Rectory, whose roof leaks, whose damp course is not what it might be, and whose solitude, it now appears, may be disturbed by a scheme, courtesy of Messrs Barratt, to build 150 much-needed new homes half a mile away.

Appleton, meanwhile, is a cosy, gossip-mongering hamlet of newly retired pensioners, which severely limits their social life. The stink from the pig farm down the road hangs in the air, and Bella's best friend at school, from whom she is naturally inseparable, lives at Cromer, all of forty-five miles away. In the winter the light goes at four and the view out over the fields is dark as pitch. As for the convenience of Nigel's commute, getting the 6.37 from Diss means rising at 5.45 and two mornings out of five the train is delayed. Last week he was forced to take part in a conference call with Tokyo from a siding near Colchester. Still, neither Nigel or Annalise would dream of putting anything other than a brave face on their sequestration. As they continue to reassure themselves, it is all worth it for the owls in the garden (the owls get in through the eaves, by the way, and create havoc in the attics) and the winter walks. Why did the Sargents come to Appleton? They came because they have a view of rural life that they acquired from glossy magazines and Boden catalogues and from watching absurd, pretentious television programmes with titles like *Escape to the Country*. They came, in other words, because they are *snobs*.

Property Snobs

'Do you know Dalston at all? They call it the Frinton of E8.'

Irene Handl, 'Shadows on the Grass' (1959)

The essence of property snobbery is this: that the area in which one lives is, for whatever reason, always more important than the size, or the attractiveness, of the house one actually inhabits. Although people have always taken an interest in the idea of property as status symbol, it is in the nineteenth century that we can detect the first emergence of the real estate snob. Victorian novels are full of impoverished dowagers clinging desperately to their bed-sitting rooms in Mayfair and City money men anxious to head west towards 'Tyburnia' – the Victorian estate agent's name for the area north of Oxford Circus. Until Thackeray's time bankers and financiers had tended to live *in situ*, often literally 'above the shop' in the East Central postal districts. Come the mid-century, social ambition dragged them westward and helped to put a squeeze on the London property market, whose fashionable quarters could no longer be contained by Belgravia, Knightsbridge and the West End. The development of Kensington, Chelsea and Pimlico was a direct response to the unwelcome fact that by the mid-Victorian age there were

The New Book of Snobs

simply not enough decent addresses to go round. ('My dear,' says a friend to a newly engaged young woman in one of Trollope's novels, 'don't let him take you south of Pimlico.') Fulham and Putney at this stage were semi-rural retreats, being built up with the kind of 'artisans' cottages' thought suitable for clerks and their broods which now change hands for three quarters of a million pounds.

If real estate snobbery has changed in the intervening years, it is because hardly any native Englishman or woman can now afford to live in what a century ago was their natural habitat (cf. the twenties socialite Brian Howard's reply to a policeman who had demanded his name during the course of a raid on a night-club: 'My name is Brian Howard and I live in Mayfair. No doubt you come from some dreary suburb'). From the 1970s onwards, in fact, the property snob was in hot pursuit not of old-style grandeur – that was unaffordable – but the up-and-coming, the newly gentrified, choice real estate truffles that it took a real snob-hound to sniff out, areas that became fashionable among certain groups of knowledgeable house-buyers before the property supplements or sometimes even the estate agents knew that they even existed and fell out of favour again almost before their trendiness had been acknowledged.

In their late fifties now, and beginning to wind down the picture-restoring business that has kept them in modest funds for the past three-and-a-half decades, Malcolm and Serena Partridge are as accomplished a pair of London property snobs as you will ever come across. They bought their first house in 1984, a period in which the migration of the middle-class tribes across the river from SW3 and SW7 and northwards from the debatable lands around King's Cross Station was in full swing and euphemistic descriptions of these new boltholes abounded. The Partridges embraced this transit with the greatest enthusiasm. They chattered to their friends about 'Bahzay' [Battersea] and 'South Chelsea' without turning a hair, and were even heard to talk about 'St Reatham'. When it came to N1 they not only knew the new districts into which Islington had now been subdivided ('Canonbury', 'Barnsbury', etc.) but were magnetically drawn to areas that it took forensic examination of the *A–Z* positively to identify. 'Just off to look at a nice little place in Halton,' Malcolm would tell admiring friends. Where was Halton? It turned out to be a confluence of tiny alleyways somewhere between Upper Street and the Canonbury Road where, mysteriously, an urban paradise seemed to beckon. In the end the Partridges settled for a mansion flat in Fulham, or 'Bishop's Park' as they called it, but their reputation as property *savants* was made, and younger friends queued up to consult them.

But the Partridges have never been mere followers of fashion. In the nineties, when the cognoscenti was nosing out hitherto uncolonised areas of Hackney and Stoke Newington and buying up unmodernised terrace houses in Bow, they began to venture west into outlandish parts of Ealing and Acton. Mysteriously, the gamble paid off. There are four BBC producers living in the street next to Northfields tube station where they set up shop in 1997, zealously converting a moribund dairy to the point where it could be featured in the *Sunday Times* 'Style' section. The Partridges were long gone by the time *they* arrived, of course. As ever, they had seen which way the wind was blowing and skipped out ahead of the pack. Just now they are living by the river in Richmond in a house whose next-door neighbour went for £1.2 million only the other month. Talking to Malcolm and Serena about property is, naturally, a real education. They are, of course, contemptuous of estate agents who have 'no idea', charge ridiculous commissions and are, additionally, 'only there to swindle you'. If there is a drawback to their consummate knowledge of the best place to live and how to find it, it lies in the fact that the houses they occupy are often inconveniently poky, lack amenities and appear to have been designed without very much regard to the owners' comfort. But then, as Serena – who has just got wind of the new-found desirability of the North End Road – will tell you, you can't have everything.

Film Snobs

Contrary to popular opinion, the film snob is not necessarily a confirmed cinema-goer, or 'cineaste' to use the preferred term. In fact, he – and it is mostly he – may not actually like modern cinema at all. There are film snobs who sincerely believe that the last great filmmaker was Pabst and the last great leading man Stroheim, who deplore the advent of Technicolor and maintain that to enjoy a film properly it is necessary to see it beamed out on a 16 mm reel-to-reel through fogs of cigarette smoke. In general, though, the film snob is distinguished by his expertise, his deeply recherché knowledge of the art-form he patronises and a range of opinions that, to the person who merely enjoys the experience of 'going to the movies', may seem simply perverse.

The perversity usually expresses itself in a fondness for films that most movie fans, and most movie critics, have found wanting. The film snob, for example, is not only likely to be an admirer of Paul Verhoeven's *Flesh and Blood* but to own a special director's cut version an hour longer than the original that was never made available to the general public. The same attitude applies to 'serious' and Oscar-garlanded actors and actresses generally thought to be at the height of their careers. No film snob will ever hear a word in favour of, say, Meryl Streep. Similar complaints are routinely levelled at such titans of the continental art-house movie as Isabelle Huppert, of whom snobs remark that 'she hasn't the least idea of how to express herself. She seems to think that all you have to do to convey emotion is put on a soulful look.'

Naturally, the film snob is more interested in 'foreign' films than in anything made in the United States or Great Britain, although the 'radical' independent director whose hand-held, monochrome representations of the English Civil War, shot in a field near Stockport, is always sure of a hearing. At the same time, there are distinctions to be made. French and Italian cinema, the film snob is keen to assure his listeners, have had their day. The future lies further afield, in Iranian cinema, Lapp cinema, Sri Lankan cinema even. The film snob will know all about the Chinese director Hoo Hee and his four-hour epic *Szechuan Confidential*. He will even have an authoritative line on foreign genre and be able to remark that the failure of all those Tamil vampire films to appear on DVD in the West is a scandal.

Of course, there is more to cinema than its locations or its directors. A certain kind of film snob, inevitably, is obsessed by technicalities, by camera angles ('I really think that freeze-frame effect Pintovsky always uses gets a bit tedious after three or films'), staging and the identities of its production staff ('That's another thing about Harbourmeister — always has a good lighting man'). Another kind, rather like the academic editors of literary texts, is concerned to establish that the artefact in front of him should be absolutely authentic ('Actually they made three versions of this and for some reason the new DVD doesn't have the scene where Boris and Katy swap their clothes in the laundromat').A third kind is beguiled by the proscriptions of the censors, will own and affect to admire the uncut version of Pasolini's *Salo* ('Yes, you need a strong stomach for that, I will admit') and possess an encyclopaedic knowledge of scenes from comparatively well-known films that ended up on the cutting-room floor.

Then, inevitably, there are the men, women and occasionally children who rather than producing, directing or otherwise orchestrating films, actually appear in them. The film snob's attitude to actors is rarely clear-cut.There are snobs who some-times seem to regard them as an impediment to the *mise en scène*, lumps of ego wedged across the path of directorial design. There are those who imagine them to be mere instruments of directorial will ('I happen to know that Malcolm McDowell was so overawed by Kubrick in *A Clockwork Orange* that he had to ask him for permission to go to the loo').And then there are snobs whose knowledge of individual CVs is calculated to enliven any screening of a thirty-year-old classic with a string of cameo identifications ('I'm surprised you didn't spot Johnny Depp in *Platoon* playing the interpreter . . .').

Most film snobs, naturally, have their favourite directors, selected from a range of criteria at which the non-snob can only guess, almost certain to be underestimated by the film-going world at large and valued for characteristics that, in other hands, would be their undoing. To the uninitiated Brian De Palma (*Carrie, Scarface, Body Double*, etc.) is simply a maker of upmarket slasher movies where, in the words of Martin Amis, 'gross insults to plausibility are routine'. To the film snob, alternatively, there is a finesse about this savagery, a Hitchcockian gloss to these deeply illogical collisions of time, place and motive. Of the voyeuristic Polish director Walerian Borowczyk, a perennial snob favourite (*Immoral Tales*, *The Beast*, *Behind Convent Walls*), film snobs invariably remark that he is 'a great artist who just happens to be a pornographer'.

To give him his due, the film snob is not always hostile to the genuinely popular, provided he can find some idiosyncrasy that the wider film-going public has missed. It is perfectly possible, for example, to talk about the 'Freudian shadings' in *Snow White and the Seven Dwarfs* or *The Lord of the Rings*'s 'homo-erotic subtext'. On the other hand, it is an article of film-snob faith that no director has more wantonly betrayed his early talent than Peter Jackson. As for his other distinguishing features, the film snob can be of any age from eighteen to eighty and drawn from any social class. He disdains nearly all newspaper film review sections and even specialist magazines as being insufficiently au fait with the 'real issues' of cinema and naturally reckons the BBC's Mark Kermode and the *Guardian*'s Peter Bradshaw the merest amateurs. It scarcely needs saying that most of his cinema visits are unaccompanied.

Henrietta Crabbe

The Progressive Snob:
Henrietta Crabbe

Henrietta Crabbe CBE, FRSL, the distinguished novelist and social commentator – see in particular her collection of essays *Broken Britain: And How to Fix It* – was born in rural Bedfordshire in 1938. The date, as she is fond of telling interviewers, was a significant one, for it meant that she became a child of the war, brought up in the atmosphere of Spam, Nissen huts, blackout curtains and rationing. She was, in addition, what was known as a 'Truby King baby', Dr King being an American child psychologist, then in vogue, who insisted on timed feeding, strictly enforced nursery routines and an absence of very much in the way of physical contact.

All these factors worked their effect, as, understandably, did the influence of her parents. Dr Crabbe, an academic historian specialising in Victorian local government, and his wife Oenone belonged to a social category which, even then, seemed on the verge of extinction: the high-minded, aristocratically descended, intellectual upper-middle class. Dr Crabbe's great-grandfather had been an earl, and his grandfather a canon of Christchurch. There was quite a lot of money, about which the Crabbes were deeply embarrassed, and a number of mementoes of this spangled past – mostly family portraits and antique silver – lying around the house. Henrietta recalled her family home as 'the kind of place where you'd be quite likely to see the Oxford Professor of Arabic stubbing out a cigarette in a Sèvres vase'.

On the other hand, no one could doubt the senior Crabbes' commitment to the causes they held dear. These included pacifism – they maintained their membership of the Peace Pledge Union throughout the war – equality, social reform and international development. Dr Crabbe always said that the proudest moment of his life came in 1931 when, after a public meeting in the north of England, he was introduced to Gandhi. Curiously, Henrietta has always harboured mixed feelings about her parents. 'They were the sort of people who'd ask the charwoman to sit down and have supper with them. Six weeks later she'd run off with the spoons, and when she did they wouldn't even be surprised. They used to say that one of the most foolish things you could do was to deny the working classes their materialism, and that televisions and expensive cars were awful and vulgar but, really, if that was what people wanted how could you stop them?'

Brought up in an atmosphere of mingled puritanism and refinement – she was an only child, aloof and rather solitary – Henrietta was sent at first to the village primary school (her father disapproved very much of private education and was fond of describing his time at Winchester as 'five years in a lukewarm bath of snobbery'). Unhappily, the experiment was not a success. Henrietta did not like the other children, and they, resenting her accent and manifestly superior intelligence, did not like her. Consequently, at the age of eleven she was dispatched to a liberally minded mixed-sex boarding school in Somerset where the amenities included embarrassed naked swimming, no-nonsense sex education lessons and nature rambles across the Quantocks. The teaching was feeble in the extreme, but, showing early signs of the determination that characterised her later career, Henrietta managed to secure a place at Somerville College, Oxford.

This was 1956, the era of Suez, Soviet tanks rolling across the Hungarian border and the Campaign for Nuclear Disarmament, in all of which Henrietta took a keen and discriminating interest. A photograph of her taken at this time, posed with half-a-dozen friends on the Somerville lawn, sometimes resurfaces in colour supplements: a small, intent girl with bobbed dark hair and a look of intense dissatisfaction. She once came to blows in the college hall during a debate with a fellow undergraduate who had expressed support for the League of Empire Loyalists, and very nearly married a Nigerian student named Eborebelosa. The Eborebelosa incident offered one of the first intimations of the finely calibrated conscience that Henrietta now discovered herself to possess.

She did not — and the realisation shamed her — like Eborebelosa, who seemed to her calculating and vainglorious. But, as she put it in a long, retrospective essay contributed to the *London Review of Books*, 'Here was this black man who wished to marry me. But I did not wish to marry him. And I extricated myself from the business with a lie. I told him that, much as I respected him — and I did respect him, for he was a clever man and not at all to be despised intellectually — I was engaged to somebody else. And yet I confess that this shamed me, for I was lying to a member of a race that had been lied to too much already, and I suspected that if he ever found out, he would take it as an insult to his colour. I wanted to spare him, but how – when it came down to it – *could* I spare him? If I had told him what I would have told a white person – "I don't love you" – then wouldn't that have been an insult too? And if he had been a white person, wouldn't I perhaps have married him?'

Happily the situation, about which even Dr and Mrs Crabbe had become faintly alarmed, was resolved when Eborebelosa was sent down from the university for stealing books from the History Faculty library. Henrietta was awarded a congratulatory first in her English finals, departed for London, where she acquired a job as editorial assistant on a magazine for young women, and began to write what became her first novel, *Born on the Midland Plain*. Like Eborebelosa, the experience smote her conscience to the core, for she believed that the small measure of success that she had now achieved was attributable to qualities that seemed to her entirely arbitrary – upbringing, heredity, an Oxford education. Why could not one of the children she had gone to school with in Bedfordshire not go to Oxford and write a novel? And why should she be esteemed for an achievement that seemed to rest on sheer chance? It was the same with her job on *Modern Modes*, which she liked but at the same time resented, because the things with which *Modern Modes* concerned itself seemed to her cheap and superficial, and the agony column, which at one point she was commissioned to edit, drove her to fury. 'All these trivial people with trivial values in search of things which are calculated to make them unhappy, and no idea of the really important issues,' she once complained to a friend.

It was almost the same with Simon, her first husband, whom she met and became engaged to at about this time, whose attractions seemed to her, when she sat down to consider them, deeply suspect. He was immensely good-looking, which naturally she appreciated, but there was an insouciance and a vanity about his manner that deeply discountenanced her. Half of her was secretly impressed and gratified by the way in which he swept into fashionable restaurants as the waiters grovelled in his wake and the other half righteously appalled. And then there was his job in some kind of stockbroking operation (Henrietta was fabulously ignorant of what went on in the City of London and how money was made in it), which seemed to her not much more than a kind of glorified Monopoly game. Nevertheless, they were married in the summer of 1962, went to live in a house in Highgate Village and produced two children, a boy named Archie and a girl named Arabella, in quick succession.

By this time *Born on the Midland Plain* had been published; its successor, *The Gilded Cage*, was nearly complete. Both were respectfully received and sold well. Henrietta's subject, the reviewers agreed, was the young woman's path through the contemporary world and her incidental themes privilege, inequality, anxiety and guilt. 'It seems scarcely possible for a character in Miss Crabbe's new novel to pick up a handkerchief without pausing to reflect on the working conditions prevalent in handkerchief factories,' wrote one of her few detractors. Invited to contribute to a newspaper symposium on how public figures intended to cast their vote in the 1964 general election, Henrietta wrote an eloquent article offering her support to 'whichever politician will do the least damage to our sense of selfhood, the least to oppress us, the least hurt, the least mischief in a world that requires honesty, tolerance and healing'. There was a slight difficulty in that the Tory candidate in her constituency was a second cousin of her mother's with whom she had attended children's parties in her youth, but, greatly to her husband's amusement, she decided to support the Labour candidate.

In her celebrated memoir *Girl in a Golden Time*, Henrietta was careful to characterise the remainder of the 1960s as her 'political years'. Indulged by Simon, who referred to the enterprise as 'Hetta's little hobby', and using the name of Etta Crabbe, she joined a women's group in a rundown part of Camden Town and lobbied the local council for better childcare facilities and greater support for working mothers. Like the Bedfordshire primary school, it was not a success. 'They *defer* to me,' she lamented to Simon. 'They call me "Mrs Crabbe" though I've told them a dozen times I prefer "Etta", and they expect me to write the letters to the councillors, and whenever there's a telephone call to be made someone always says "Let Mrs Crabbe do it. She knows how to talk on the phone." Why do they have to be so subservient?' 'Easy,' Simon replied. 'They know a good thing when they see it. It's surprising how respectful the working classes are, even in this day and age. Are any of them looking for part-time work, by the way? We could do with a new cleaner.'

Shortly after this exchange, Henrietta moved out of the house in Highgate Village and, together with Archie and Arabella, established herself in a terraced property in Somers Town. Her third novel, *Women and Children Last*, published a year later, was thought to display a maturity that its predecessors had merely hinted at. A BBC2 arts programme conducted an interview at the kitchen table in Somers Town in which, crop-haired, her fingernails painted purple and wearing a dress by Biba, she spoke feelingly of the conditioning to which today's young women were subject and the barriers thrown over their path to self-improvement. 'I am an old-fashioned liberal,' she declared. 'I believe in giving people choices. I believe that they should be constrained as little as possible and given the space in which they can become themselves.' It was odd, then, that most of the characters in the fiction she now began to publish – see, for example, *Puppet on a String* (1971) – seemed to have no choice at all. Oppressed single parents, middle-aged women trapped in loveless marriages, girls smitten by awful misogynist men, they were, all but her most strident female supporters insisted, merely there to authenticate various beliefs that Henrietta held about modern society.

As well as being an old-fashioned liberal – whatever that meant – Henrietta was also a mother. By now, on the back of a lucrative film deal for *Puppet on a String*, she was living in Holland Park and Archie and Arabella were sent to an immensely fashionable comprehensive school, famous for educating the children of Labour cabinet ministers. Like her own schooling, and the Camden women's group, this, too, was not a success, and Arabella, thought to be 'posh' and 'stuck up', was regularly waylaid by girls in her class, robbed of her lunch-money and sprayed with the dregs of fizzy-drink cans. All this led to several anguished conversations between mother and daughter, over which hung what Henrietta liked to call 'the spirit of social justice'. 'I'm sure Mandy is every bit as awful as you say, darling,' she remarked on one of these occasions. 'But why not try to have some kind of rational conversation with her about why she doesn't like you?' 'Honestly, Mum, Mandy isn't the sort of person you can have a rational conversation with.' 'Well, she sounds to me, darling, like a very unhappy girl who's rather aware of the fact that she doesn't have your advantages.' 'What you're saying, Mum,' Arabella told her, 'is that I have to have my head stuck down a toilet twice a week so that you can feel good about yourself.' Shortly after this, Arabella jumped ship, took refuge in Highgate and was later entered for St Paul's Girls' School. Henrietta, as she once put it, 'never forgave' her ex-husband for this act of treachery.

But there were other signs that the later 1970s, and the years that were to follow them, might not be a hospitable place for Henrietta and her kind. She supported the trades unions in their confrontations with the Callaghan government, but felt that their aims were seriously misguided ('All they want is more money to buy rubbish with, so they can live hedonistic lives. They haven't the least idea of what really needs to be done to change society for the better'). The advent of Mrs Thatcher, on the other hand, she regarded as a personal affront and she wrote a notorious article for the *New Statesman* claiming that a picture of the Conservative leader buying groceries while out on the campaign trail made her feel physically sick ('her small-mindedness, her intellectual nullity, her clothing, her suburban values – all these should be abhorrent to any civilised person'). She was married again, by this time, to a highly innocuous Labour MP who deferred to her in all domestic matters and, to certain degree, emotionally content, but the critics had begun to snipe at her novels, whose characters, they alleged, attended dinner parties at which they eschewed plausible conversations for the kind of topics ventilated in the letters page of the *Guardian*. There was a regrettable incident at a book-trade *conversazioni* which ended with her throwing a glass of wine over a young man who had declared that the heroine of *The Last of England* 'had no individual life of her own' but merely embodied 'all the desperate neuroses of a certain brand of superannuated upper-bourgeois sensibility'.

All this was deeply upsetting. Yet worse was to come. In fact, Henrietta's life may be said to have changed irrevocably on the morning after the Labour Party's election victory in the early summer of 1997 when, having finished an article for the *Observer* that set out what she expected Mr Blair and his associates to achieve ('an opening of windows, an opening of minds, a generosity of spirit, an assault on vested interests, an enlightened policy for the arts'), she tore open a newly delivered parcel to discover a proof copy of a book entitled *A Voyage Round My Mother*. The author was Arabella. The mother was her. All that long May afternoon, as the shadows lengthened and the television brought news of the new Prime Minister's triumphal arrival in Downing Street, Henrietta read on in a spirit of mingled fascination and horror. It was all there – everything – from the instructions on how to eat asparagus properly ('fingers, darling, never a knife and fork'), to the enforced attendance at CND marches and being taken to the family planning clinic at the age of fourteen.

Her husband, coming home in the early evening with the news that he had been appointed a junior minister at the Department of Transport, found her collapsed on a beanbag in the corner of her study. 'It's a foul, disgusting, disloyal, *immoral* book,' Henrietta tearfully complained, when she had been brought a cup of coffee, 'and terribly badly written, too. I shall certainly sue.' But Henrietta did not sue. She could not take legal action because she knew, and Arabella knew she knew, and she knew that Arabella knew she knew, that what her daughter had written was the literal truth. She contented herself with publishing an impassioned defence of herself in the *Guardian* ('Cast aside by the daughter I loved – a mother's tale') and never speaking to the managing director of the firm who had published the book again.

All that was nearly twenty years ago. To those who do not know her well Henrietta is, to all intents and purposes, exactly the same: older, greyer, bonier – she is in her late seventies now – but outwardly as vigorous as ever, and still eager to file her 800 words of newspaper comment whenever the occasion demands. Her husband, on retiring from Parliament after the general election of 2010, was sent to the Lords so she is technically 'Lady Fullbrook', although any attempt to address her by her title is greeted with gales of laughter. On the other hand, friends insist that some vital spark has gone out of her, that the asperity and the self-confidence that characterised her contributions to public debate have largely disappeared. Certainly she has not written a novel for a decade and a half and, when questioned about this drying up of her muse, will only say that the present age is not a good time for fiction, 'and besides, I don't think that people are really interested in the things I want to write about any more'. Asked about her political views by earnest young female interviewers, she has been heard to say that she is 'a petrified Dodo's egg, my dear, washed up on the Mauritian strand. You see, I am a genuine egalitarian, and we all know how unpopular they are.' To do her justice, the confusions of her social background and her political views seem scarcely to have occurred to her. Their exposure was left to Arabella.

The City Snob:
Mr de Lisle

Geoffrey de Lisle FCA is a partner at one of the 'Big Four' City accountancy firms – Tender & Mainprice, let us call it – a herculean concern employing upwards of 4,000 people which occupies most of a tower-block near Ludgate Circus, with satellite offices in Glasgow, Edinburgh, Bristol, Birmingham and a dozen other regional population centres besides and is always being featured in the newspapers for the 'aggressiveness' of its tax avoidance schemes. The business has been going for upwards of 150 years, ever since old Ezekiel Mainprice, its founder, left his native Dundee and headed south to establish an insolvency practice in Gutter Lane, EC, and nothing can exceed Mr de Lisle's pleasure in watching the ancient equipage of which he is a component part, now modernised and otherwise brought up to date, go rattling through the first decades of the twenty-first century. He is always bragging about the legendarily exigent obstacle race that is the current firm's recruitment policy, the hundreds of aspiring graduate trainees who perish on the rocks of its interview process and the enviable acumen of those finally offered a job at the end of it. It is the same with the partnership – 600-strong now – which, to hear him talk, you would think a combination of the Order of Merit and the British Academy rather than a collection of reasonably intelligent men (there are very few women partners) with a moderate amount of technical and statistical ability.

Curiously, Mr de Lisle's own licence to roam the Elysian Fields of Mainprice House, on whose sixth floor he now sits in splendour, granted him in the early 1980s, was a much more prosaic affair. A graduate of the University of Exeter, with a mediocre degree in English Literature, he applied to T & M having been turned down by every stockbroking firm and merchant bank from Lothbury to the Strand, and was finally taken on after his uncle, at that point the firm's partnership secretary, had 'put in a word'. On the other hand, there was no doubting the newcomer's enthusiasm for his work. While the other trainees found the atmosphere of Mainprice House stuffy and absurd, Mr de Lisle immediately took to the place. He liked the little, secret dining rooms where the partners assembled at lunch-time, with their rows of portraits of deceased predecessors and their clinking decanters, and he pined to luxuriate in them himself. He liked the studied air of formality, the sober suits, the black Oxford shoes and the elderly tax specialist he once witnessed rebuking a secretary for having the temerity to eat an ice-cream in the street. Time, professional examinations and the lure of commerce have whittled away this group of early colleagues – they went off to work in commodity broking or to financial directorships in industry – but Mr de Lisle hung on, to the point where he is as much a fixture as the Henry Moore sculpture that now stands in the vestibule or Ezekiel Mainprice's original silver-nibbed pen, kept for posterity and displayed in a Perspex box on the wall outside the senior partner's office.

'The partner is always right,' the young audit trainee once heard a grand old gentleman, F. C. A., instruct a public relations manager who had made the mistake of disagreeing with him over the use of a subjunctive in a press release. This seemed to him an excellent maxim for anyone who wished to prosper at Tender & Mainprice and he adopted it forthwith. Ask how Mr de Lisle 'got on' at T&M and the answer is through thorough-going obsequiousness. He called everybody 'sir', even the audit managers. He volunteered for weekend work. He bought the *Financial Times* every morning, sat ostentatiously reading it at his desk and circulated articles that he thought interesting around the department. He was once heard remonstrating with a fellow trainee who had presumed to use the photocopier for reproducing some rugby-club subscription forms. When he was on the point of marrying Mrs de Lisle, formerly his secretary, he happily agreed to postpone his honeymoon so as to work on a proposal for the audit of a chain of grocers' shops.

To obsequiousness was very soon added loyalty. Fellow workers who departed the firm for jobs elsewhere invariably got short shrift from Mr de Lisle – fancy rewarding a concern that had trained them up and nurtured the skills they now had at their disposal with such ingrate behaviour! If his own loyalty was never called into question, it was perhaps because no competitor or commercial concern, doubtless for reasons best known to themselves, ever tried to entice him away. Still, the attributes he brought to his work for Tender & Mainprice could not be ignored and, after passing his final examinations (at the third attempt) and serving for some years in a managerial capacity, he was, at thirty-five – rather late, perhaps, compared to some of his contemporaries – promoted to the rank of partner in one of the audit divisions. The day on which this announcement was made public was, it is safe to say, the happiest of Mr de Lisle's life. He began – something he had never done before – to refer to the firm as 'We'. When he told one of the clients whose financial affairs he supervised or an upstart junior whose forwardness he was attempting to quell what 'we' thought' or 'we' believed, the tone of his voice dropped half an octave, such was his awe at the position in which he found himself and his consciousness of the debt he owed to the hundreds of T&M partners – a little ghostly now, but still potent in his mind – who had gone before him and into whose collective ranks he was now subsumed.

Just now, having previously served in Corporate Finance and Investigations, Mr de Lisle has charge of the Marketing Department, with a palatial office, a roll-top desk 40 feet square and a business card that reads *Geoffrey de Lisle FCA, Head of Marketing, External Affairs and Corporate Sponsorship*. He cannot tell a Degas from a Sisley, but still enjoys wandering around the Royal Academy or the Tate at the various exhibitions that the firm thinks it good for its image to underwrite. Alas, then, that a faint shadow should have begun to hang over the remainder of Mr de Lisle's career. In his early fifties now, he is all-too conscious that he will not now make senior partner or even be elected onto the firm's executive committee (the younger partners for some reason think him rather pompous and insufficiently instructed in the techniques of modern accounting). Marketing, alas, has the reputation of a professional graveyard. Happily, there are other ways in which ageing City men can advance their reputations. One of them is by taking an interest in that fine old anachronism, the Corporation of London, and Mr de Lisle has already taken steps to join the boards of several livery companies and get himself voted in as an alderman for some tiny district east of Leadenhall market. In five years' time, if all goes according to plan, and on the principle of Buggins's Turn, he will be Lord Mayor of London, with all manner of antiquated flummery to enjoy and an *ex officio* knighthood.

All this imparts a welcome air of anticipation to his last decade in the City and gives a sense of purpose to his tread along the corridors of Mainprice House. Meanwhile, he is very keen on junior members of staff working late on tasks that could very easily be left until the morning and very loud in defence of the firm's much-criticised tax strategies – the fault, you see, lies with the complexity of modern tax legislation and the inadequacies of Her Majesty's Revenue & Customs, not with the highly trained specialists who sit devising ways in which Messrs Google shall remit 3 per cent of their receipts to the Treasury when everyone else pays 20. Mrs de Lisle, who sits at home in Beckenham, is disposed to think of him as very nearly a genius and regards his exploits with almost sacramental awe.

Sporting Snobs

In no other department, perhaps, has the snob world changed quite so much over the past thirty or forty years as in its attitudes to sport. Until at least the 1980s it was not only possible to demarcate certain sports from each other on social grounds, but to draw further distinctions within the sports themselves based on the particular codes employed. Thus rugby union was a game for public-school educated gentlemen and rugby league the diversion of barbarous northern orcs. Elderly middle-class bowls players joined clubs affiliated to the EBA (the English Bowling Association), while their working-class equivalents inclined to 'Federation' rules, or in the north of England the variant known as 'Crown Green', played on a curious sloping pitch. The elemental separation between 'gentlemen' and 'players', reflecting the ancient amateur–professional divides of cricket, extended to everything from angling (fly fishing versus coarse), to tennis (court or royal tennis versus lawn) and horse racing (National Hunt versus flat).

Here in the twenty-first century, in response to both demographic and economic pressure, many of these forms of sporting apartheid have largely disappeared. England rugby

XVs, for example, are full of people educated at comprehensive schools. It is no longer possible to categorise the England cricket team by way of the contending stereotypes of gentlemanly tactician (J. M. Brearley, say) and beefy proletarian slogger. In fact, cricket, though long characterised as a snob sport, has always been a much more democratic pastime than it may once have appeared. It was Orwell, reviewing Edmund Blunden's *Cricket Country* (1944), who pointed out that as it needs approximately twenty-five people to make up a game, the inevitable consequence is a good deal of social mixing. To Orwell, alternatively, the inherently snobbish game was golf 'which causes whole stretches of countryside to be turned into carefully guarded class preserves'. But golf, too, has prudently extended its catchment areas. The comic actor David Mitchell, paying a visit to the Chipping Sodbury club for BBC Radio 4 not long ago, discovered a world in flux, with dress regulations and language codes being relaxed as a means of attracting new members.

Naturally, sporting snobbery still exists, but it tends to migrate to more rarefied levels where, detached from public gaze, it can luxuriate in its own protocols. MCC snobbery, for instance, is as old as the Ashes, if not older. Alec Waugh, elected to membership of the club in the 1930s and proudly ordering up one of its distinctive red and yellow blazers, was soon made to realise that he had perpetrated a gross solecism, when the captain of the MCC touring side for which he had been selected informed him before his fellow players that he would cause grave offence to certain veterans who had worn Marylebone blazers in the days of W. G. Grace. Similarly, the old gentleman-amateur conception of sport as essentially a moral activity in which the ethically salubrious are encouraged to display qualities of doggedness and pluck only survives in a handful of old-fashioned prep schools.

Nonetheless, sport remains a valuable focus for that age-old confraternity between upper-class and lower-class people bent on excluding pushy bourgeois intruders. Even now, field sports are distinguished by their lack of middle-class affiliates – see, for example, the gatherings of the Countryside Alliance, which tend to be populated either by those who own land or those who work on it. Horse-racing, too, has more or less retained its Victorian character as a sport largely kept going by the proletariat but sustained at its upper levels by aristocrat patronage. On the other hand, if the recent history of British sport has been distinguished by the breaking down of social barriers, then there are still sports that come decked about with an irrevocable air of class privilege (polo, yachting, rowing) and those which 95 per cent of the population can enjoy itself patronising. There are, sadly, very few upper-class darts players, and Martin Amis once wrote an amusing essay noting that, however avid the urge to send the pasttime upmarket, all you were left with was an exercise so elemental in its dimensions (the shaft, the hand propelling it, the board, a series of mathematical formulae that could be grasped in minutes) as to defy anything in the way of subtlety and sophistication.

Does sporting snobbery have a future? The faint hope that remains for it lies in the field of novelty, the invention of new sports that insiders can colonise before the rest of the sporting world wakes up to the fact of their existence. Go-ahead sporting snobs, these days, are probably fans of Korfball or Pelota.

They have doubtless already given up on women's football or beach volleyball on the grounds that these are just 'too popular'. Meanwhile, old-style sporting snobs are still widely distributed. They can be found at cricket grounds applauding 'exquisite' late cuts, well-wrapped in scarves and overcoats on the freezing margins of hockey pitches shouting 'Hard in for the last ten minutes, Hoppers', at independent school rugby fixtures offering the sage advice 'tackle him low', on golf courses advising novices that they should 'hit into the wind', at swimming galas explaining how such-and-such an exponent of the butterfly stroke has just executed an illegal turn, at Henley fingering Leander ties and referring to individual competitors not as 'rowers' but 'oars', and at the Queen's Club tennis tournament debating horribly abstruse points of 'technique'.

The football snob, alternatively, is distinguished by an altogether primitive loyalty. He genuinely does believe that his club – as likely to be an ornament of the Vanarama National League as the Premiership – is the greatest in the world and denied preferment by jealous rivals and conniving referees. He collects its programmes as if they were new instalments of the scriptures brought freshly down from Sinai, knows where the manager lives and the pub he drinks in, takes any piece of gossip about transfers or boardroom intent as gospel, assumes that any player who declines to sign for it is a rogue and an incompetent, and that any regional rivalry it espouses is the modern equivalent of the Montagues against the Capulets. To this end, he is capable of astonishing feats of memory. Neutral observers are sometimes alarmed by the habit of a small section of a football crowd's home supporters to begin booing one of the opposition's players for no apparent reason about ten minutes into the match, but the explanation is a simple one: the discovery, by twenty or thirty football snobs, that a dozen years ago, at the dawn of his career, the man in question played half-a-dozen games for their great local rivals, Fulchester United.

School Snob

School Snobs

There are several peculiarities about fat, gone-to-seed forty-something Roger Strivens. One of them is the fact that he looks at least ten years older than his actual age. Another is his habit of turning up for work, day in, day out, in a distinctively patterned salmon and azure tie. A third, and perhaps the most peculiar of all, is his tendency to draw further attention to this piece of neckwear by constantly taking off his jacket, the better to reveal the colour scheme in all its ghastly, Turner-sunset glory. Sadly, in the contest of Roger's life, labours and professional regimen this is a futile gesture, the equivalent of displaying an installation by Tracey Emin at a roadside stopping point in the Gobi Desert for passing caravan trains to admire. For it is a very rare visitor to the insurance-broking office near Birmingham's New Street station who recognises the garment for what it is − the old boys' tie of Fernhurst College.

As private schools go, Fernhurst − very old former pupils sometimes call it 'the Hurst' − near Tunbridge Wells, Kent (497 pupils, motto *primus inter pares*, girls admitted to the sixth form, fees on application to the bursar), is a very modest establishment.

If the categorisations offered by Mr Levy of Church and Gargoyle, scholastic agents, in Evelyn Waugh's *Decline and Fall* still stand ('We class schools, you see, into four grades: Leading School, First-rate School, Good School, and School. Frankly, School is pretty bad'), then it probably falls somewhere between 'Good School' and 'School'. It has never, in the course of its unexceptionable eighty-year history, sent an embryo statesman, industrialist or sporting hero out into the world. Its artistic talent is limited to the now forgotten novelist Alaric Upjohn (Benson's, 1939–1946), whose debut *Not That Kind of a Girl* (1957) had him briefly classified as an Angry Young Man. Its headmaster, C. H. Wrigglesworth MA (Loughborough), is never interviewed on the radio about government education policy and never writes a letter to *The Times*. And yet in Roger, who spent five years on the premises in the 1980s, it has found its most devoted son.

The most common misapprehension about school snobs is that they will invariably have attended what Mr Levy would have called a 'Leading School'. In fact, this is rarely the case. Unless there is something altogether exceptional about the social ascent that brought them there, Wykehamists, Carthusians and Salopians tend to take the circumstances, and the comparative lustre, of their education for granted. In the inter-war era, for example, it was considered bad form by the stiffer kind of Old Etonian to wear an old boys' tie at any other occasion than a return visit to the school. It is, alternatively, the boy from the second- or third-grade establishment who likes to brag about the time spent in its classrooms, air the esoteric slang he picked up in its corridors and keep up with the cronies he accumulated on its playing fields or, in the case of boarding schools, its dormitories and study bedrooms. Certainly there are professional Old Etonians still insouciantly at large in Oxbridge quadrangles and City dealing rooms, but the professional Old Radlean is commoner and the professional Old Fernhurstian commoner still.

Evidence of Roger's fixation with his alma mater – it is not overstating the case to call it that – can be found in nearly every department of his not especially eventful life. The annual old boys' dinner is held 150 miles away, but distance has never stopped him attending: he once left his sister's wedding halfway through the toasts to be sure of getting there. The dinner itself is a riot of maudlin speeches, inexpertly flung bread rolls and middle-aged men trading fragments of school jargon (the annual cross-country race is called 'the Double Grinder', half-holidays were known as 'rekkers' – that kind of thing) or recalling the famous afternoon on which 'Mad Tuppy' Headlam, the veteran Physics master, started foaming at the mouth when someone let loose a pet gerbil in the laboratory. When the publication of an official history (*Fernhurst: An Eternal Golden Braid*) was advertised on the school website, he was the first subscriber. The school's Facebook page is full of little notes from him congratulating the Under 13 rugby team on their progress in the county championships or enquiring if anybody knows the precise linguistic origin of the Fernhurst phrase 'galoshing', meaning to abscond from the premises after lights out.

Naturally, all this esteem, all this *love*, all this fervent belief that Fernhurst was the best school in the world, and is likely to remain so, has a moral basis. It was Fernhurst, he sincerely believes, that made him what he is; Fernhurst that erected the ethical turret from which he surveys the world; Fernhurst that taught him everything from how to bowl an off-break to construct a syllogism. If you didn't go to Fernhurst then you are lacking some vital part of what makes you a human being, and it is the want of a Fernhurstian education that makes so many of our leading public figures the nonentities they are. A shame, then, that Roger – unmarried and likely to stay that way – is childless, otherwise a tribe of little Strivenses might have been despatched south to follow the ancestral trail. The very few of his colleagues who know the provenance of the tie sometimes wonder what mighty deeds he performed at Fernhurst that the place should have inspired such affection in him. A glance at the *Fernhurst Register* (£8.95 on application to the school secretary) reveals only that R. J. Strivens (Podger's) was a junior house prefect and represented the school Third XI at cricket with a bowling average of 57.93. But then loyalty, like the Old Fernhurstian tie, is a very curious thing.

There is, of course, another kind of school snob. This is the inverted kind, who went not to Eton, or Radley, or even to Fernhurst, but was negligently or punitively educated by the state and whose scars – emotional and actual – are as proudly born as a public school boy's First XI cricketing colours. It was all pretty bloody tough, they imply, but, as with Roger, it made us the men we are. 'They had to take the maths master out on a stretcher,' state-school snobs will darkly reminiscence – all too conscious of the effect they are producing on more genteelly educated dinner guests – 'After all, you didn't mess with Gary Blackhead. Not after he came out of Borstal the second time. I mean, there were fourteen-year-olds in my class who were dealing speed out of buckets.' It is not quite certain, again as with Roger, who they are trying to impress.

The Broadhursts and Lucy

The Broadhursts are one of those big, philoprogenitive 'county' families of whom rather less fuss is made these days than used to be the case. Mr Broadhurst's grandpapa was Lord Lieutenant of Lincolnshire in the dying days of the Macmillan government, and Mrs B once had her photograph taken for *The Field*, standing on the steps of some stately home and staring rather severely at a brace of dead pheasants. In the meantime, the clan's fortunes have been steadily on the wane. A couple of fields had to be sold to pay death duties after Mr B's father died and the big estate not far from Sleaford is greatly reduced in size. The paddocks are overgrown, the stables empty and the ornamental lake, in which a Victorian parlour-maid was once supposed to have drowned herself, clogged up with silt. True to the traditions of their class, the Broadhursts were not distressed by these intimations of decline. They had prospered before, and assuredly they would prosper again: all this – the paid-off gardeners, the cow parsley growing up eight feet high in the meadows with no one to cut it, the mothballing of the north wing and the disappearance of its furniture beneath hessian covers – was merely a temporary becalming, here on the slack and unprepossessing modernist tide. Mr Broadhurst greeted the absence of a male heir with the same stoicism that he had greeted his losses at Lloyd's ('Wouldn't have been much for him to inherit anyway') and instead resolved to concentrate his energies on his daughters.

The first four of these were all of a piece: bright, bold, lissom girls named Camilla, Arabella, Louisa and Xanthe, with corn-coloured hair, high cheekbones and fresh complexions, who oozed charm and social adroitness as their father's bank account oozed debt. It could not be said that Lucy, the fifth, was an accident – no such word was ever admitted into the Broadhursts' genealogical vocabulary – but she certainly counted as an afterthought. Xanthe, the sister nearest to her in age, was seven at the time of her birth, and Camilla, the eldest, already at Bedales. Neither, at this remove in time, was it expected that the ancient structures of Broadhurst child-rearing – nannies, nurseries, the search for exalted godparents – could be instantly wheeled back into place. Still, no one could have said that the Broadhursts ignored their manifest social duty. Mrs Broadhurst gave up the psychology class in which, greatly daring, she had recently enrolled and noted with a sigh that her original stock of maternity dresses were all horribly out of date. The old day nursery, since pressed into service as an extra guest bedroom, was hastily recommissioned, while Mr Broadhurst resigned the membership of the solitary London gentleman's club to which he still belonged and invested the capital sum thereby released in a building society account known, without the faintest conceivable irony, as the Save the Children Fund. For her part, Mrs B endured a fretful pregnancy and on more than one occasion claimed to have seen the ghost of Sarah, the drowned parlour-maid, gliding restlessly around the lakeside.

If these were hardly promising signs, then it could not be said that Lucy's upbringing was in any way neglected – a marchioness hovered over the font at her christening in the local parish church and the nanny who helped raise her for the first year of her life came direct from Chatsworth – it was merely that family life had moved on. There was also a lot less money. And so the Sleaford and District Pony Club, where her sisters had made the first of the friendships that would sustain them through their adolescence, was exchanged for the Girl Guides ('They do such very interesting things,' Mrs Broadhurst enthused, 'not at all like when I was a girl') and the day school outside Grantham where Arabella, Louisa and Xanthe had been educated for the 'very good' village primary. To do Lucy justice she was not at all put out by this apparent diminution in status, and appeared to enjoy the litter-picking excursions and the visits to old people's homes in which the Guide troop seemed to specialise. On the other hand, there was an embarrassing moment when one of the friends she brought back from school turned out to be a girl called Mandy Atkinson. 'Isn't that Sandra Atkinson's youngest?' Mr Broadhurst nervously enquired, catching sight of the carroty curls of his daughter's guest across the tea table. 'I really don't like to go into these things,' his wife replied, perhaps not wanting to recall that until a year or so ago, when financial constraints had urged the abolition of the post, Mrs Atkinson had officiated as the Broadhurst's daily 'help'. *A pleasant, helpful girl who seems to easily make friends* ran her headmistress's final report, over the inexactitude of whose grammar Mrs Broadhurst sadly shook her head. *We wish her well for the future.*

As to what that future might hold, Mrs Broadhurst, when, two or three years later, she came to reckon up her daughter's prospects, was not exactly sure. Admittedly, Lucy – now at the local comprehensive – was markedly less neurotic and highly strung than her sisters, which could only be rated a bonus, but she was also – this had to be acknowledged too – much less bright, bold and lissom. There was, as Mrs Broadhurst matter-of-factly conceded, no point in invoking that great upper-class shibboleth 'Hair out of the eyes, darling', for Lucy's sallow slab of a forehead looked a great deal better when covered with a fringe. There was also no point in trying to wheedle her into the handed down Loden coats and Laura Ashley frocks that had set off the figures of the older girls to such advantage. But the first real sign that Lucy might not be cut from the same ancestral cloth as her predecessors came in the summer of her fifteenth year when, ascending to the upstairs landing of the house and loudly demanding where on the premises daughter might be, Mrs Broadhurst received the reply: 'Moom, ah'm in me rume.' Mrs Broadhurst knew that accent. She had heard it in the streets of Sleaford, at Louth market, at point-to-point meetings from Gainsborough to Carlton Scroop. Game dealers had cheerfully directed it at her as they wrapped up her partridges and floor-walkers breathed it as they waved her out of the Stamford department stores. But never, in all her thirty years in South Lincolnshire, had it been addressed to her by one of her own children.

Life was hard, Mrs Broadhurst thought, one foot planted squarely on the topmost stair, the other hovering uncertainly over the drugget carpet of the landing, life was very hard. But if there was one rule that three decades of child-raising had taught her, it was that nettles of this kind had to be grasped, and the more firmly the better. 'Lucy,' she quavered – and the agitation in her voice imparted a curious, hissing sound to the sibilants – 'have you seen my secateurs?' 'They're in the kubbud, moom,' Lucy briskly returned. After that Mrs Broadhurst went downstairs and spent the rest of the morning grimly poring over a Countrywear Casuals catalogue, whose expensively dressed models seemed to mock her with each fresh garment in which they came arrayed. By supper-time, when Lucy had made mention of a friend who was 'at uni oop in Notts' (trs. 'studying at the University of Nottingham'), it was clear that something would have to be done.

'Do you think' she enquired of her husband later that evening, having cornered him in his study, 'that we could find the money to send Lucy to St Chad's for sixth form rather than carrying on at that dreadful place she is now?' But the income on which Mr Broadhurst had predicated his domestic expenditure for the next three years did not allow for private education. 'Quite out of the question, I'm afraid,' he declared. 'Anyway, I thought you said Lucy was doing very well at the Academy and liked being there?' It was on the tip of Mrs Broadhurst's tongue to explain about the *rumes*, *kubbuds* and the friend *oop in Notts*, but the triviality of these objections could not be gainsaid, and so she contented herself with the observation that it was a pity that Lucy lacked some of the advantages that had been accorded to her sisters. 'Yes, it is a pity,' Mr Broadhurst agreed and went back to reading a book called *With Rod and Gun Through Roxburghshire*. Outside the rain fell on the sodden Lincolnshire grass.

Worse, alas, was to come. For all her progress at the Academy, it was clear by this point to all objective observers – even to

Mrs Broadhurst, for whom, necessarily, all her geese were swans – that Lucy's intellectual attainments were of a rather modest sort. 'She's not at all academic,' her mother told her friends, occasionally adding the coda, 'I'm very pleased to say. We think she may want to do something in child-care, or occupational therapy.' With this aim in mind, having acquired four GCSEs, Lucy proceeded to a course at the local technical college, combining her attendance with a part-time job at a nearby stables. Mrs Broadhurst heartily approved of the stables. 'Very nice people,' she explained, 'and of course Lu has always been good with animals.' With a vision of the Countrywear Casuals catalogue and its immaculate girls before her, Mrs Broadhurst spent money she could not afford on a Barbour jacket and several pairs of jodhpurs, but the experiment was not a success: after a fortnight Lucy went back to jeans and trainers. 'Mum,' she remarked one morning, prior to her departure to the technical college. 'Is it OK if Wayne comes to supper this evening?' 'Wayne,' Mrs Broadhurst echoed, with the faintest perceptible emphasis. 'Who exactly is Wayne?' 'He's a friend of mine, Mum. You know. Can he come to supper?' 'Darling, of course your friends are welcome to supper,' Mrs Broadhurst said, who did not know. As it happened, Mr Broadhurst was away that evening, at a meeting of the County Landowners' Association, and so they dined à trois.

Wayne, seated with his back to the photograph of Grandpapa Broadhurst in his Lord Lieutenant's robes bowing to the Queen on the steps of Lincoln cathedral, turned out to be a small and rather weasel-like boy with an overlong nose dressed in what could only have been a tracksuit. He said awreet when offered condiments, champion when given one of Mr Broadhurst's cans of beer to drink, and clearly found the venison sausages and caper sauce rather hard going. Afterwards he and Lucy repaired to her room, from which the sound of loud music, and other noises, rapidly began to emanate. Later, at Lucy's urgent request, Mrs Broadhurst took the Land Rover and returned him to a small terraced house on the outskirts of Sleaford. 'Who's this Wayne I've been hearing about?' Mr Broadhurst jovially enquired the next morning – the meeting of the County Landowners' Association had put him in a good temper – 'What sort of a chap is he?' 'Well . . .' and here Mrs Broadhurst hesitated, 'he's rather . . .' Twenty years ago she would have used the word 'common', but even Mrs Broadhurst, stickler for tone, protocol and *politesse* that she was, did not think that you could decently call anyone 'common' here in the second decade of the twenty-first century. 'He's rather . . . *uncouth*,' she temporised. 'Uncouth?' 'Well, you know. Not much in the way of airs and graces.' 'Nothing wrong with that,' Mr Broadhurst declared – he could be very odd at times. 'But Lucy likes him?' 'Oh, besotted,' Mrs Broadhurst told him, and went off to write a cross letter to the IEC Wine Society for supplying her with a bottle of champagne that had blown up when extracted from its crate.

In the course of the next few weeks, the Broadhursts were to see a great deal of Wayne. He came to supper again and to Sunday lunch. The sound of his moped puttering along the gravel drive was as regular an occurrence as the noise of the beet lorries or the cries of the gulls. There was a day – a terrible day, etched in the annals of Broadhurst family history – when Mrs Broadhurst came downstairs to find him sitting at the breakfast table, having clearly spent the night on the premises. His shell-suits appeared in the laundry basket alongside

Mr Broadhurst's shirts from Charles Tyrwhitt and his debased and soil-encrusted footwear lay in the vestibule next to his host's golfing brogues. It was at this point that Mrs Broadhurst – an essentially rational woman, who always thought that there should be a reason for her likes and dislikes – sat down to consider why it was that she held Wayne in such utter contempt. Most obviously, there were the things that he was – spotty, shifty (or so she inferred), unkempt, ignorant, jobless and, above all, the ravisher of her daughter. But to add to these disqualifications were the things that he patently was not. Specifically, Mrs Broadhurst would have liked him more, or rather disliked him less, had he been abashed by the circumstances in which he found himself: the picturesque lake, the rolling lawns, the big house with its wall of departed Broadhursts leering from their frames, the crowded mantelpiece with its line of pasteboard invitations.

Wayne, on the other hand, so far as she could tell, was not in the least humbled, or impressed, or embarrassed, by the comparative grandeur of the locale in which he had now fetched up. It was simply the house in which his girlfriend lived. He could take it or leave it. Then there was the fact that, despite the spots and the ignorance and the shiftiness, there was no real context into which she could locate him, no touch-paper she could light to spark him into life in her imagination. Had he fallen into the category of what Mrs Broadhurst called 'country boy' – had he even been the kind of canny rural peasant who coursed hares over the fields or went poaching game in Mr Broadhurst's copses – then she could have had some kind of conversation with him. But no, he was merely a dull, stolid, unambitious seventeen-year-old from Sleaford, and so Mrs Broadhurst hated him with all her heart, conscious all the while that the hatred was unworthy of her, and him, but unable in the circumstances – this being her own flesh and blood, after all – to establish how else she was supposed to react to this trifling with every value she held dear.

Christmas came, and with it a card with a Sleaford postmark, the address on its square buff envelope inscribed in outsize capitals. 'Who are Gary and Melissa?' Mr Broadhurst wondered, when he came upon it amid an assortment of messages from men with whom, forty years before, he been at Eton and fellow underwriters in whose boxes he had hobnobbed at Lloyd's. 'I think they must be Wayne's father and step-mother,' Mrs Broadhurst told him. 'Well, that's very nice of them.' 'Yes, isn't it?' Mrs Broadhurst said, bending two prongs of a silver-plated fork by stabbing a chopping board with them. Mrs Broadhurst had never been confidential with her elder daughters. Their dialogues had tended to consist of the girls offering information on what they intended to do or wear, in whose company, and until what hour, and Mrs Broadhurst either approving, acquiescing or wearily remonstrating as circumstance demanded. Her attempts to cross-question Lucy about Wayne were, consequently, doomed to failure from the start. 'I know you don't like him [*doont lakh im*], Mum, so there's not much point in talking about it, is there?' Lucy had remarked at an early stage in the proceedings. 'I never said I didn't like him, darling,' Mrs Broadhurst returned, which was, strictly speaking, true. 'It's just that . . .' But whatever it was trailed off into silence. There was no language in which Wayne could be discussed, no conceptual backdrop against which he could adequately feature, no Broadhurstian frieze in which his figure could get any kind of a look-in. He was simply Caliban, and she Miranda, with no Prospero on hand to bring him to heel. And so the conversation lapsed.

There had been a time when Mrs Broadhurst had been gripped by the delusion that her daughter's *mésalliance* – and that was the only word for it – could be hushed up, or at any rate kept from the world at large. But the thing had gone on too long now; the secret could no longer be hidden, certainly not from Mrs Broadhurst's more intimate friends, or from her daughters, all living in London, each married or otherwise partnered off but eager to return home for country weekends. Again, Mrs B might have been able to comfort herself had there been any unanimity in their response, but there was not. The sisters varied between finding Lucy's behaviour 'a scream' to thinking that she ought to 'pull herself together' or be 'sent off somewhere to do something'. 'What do you think about Wayne?' she demanded once of Louisa, always reckoned to be the kindest and most dispassionate of the four. 'He's all right, Mummy,' Louisa replied. 'Thick as a plank, I daresay, but he's all right. What does Daddy make of it?' 'I sometimes think,' Mrs Broadhurst bitterly reflected, 'that your father never notices anything at all these days.' 'Well, he can hardly throw him out of the house, can he?' 'Geoffrey Falmer told one of Hermione's young men that if he ever saw him on his property again he'd call the police.' 'More fool Geoffrey Falmer, Mum. What are you going to do? Get Lu made a ward of court?' There was no answer to this, and Mrs Broadhurst left the sheaf of spring lilies she was daintily arranging in a bowl, climbed the stairs to her bedroom, concealed herself under a blanket and actually wept. Coming downstairs again half-an-hour later she bumped into Wayne in the hallway. "Allo, Missus B,' he remarked.

Contemplating the deeply unpromising hand that fate had dealt her, Mrs Broadhurst decided that a single trump card remained. 'Lucy, dear,' she artlessly enquired, on finding her daughter loitering in the hall one morning, 'it must be awfully dull for you here at the moment, even with the Tech' – Mrs Broadhurst quite startled herself with the breeziness with which she brought out this abbreviation. 'How would you like to go to New Zealand for six months? Only I just had a letter from cousin Lottie and she's simply *desperate* for an au pair to look after the children for a bit while she and Toby get their affairs into shape. Apparently there's an annexe on the ranch where you could stay, and afterwards I'm sure you could go travelling somewhere. Shall I email her and say that you'll think about it?' 'Why would I want to stay with cousin Lottie in New Zealand, Mum?' Lucy replied, who by this time had manoeuvred herself into a raincoat and a pair of waterproof trousers and looked, her mother thought, like an exceptionally sullen and overweight elf. 'Anyway, I thought you said the children were the ghastliest pair of brats you'd ever come across last time you saw them and no civilised person could spend three days in a house [*in a nowce*] with Lottie without throwing a water-jug at her?' There was no answer to this, and Mrs Broadhurst slunk cravenly away.

Shortly after this, a crisis blew up. 'He can't be here when Kitty comes. I absolutely forbid it,' Mrs Broadhurst announced. Kitty was the Marchioness of Auld Reekie and Lucy's godmother, whose annual visit now loomed. 'What are you suggesting?' Mr Broadhurst enquired. 'A kind of *cordon sanitaire*? I can't see Kitty liking that.' 'If it comes to it,' Mrs Broadhurst riposted, 'I shall ring and put her off. Tell her we've all got flu or something.' In the end, however, reason prevailed, and there was no *cordon sanitaire* or phantom influenza. Kitty, who drove herself to the Broadhursts in an antique Rolls-Royce shooting brake, was a grave and stately lady in late middle age, with a glacial eye, something of whose grandeur rubbed off even on the hitherto unimpressionable Wayne. He could be seen watching her during luncheon like a rabbit caught in a car's headlights. When the party returned to the drawing room he went so far as to hold the door open. Mrs Broadhurst, who had passed the meal in a state of silent anguish, was very faintly consoled.

In the afternoon hostess and guest, well wrapped up against the equinoctial gales, went for a walk around the estate. 'So that is the famous Wayne,' Kitty remarked. 'Well, Lucy certainly seems very happy.' 'The whole thing is a *disaster*,' Mrs Broadhurst told her. 'I don't doubt that you're right,' said the chatelaine of Auld Reekie Castle. 'But that's how it is these days, Fenella. Why, Kirsten is very nearly engaged to a man who, as far as I can make out, sells photocopying equipment. They live in a maisonette near the Greenwich Observatory. He calls me Katherine. I didn't ask him to. I suppose I should be grateful they're even thinking of getting married. And John Troutbridge's son – you remember that nice young man who used to come to Annabel's parties? – manages a caravan site somewhere on the Yorkshire coast. The Troutbridges have even been and stayed there, I gather. That's how it is, you see. *Eppure si muove*, my dear.' Mrs Broadhurst was not quite sure what *eppure si muove* meant, but she dutifully inclined her head. 'Do you know,' she said, 'it almost makes me wish I'd married Tony Wiltshire all those years ago. I mean, he did ask.' 'You can be very grateful you didn't,' Kitty assured her friend. '*Very* grateful. They've had to sell the dower house and the last I heard half the land was being turned into a golf course. How are your aconites doing?' And Mrs Broadhurst saw that the material part of their conversation was at an end. 'Oh, it's been rather a good year,' she conceded. Silently, yet companionably, through runnels of liquid mud, heads carefully angled against the wind, with the rooks cawing in the elms above them, they returned to the house. Here they came upon Lucy and Wayne, rumpled and affectionate, emerging hand-in-hand from one of the outbuildings. 'I know I shouldn't say so, Kitty,' Mrs Broadhurst murmured, 'but it's *exactly* like *The Darling Buds of May*.'

All this took place nearly a year ago. Just now Lucy and Wayne are living in the newly reconditioned stable-block at the back of the house. The reconditioning was set in train by Mr Broadhurst on the grounds that he would sooner his daughter were comfortable than not, and involved the selling of another field to the developers. Lucy, as it happens, is six months pregnant. In this capacity she attends ante-natal classes at Sleaford Town Hall where 'if you can believe it', as Mrs Broadhurst has more than once observed, the principal language spoken is Polish. Three of her sisters have already sent knitted gifts in advance of the birth, and the Marchioness of Auld Reekie a cheque for £100 and some linen thought to have come from Balmoral itself.

Wayne leaves the stable-block on his moped at seven o'clock each morning for a job in the potato fields. To Mrs Broadhurst, who sometimes watches this transit from her bedroom window in the aftermath of one of her many sleepless nights, a host of more or less unanswerable questions have already begun to present themselves. What will the child be named? (Wayne's patronym, alas, turned out to be Higginbotham.) How are they to stage the christening, and who will be invited to it? It is a provisional life, Mrs Broadhurst feels, to which the marchioness's consoling words — *eppure si muove* indeed! — scarcely do justice. Mr Broadhurst, meanwhile, is talking gloomily about 'downsizing' and the advantages of a smaller house nearer Sleaford. One of the Labradors is dead of distemper and the paddock was under water for a month after the spring floods. Outside the long Lincolnshire days lengthen into dusk.

Lucy

A Little Dinner at the Perownes'

I hadn't set eyes on Henry Perowne since the day we graduated from college, but there he was again, looming out of
the crowd of faces in a Chancery Lane wine-bar – very sleek
and well-fed faces they were – the red hair of which he was
so proud still furiously a-glint and not looking a day over
thirty-five. 'Very odd that we never managed to keep up,' he
declared. (I don't suppose we exchanged more than a half-a-
dozen sentences at university.) 'Of course I still see x and y
now and again' – and here he named a newly elected
Conservative MP for one of the Sussex constituencies, and a
well-known venture capitalist. 'What have you been doing
with yourself?' As I gave some account of my accomplish-
ments, such as they were, the mobile phone in the pocket of
his pinstripe suit began to judder. 'You'll have to excuse me,'
he explained. 'That's the trouble about being in media law.
They *will* ring you up after hours.' I tried not to eavesdrop on
the rather emphatic conversation that followed, but I am
pretty sure it contained the words 'I don't think she can be
expected to settle for less than five mill.' Outside the rain fell
over the grey streets and the lights from the taxis shone up

through the murk. 'Sorry about that,' Henry went on. 'Client of mine in desperate straits – husband gone off with another woman – found a note on the mantelpiece when she came home one night – prepared to give her the cottage on the Northamptonshire estate and half the trust-fund – she wants the townhouse – school-fees not paid – terrible mess all round. Did you say you were writing a book about . . . Cyril Connolly, was it? I'm afraid I don't get much time for reading.'

It was all very different, I thought, from the Henry Perowne of Oxford days, who went around in a Dead Kennedys T-shirt, painted his fingernails black, edited a magazine called *Radical Action Now* and was sometimes seen ostentatiously browsing through Jacques Derrida's *De la Grammatologie* in the college library. He was wearing what looked very like an MCC tie, only that the width of the stripes was half an inch too short, and the neatest little leather briefcase with the initials *H. de la C. P.* embossed on it in curlicue silver italics lay at his expensively shod feet. 'We ought to have lunch,' he said, 'that's if you feel you can stand the food at the Garrick. Middle of the day no good? Well, why not come and have supper with us one night? Fleur will be delighted to see you.' Nothing loath, I agreed on a date a fortnight hence. There was some further professional small-talk about the signal services he had recently rendered 'Ken' and 'Kev' – I think he meant Kenneth Branagh and Kevin Spacey – and then, having ascertained my telephone number, and given a little pat to his lambent hair, he walked out into the November night, where the taxis slewed and concertina'd to a halt the moment he raised his arm.

One's wife, I find, tends to be suspicious of people one knew at college of whose existence she was previously unaware. Mine was unimpressed by both Perowne, his connections and the invitation to Hampstead. 'Fleur Perowne? Isn't she some kind of interior designer? I'm sure I read a piece about her in *Vogue*. We're not staying any later than eleven, I can tell you that.' To all this I meekly acquiesced. Just to assure myself that the whole thing – the wine-bar, the shining red curls, the designer brief-case, the five million – had not been an illusion I went up to the loft and pulled out the freshman's photograph from beneath a pile of programmes from old college revues and some copies of the *New Oxford Magazine,* but there he was, standing between two boys with long hair and spotty complexions whose names, at this remove in time, I could not even remember. Then, intrigued by the thought of his interior-designing wife, I goog-led her name and found a picture of the pair of them, together with a pair of splendiferously toothed red-headed children, arranged, together with a Labrador and a brace of cocker span-iels, in a kind of gazebo hung about with exotic plants and creepers. *Henry and Fleur Perowne*, the caption read. *A very mod-ern metropolitan couple*. After that I forgot about them until the day of the dinner.

Henry's text message   *really up against it, what with the Pearson reconfiguration, but looking forward to seeing you*   had stated 8 p.m. To allow ourselves plenty of time we set off at seven. Even as we left the tube station, alas, a difficulty arose. 'I can't find their street anywhere in NW3,' my wife said, pausing under a lamp to examine the *A–Z*. 'I'm sure he said Hampstead.' Closer inspection of the map revealed a location on the westernmost edge of that genteel borough, specifically one of those rather elongated roads that run off Cricklewood Broadway. Luckily we managed to find a taxi to take us the last half-mile. Sink Street NW6 turned out to be a winding and dimly lit thoroughfare full of double-parked cars and abandoned supermarket trolleys. Teenagers in beanie hats scurried here and there to the accompaniment of distant sounds of breaking glass. 'Bit noisy out there,' I remarked to Henry, who answered the door with such punctiliousness that he might have been purposely waiting behind it. 'Oh, we like living in a mixed area,' he said. He was wearing a velvet smoking jacket and a pair of red corduroy trousers. 'Can't shut yourself off from real life, you know. I've got partners who live in gated communities up in Hendon, but it's a multicultural world these days. Just excuse me a sec, will you, while I nip out and check the car's security system is on.'

There was no one about in the draughty hallway, though children's voices could be heard somewhere above our heads, so, having hung up our coats, we wandered into the drawing room. Compact, clutter-free and chastely furnished, this, too, was empty, and I amused myself by admiring the long line of invitations that ran across the mantelpiece. Was anyone's company, I asked myself, quite so valued as that of 'H. Perowne Esq.', 'Mr and Mrs Henry Perowne', 'Henry' or 'Hezza' over the festive season? The partners of the Entertainment and Media Group of Messrs Ernst & Young invited him to a drinks reception. The Prime Warden of the Worshipful Company of Dyers urged him to mulled wine, minced pies and choral singing. The BAFTA trustees were anxious for him to attend a charity screening of *It's a Wonderful Life*. He was wanted at the Guildhall, in Lincoln's Inn, at Hatchards bookshop, the Royal Academy, the British Library and half-a-dozen places besides. I was still happily engrossed when Henry came back from attending to the car. 'Little bastards,' he said crossly. 'Have the hubcaps off before you know where you are ...' The line of invites caught his eye and he made a deprecating gesture. 'Don't know why we put all these up, really. Shan't be able to find the time to go, in any case. Although you do get a very good supper at the Dyers. People are always sniffy about the livery companies, but they do very good work in their way ... I hope you like the room. Fleur did it herself.'

We said we thought the drawing room was very nice. 'Very contemporary,' my wife said, which always seems a safe word on these occasions. It was certainly very contemporary The walls had been got up in bright crimson and the fabric of chair backs was the colour of mint humbugs. Here and there hung photographs: Henry in a tweed suit holding a shotgun; Henry in peaked cap at the prow of a motor-boat; Henry amid a throng of dinner-jacketed party-goers. 'Isn't that Stephen Fry?' I enquired. 'Stephen?' Henry stared at the photograph as if he had never seen it before. 'We do a little work for him now and again. Actually it's his husband we see more of ...Ah, there you are, darling' – this as a small, dark-haired and immensely cross-looking woman came through the door – 'I was just explaining that you did the room yourself.' 'The dishwasher's not working,' Mrs Perowne said, without introducing herself. 'You'd better go and see about it.' 'Couldn't it wait?' Henry enquired, with a last intent look at Stephen Fry. 'I mean ...' 'If you don't go and look it there won't be any plates to eat off,' Mrs Perowne told him. When Henry had gone I explained who we were. 'Oh yes,' she remarked, a touch more graciously, 'Henry has spoken of you often. It's always nice to meet his old friends. Really, some of the people one has to put up with in his line of work ...'

There were clearly other things to be said about the kind of people one had to put up with in Henry's line of work, but she left it at that.

There was something about Mrs Perowne – Fleur – that did not invite small-talk, but she thawed a little when my wife admired the displays of dried flowers on the occasional tables. 'You see,' she explained, 'nobody can arrange flowers these days. It is an art that has quite vanished. But in my profession you appreciate the importance of these things.' 'And where did you meet Henry?' I enquired. 'Oh, we were at Oxford together,' said Mrs P coyly. 'Which college were you at?' my wife duly followed up, whereupon there was an icy silence. Could Mrs P have attended Oxford *Brookes* University, or did she not think the matter worth bothering with? It was hard to tell. All this time our hostess was making furious little assaults on the ornamentation of the room, minutely adjusting chair cushions and restoring symmetry to the line of party invites that Henry and I had so wantonly despoiled. 'I always believe that a drawing room should be a kind of *sanctum*, don't you think?' she blithely remarked. 'I never let the children in here unsupervised, much less the nanny.' This was clearly a cue for polite enquiries about the Perowne juniors, and while my wife attended to a description of the very good Church of England primary school at which Felicity and Hugo had been enrolled (as a preliminary to St Paul's Girls' School and Latimer Upper, naturally), I went off in search of the bathroom. Clearly the Perownes were much more intellectual than they let on, for this contained back numbers of the *London Review of Books*, the *Times Literary Supplement* and *Spectator*.

By the time I came back into the drawing room, Henry had returned from mending the dishwasher and was standing on the hearth-rug next to a young red-headed woman in a poncho and a pair of top-boots. 'Now,' he said in an avuncular manner, 'I think you'll agree that Daisy needs no introduction at all.' 'Absolutely,' I said, which seemed the best way of disguising that I had no idea who she was. Happily my wife sometimes sees snatches of E4 when she is forbidding the children to watch it. 'You're Daisy Trefoil, aren't you?' she exclaimed. 'From that series about the students in the technical college near Taunton?' It turned out that Ms Trefoil did indeed play the female lead in *Cider Kidz*, and together with her co-star 'Dummer' was about to open in *Puss in Boots* at the Civic Centre, Guildford. She was a nice girl, but rather quiet, although perhaps somewhat exhausted from her day's labours, which, as Henry assured me in a whisper, had involved opening a garden centre in Epsom and the furious denial of a story thought to be appearing in the following day's *Star on Sunday*. 'I'm afraid the press just won't leave Daisy alone,' he said loftily. 'As for the episode where she deep-fried the tampon by mistake, I never thought we'd hear the last of it.' By now two other men had arrived, one of whom was described by Henry as 'a man who knows more about the copyright law of mechanical reproduction than anyone in England'. The other introduced himself by saying, 'I think your car's been scratched again, Henry. It certainly looked like it as I came by.' Shortly after this, at about twenty past nine – I could already see my wife staring frostily at her watch – the seven of us went in to dinner.

It was quite a nice meal, if you like wood sorrel, 'foraged' mushrooms and aubergines, none of which, alas, I have much of a taste for. Henry, who presumably had been present at the dinner's devising and construction, pretended not to know what its separate elements were, rubbed his hands together and exclaimed 'My, what have we here?' whenever a new dish appeared, rather as if it were a Barmecidal feast descending from the rafters. Fleur very helpfully itemised the ingredients, and confided to us the name of the celebrity chef who had given her the recipes. There was rather a noise of music coming through the party wall, but not nearly enough to inhibit conversation, which was, of course, very lively. During the meal, Mrs Perowne talked about:

- Her interior decorating business, the sitting room she had designed for the former Chancellor of the Exchequer's wife ('Such a nice woman, when you get to know her, and he's really much more charming than he seems on the television') and the difficulties of working for wealthy Russians who, though punctilious in settling their bills, were sometimes 'not very civilised'.

- Where she had been and intended to go on holiday, the regrettable fact that Brittany was 'quite dead these days' and the dreadful falling off in quality of Breton-ware available in the shops in Quimper, and the relative advantages of Venice in season and out of it.

- The curious fact that Bulgarian nannies were more reliable, and seemed content to be paid less than Polish, Estonian or Latvian nannies. 'And the Bulgarian ones are better looking,' Henry jovially remarked. This got him a ferocious kick under the table which only I saw.

I glanced at Henry's face once or twice as these monologues continued, and it bore a look of absolutely slavish admiration. He is clearly a very lucky man.

Towards the end of the meal, when we were eating *glace à la framboise avec chocolat* (strawberry ice-cream with a light dusting of cocoa powder) the following things happened:

- Ms Trefoil, who had drunk at least five large glasses of Beaujolais, burst into tears, said that she wished she had never seen the script for *Cider Kidz*, that her appearance on *Celebrity Strictly Come Dancing* had been a terrible mistake, and that she wished she were dead, before locking herself in the lavatory. Fleur, whom Henry begged to intercede, declined on the grounds that she had 'had quite enough of that ghastly little tart'.

- There was a scurry of footsteps across the hall floor and a loud slamming of the front door, advertising what enquiry revealed to be the final departure of the nanny, of whom Fleur remarked that she was a thoroughly nasty girl and she hoped she would be deported.

- Henry's car-alarm went off several times, investigation revealing that someone had broken into it and stolen the stereo system.

One had, through all of this, to admire Henry's spirit. He brought the coffee in himself – Fleur had gone upstairs to see to the children – and told several amusing anecdotes about batting with Hugh Grant and Colin Firth in a charity cricket match. 'I very much hope we'll see more of each other,' he said as we left. I said I hoped so too, and that I hoped Ms Trefoil would be all right. 'Between you and me, she's one plate short of a dinner service,' Henry remarked. It was about a quarter to midnight now, and the teenagers in beanie hats were still rampaging around. Halfway down Sink Street we were passed by an ambulance with its lights flashing. 'I expect it's come for Daisy,' my wife said. We missed the last tube and had to take a taxi.

A day or so later I had a text from Henry. *Delighted to see you. Fleur charmed. Daisy now at Priory and doing well. V. busy with HMV but be in touch.* Only one – or rather two – questions remained. Why on earth had the Perownes invited us to their little dinner, and why on earth had we gone?

The Perownes

The Story of Harriet Silver

Trim, grey-haired, expensively though unobtrusively dressed, in her late sixties and recently widowed, Harriet Silver – Mrs N. E. A. Silver as she still punctiliously styles herself – inhabits a grey stucco townhouse in one of the Kensington squares. Here she subscribes to the *Daily Telegraph*, the *Lady*, *Country Life* and the *Tatler* (although she considers the latter 'rather vulgar'), deplores the colonisation of the area by European plutocrats, and plays an active part in the capital's social life, or rather that part of it suited to her age, habits and social class. The Chelsea Flower Show knows her well, as does the Royal Academy Summer Exhibition, the second week of Wimbledon and events of a ceremonial nature at which royalty are likely to be present. Twice a year she takes what she calls a 'little holiday', rents a chalet at Menton with a similarly situated friend or goes on a cruise around the Scandinavian fjords.

It is a busy but somewhat circumscribed existence, consisting in the main of coffee orgies, bridge nights in the Kensington drawing room where the light gleams off the silver tea service and the late Mr Silver's portrait stares from the wall, dinners, classical concerts, a little light weeding in her small but elegant garden and a great deal of sober recreation. Such is the assurance of her manner that anyone who saw her conducting it – watched her lunching with a friend at Fortnum & Mason, say, or haggling over a piece of statuary at one of the antique shops in the Pimlico Road – might reasonably assume that it was in her blood, that her ancestors had lived in Kensington squares since Kensington squares were there to be lived in, that the ghosts of generations of well-conducted gentlewomen stood at the door of Hatchards bookshop as she emerged from it with one of her genteel travel books or something about the Mitford sisters to cheer her on. In fact, nothing could be further from the case, for Mrs Silver's progress through life turns out to be both a case study in social advancement and a testimony to her determination to exchange the world into which she was born for something more befitting to her tastes and ambitions.

As to what that world had consisted of, Harriet's father had been a solicitor in a small town in North Yorkshire, with premises in the high street and a plastic sign bearing his name in the upstairs window. There was nothing intrinsically suspect about this occupation – the father of one of the girls in her class ran a fleet of motor coaches – but it did not inspire confidence, either in the matter of immediate advice, of which Harriet felt herself to be in urgent need, or ultimate horizons. She was a shy, pale, clever and rather isolated girl – there was a solitary sister, some years older than her – who disliked the North Yorkshire town and the (rather good) girls' day school just outside it not because anybody in them was unkind to her or failed to appreciate her considerable intelligence, but because each of them fell so horribly short of the mythological yardsticks that she had already begun to contrive for herself. Didn't somebody once say that there comes a moment in childhood when, out of the blue, instantaneously and irrevocably, we get a glimpse of the people we should like to be? Didn't the literary critic Cyril Connolly's life change when, loitering on a bridge in Berkshire, he overheard one swaggering Etonian tell another that the boy labouring in the rigger beneath them was 'rather a good oar'? There were no moss-clad Berkshire bridges or swaggering Etonians in Harriet's childhood. On the other hand, the little house on the edge of the moor harboured other talismans that were quite as potent, and one of them was a complete set of the Chalet School books written by that celebrated authoress, Miss Elinor Brent-Dyer.

It is no exaggeration to say that to Harriet the advent of the Chalet School into her life was as lightning from a clear sky and that the adventures of Robin, Daisy, Bride and their chums were as real to her, if not more real, than what went on around her. She sat with them as they brewed their cocoa, ate their 'ripping teas' and discussed the shortcomings of their gym mistresses. She journeyed with them when the school relocated from the Austrian Alps to the Channel Isles, and when they plotted the reclamation of some non-conforming new bug she was censoriously at their side. The Chalet School was her solace, but also the phantom that pursued her through her dreams, for she knew that she would never go to boarding school and that Robin, Daisy, Bride and the others were lost to her, bright, seraphic ornaments of a paradise that she herself could never hope to penetrate. Sustained and also chastened by this personal myth, largely indifferent to the landscapes in which she was compelled to wander, she applied herself to her school work, passed her A levels in a blaze of glory – her two 'best friends' were set to become, respectively, a legal secretary and a trainee veterinarian – and rather to her own surprise was offered a place at Newnham College, Cambridge, to study Modern Languages. Here, even more to her surprise, she discovered that, far from being hurled towards extinction by the servants of a debased modern age, the spirit of the Chalet School was alive and well.

It was a strange time to be a student, here in the late 1960s. The newspapers were full of stories about the Summer of Love and Vietnam, and the shops full of cheesecloth shirts and Granny Takes a Trip sunglasses, but King's Parade was still awash with well-scrubbed men in sports jackets who looked as if their immemorial destiny was to return home to Perthshire to manage their fathers' estates. It sometimes seemed to Harriet, browsing through the junior common room copy of the *New Statesman*, that the 1960s were only happening in two or three miles of central London: there was precious little sign of them here. The two great Newnham scandals of the year were a girl who ran off with one of the porters and a Commonwealth Scholar from Antigua who was brought out of her room on a stretcher, having very nearly starved herself to death. And if the decade – on the one hand so bright and tantalising, on the other so dense and rebarbative – seemed to be dissolving under her hand, instantly reconfiguring itself whenever she reached out to embrace it – so her own life seemed subject to the same paralysing incongruities. The compass of the age was set in one direction and she was pointed in the other. Most of the blame for this could be attributed to a girl called Amanda Hockering, with whom she fell in at the end of her second year and whose symbolic importance hung over the rest of her Cambridge days like smoke from a bonfire. Even at Cambridge, here in the late 1960s, there was an assumption that girls like Amanda did not actually exist anymore, that they were the human equivalent of the dodo or the passenger pigeon, but nevertheless there she was: a tall, odd, black-haired girl, two years out of a Wiltshire convent school, who had once been photographed for *Country Life* and whose parents were reliably reported to have dined with the Queen, and if she was not Cambridge's Zuleika Dobson she was certainly its Lady Catherine de Bourgh.

Perhaps the most extraordinary, and enticing, thing about her was her manner. This was not only entirely ironic but hinted at ulterior knowledge. Seizing on Harriet in the lunch queue one day, she contrived to suggest that she knew all about her, even the discreditable bits, and was prepared to put up with them in exchange for her delight in a personality of whose true worth Harriet could not possibly be aware. All this, needless to say, was very flattering, and so too were its practical consequences, which were invitations to tea in Amanda's room, suppers in out-of-the-way Cambridge restaurants of which most undergraduates had never heard, and, once, a fully fledged weekend at the Hockerings' house ('It's fearfully small, I'm afraid. You'll probably have to sleep in an attic') in Leicestershire. The people Harriet met here – the women especially – were a decided novelty. It was not quite how they talked, and it was not quite how they dressed. It was not even where they had been to school, merely that something in their spiritual get-up seemed to set them apart from anyone else she had ever met, both inside Cambridge and beyond it. In fact, they were so exclusive, so rarefied in their connections, that the exclusiveness scarcely mattered to them, was regarded, alternatively, as something intrinsic, accepted without having to be thought about. Harriet had once been lounging on the bed-sitting room chair of a girl called Penelope Shuttleworth – The Honourable Penelope Shuttleworth, a glance at the envelope of a letter sent to her that morning by her mother confirmed – when the subject of Penelope's plans for the summer vacation came up. 'I dare say,' The Honourable Penelope had remarked – she was sewing sequins into a ball gown with a practised hand – 'that I shall go to Ithaca with Uncle Mark. On the other hand, Peter's leased a cottage on Islay. And then again, it might be rather fun to stay in Knightsbridge with Cecily Faulks and be a girl about town, whatever that is.'

A year ago Harriet would have thought this brisk canvassing of alternatives, each of them desirable beyond measure, quite hopelessly affected, the last exhausted gasp of a *rentier* sensibility which the social forces of the age seemed bent on destroying. But she had endured enough of people who might have been considered her natural allies, and the effect of coming upon Amanda and her gorgeous satellites, conversing in their artful, peacock voices, having their young men deposit them outside college gates in sports cars, not caring how they performed in tutorials or exams, was wholly exotic: like finding a herd of deer unknown to Linnaeus deep in the heart of the Prussian forests. Curiously, or perhaps not so curiously, the girls liked Harriet. They thought, or affected to think, her 'sensible', and having heard of her upbringing in the shadow of the solicitor's office they presumed to find in her a degree of practical knowledge to which they could not themselves aspire. 'Harriet will know all about *that*,' they would say – it might be a defective electrical plug or an extra charge on the college battels – and

Harriet, ever obliging, would see what she could do. The girls were careful not to patronise her, Harriet was equally careful that she was not taken for granted, occasional sharp words were smoothed away by the pleasant thought that 'Harriet can be very outspoken' – outspokenness sometimes, but not always, being a point in your favour – and in general everybody got on very well.

All this produced certain refinements in Harriet's character and appearance of which she was probably not wholly aware. Her clothes became even more detached from the tenor of the time, and her vowels slightly more elongated. Mrs Baird, to whom evidence of these new-found affiliations was presented in the holidays, was mystified but not unresponsive. She was not alarmed at the prospect of her daughter being turned into a more exotic version of contemporary girlhood: rather, she seemed to think that its roots might have something to do with an influence she could not, mysteriously, remember having wielded in the first place. Gratifying as this was, it came accompanied by a suspicion that there was no future in Amanda, Penelope and the others. How could there be? After Cambridge they would surely retreat into more or less unimaginable worlds where Harriet, a refugee from her class, feared she could not follow. In the meantime, there was a certain amount of pleasure to be gained from spending time with them, learning their language – a fearsome instrument in which understatement predominated – and cracking their codes.

Years later half-a-dozen phrases from this period stuck in her head like burrs: *rather an awful man*; *one of our ancient retainers*; *someone of Mummy's*. None of them meant precisely what it said – *one of our ancient retainers* was longhand for 'cleaning lady'

– but their fascination could not be denied. Finals came and the alliances of the Newnham corridors broke up and dispersed. Amanda, Penelope and co., who had got third-class degrees, went off to do nothing in particular, to ornament Mayfair galleries, or in Penelope's case to marry a real live viscount who was supposed to own half the upper reaches of the Tweed. Harriet, who had got a rather good second, migrated to London and a job in a public relations agency in Newman Street. And it was from this address that she allowed herself to be taken to a champagne reception at the Guards Club, sponsored by one of the firm's clients, where at a late hour, in a billiard room crammed with red-faced and square-jawed young men, among whom he seemed the most red-faced and square-jawed of all, she met Nigel Silver, who had just exchanged a captaincy in the Blues and Royals for a job in a stockbroking firm in Throckmorton Street.

There was some doubt, at the outset of their relationship, as to whether Harriet would 'do'. Happily, Mrs Silver, a terrifying old lady in pearls and twinset with a nutcracker face, run to earth in an Elizabethan manor house at the end of nearly half a mile of gravel driveway somewhere in Warwickshire, pronounced her 'a nice girl', later amending this to 'a very nice girl, and' – to Nigel – 'clearly very fond of you', and further remarking that 'She seems to have been very well brought up.' 'I think Mother's rather taken to you, Hatty,' Nigel confided on the way home from a weekend spent perambulating Mrs Silver's rose garden and reading the newspapers in her chilly drawing room, the implication being that there were many more proto-Harriets to whom Mrs Silver had manifestly not taken.

The Silvers, Harriet discovered, were an ancient Warwickshire family, so ancient, it was alleged, as to make the Plantagenets look like parvenus, and there was a real-live parlour maid in cap and Lisle stockings to bring in the tea. Another girl would have wandered in stark bewilderment through this mausoleum to a vanished age, its photographs of Nigel, in gaiters and a knee-length scarf, heading off to play the Wall Game, its cuttings book filled with reportage from the debutante dances of Mrs Silver's youth, but Harriet thought that she liked it. They drove back to London with a Sunday paper across their lap bringing news of Saigon, Mr Heath and Mr Wilson and no hint of incongruity ever occurred to her. It was Mrs Silver, snug in her lair of Turkey carpets and Sheraton furniture and the little tinkling bell she rang to summon her domestics, who was real.

They were married in the summer of 1972 in the parish church in Warwickshire − at Mrs Silver's insistence − a rather grand affair, with a guard of honour composed of Nigel's old military comrades holding up an arch of swords and half-a-dozen bridesmaids in antique taffeta dresses. Harriet's mother and father looked on proudly, but the rest of her relatives followed the proceedings with a faint air of suspicion. It was not their kind of occasion, and her sister, who had grown very left-wing and married a teacher at a comprehensive school, said that Hatty's head had been turned. There was an unfortunate moment when Harriet's father, who had volunteered to pay for the wine, heard Mrs Silver murmur the words, 'But my dear, isn't cheap champagne hellish?' to one of her cronies when she thought no one else was listening, but everyone said that the bride looked radiant.

In the months that followed it was a source of gratification to Mrs Silver that, in terms of the life the young couple intended to lead, it seemed to be Harriet who made most of the running. For all the rigour of his upbringing, Nigel was an easy-going type who would probably have been content with a maisonette off the Fulham Road and semi-bohemian laxity. It was Harriet who negotiated with her mother-in-law for the release of sufficient capital to purchase the freehold of the house in the Kensington square, who lobbied for the Hurlingham Club subscription on the grounds that 'We need somewhere to see our friends at the weekend', who got the children into an immensely old-fashioned pre-prep school in Sloane Square where the boys wore corduroy knee-breeches and the school hymn still contained references to 'the Empire's vast expanse'. Old Mrs Silver, watching all this, was both charmed and impressed. She could be heard to say that Harriet was not only a 'nice girl', but a 'capable girl' and on one memorable afternoon when a duchess was staying in the house and the cook, stung by a bee, had an anaphylactic attack, a 'reliable girl'.

There were even times when Harriet could have been thought to have overplayed her hand, such as the moment, sometime in the early 1980s, at which Nigel, inspecting the Norfolk jacket and miniature plus-fours in which his eldest son was attired as they sat picnicking at the Round Pound, declared, 'Hatty, you can't possible let Raife go around dressed like that. He looks like one of Edward VII's gamekeepers.' And Harriet, one hand delving into the picnic basket, the other manoeuvring her daughter's Alice band back into place, her mind searching for reasons as to why they could not go to North Yorkshire for the August Bank Holiday, humbly lowered her head in the realisation that for once, in her dealings with the Silvers, she had gone too far.

But then there was always an excuse for having gone too far, which was that so many people, here in an age of social confusion and behavioural drift, had not gone far enough. The late 1960s and early 1970s had rather passed Harriet by: Cambridge, Nigel, the Hurlingham Club and old Mrs Silver in her Warwickshire eyrie had insulated her from the chill winds blowing in across this ever more egalitarian landscape. It was only when her offspring began to grow up that she realised quite how much the world had changed since her own childhood and quite how much she hated the transformation. Raife, Felicity and Bella were nice, dutiful children ('rather neurotic,' Mrs Silver had been heard to say, 'but that's what comes of living in London, and I don't blame Harriet *at all*'), but they had an irritating habit, once advanced into late teendom, of interrogating their mother over the plethora of niggling social judgements that had, some years before, descended on their unquestioning infant heads.

'When we stayed that time in Herefordshire, Mummy, why weren't we allowed to play with the children in the lodge next door?' 'I really don't remember, darling,' Mrs Silver would reply, who remembered all too well the twanging Estuarine accents that broke upon the early morning air. 'Weren't they rather ragamuffins?' 'And why was it that you didn't like Mr Hopkinson who lived at Number 23?' 'Did I say I didn't like him?' Mrs Silver would mildly demur. 'I don't really remember the man. Didn't he sell cars or something?' And so the memory of poor Mr Hopkinson, with his car dealership, his brown suits and his Holland Park Comprehensive-educated children, whose suitability for the ownership of a house in Kensington Mrs Silver had loudly questioned over the breakfast table and whose sherry parties she had flatly refused to attend, was sent swiftly on its way. 'And why did we always have to watch the children's programmes on the BBC and never ITV?' And here Mrs Silver would hesitate, because she knew that she could not decently say that she found the presenters employed by the commercial channels vulgar in comparison with the wholesome young men and women operating out of Broadcasting House, never mind that Susan Stranks on *Magpie* was clearly not wearing a brassière . . . 'Oh, I don't know,' she would temporise. 'I don't think it was anything to do with me. Anyway, I always thought you liked the nice competitions they had on *Blue Peter*.'

All that, of course, was nearly a quarter of a century ago. The children are grown up now, with children of their own, on whom Harriet 'dotes' as she puts it, and whose school fees she discreetly subsidises. That she can afford to do this is mostly down to the acumen of her late husband, who, defying the gloomy prophecies of his Winchester reports, made rather a success of his career in the City and, on dying at the early age of sixty-five, was discovered to have left his widow several million pounds expertly tied up in a series of tax-friendly family trusts. And there in the house in the Kensington square, now worth nearly as much as her trust funds, surrounded by Russian oligarchs and anonymous tribunes of the European super-rich, she sits, hale, respectable and indefatigable. For, when not seeing her friends or attending to her round of seasonal pursuits, there is a great deal for Harriet to do, her grandchildren to see (the latter are fond of 'Granny' while finding her somewhat demanding in the area of 'manners' and, in the girls' case, deportment), her lawyers to consult and her financial holdings to consolidate. Here in her widowhood she has become rather interested ('fascinated, actually') in genealogy, to the extent of pursuing her own clan, the Arkwrights of Pickering, to the uttermost tendrils of their family tree. It was a rewarding exercise, which not only turned up a certain Josiah Arkwright, an eighteenth-century industrialist who became a freeman of the city of Leeds, but also a Victorian poetess, Susannah Arkwright, author of *Plant of Plinlimmon* and other works, who married the younger son of a baronet. Harriet procured a copy of *Plant of Plinlimmon* at considerable expense from a rare book dealer and read it in an ecstasy of ancestral pride.

What else is there to say about Harriet? She is, naturally, a supporter of her local Anglican church, a number of faintly obscure charities, and the Kensington and Chelsea Conservative Association, while fearing that its parliamentary representative is not really what she calls a Conservative. She enjoys watching period dramas on the television, not so much for the quality of the acting as for the frequent opportunity to criticise some of the historical detail ('Lord Mountstuart would simply not have spoken to the parlour-maid like that, and as for the butler pinching the governess's bottom . . .'). An exception to this rule is *Call the Midwife*, whose 'very nice girls' go about their work in the right spirit and are clearly happy with the situation in which providence has seen fit to locate them.

The world would be a much better place, Harriet feels, if people complained less, were more mindful of their duty, attentive to the needs of others and not constantly striving to outdo each other in the matter of personal prestige and material comfort. Her own extraordinary march through the upper reaches of the English social world, much less the wholesale personal reinvention that accompanied it, has probably never occurred to her. Meanwhile, as she is delighted to inform her friends, the potted shrimps at the Hurlingham Club are as good as ever.

A Note on Names and Titles

Titles

It is not snobbish to possess a title. The snob is a person who uses a title ostentatiously. See, for example, the Nobel Prize-winning author William Golding, who not only instructed friends to lobby for his knighthood but had his and his wife's passports altered to 'Sir William and Lady Golding' within days of its being gazetted. Extrapolating from the Thackeray principle (see Chapter 3) Sir William's actions may be said to have demeaned both himself and the award to which he aspired. At the same time, if it is snobbish to glory in your advancement, then it is equally snobbish to make a fuss about not glorying in it. A journalist who declines the offer of a CBE and then writes an article in the *Guardian* about his principled stand against the tyranny of the honours system is quite as much a snob as the author of *Lord of the Flies*.

Professional qualifications

Ideally, the use of a professional qualification should be limited to the professional beat in which it applies. Styling yourself 'Dr

John Smith' in the residential section of the telephone book when the doctorate happens to be in animal husbandry is snobbish. So is introducing yourself as 'Professor James Bond' at a rehearsal of the Chertsey Chorale. A Fellow of the Royal Society of Literature should only expect to be addressed as 'FRSL' in communications from that body. The same rule applies to the ex-officer's habit – much rarer now than it used to be in the inter-war era – of transferring a military rank into civilian life. The House of Commons of the early 1950s, for example, was stiff with moonlighting Wing Commanders and Brigadiers. These days it is a brave man who signs the correspondence of the golf club at which he officiates as secretary 'Major Giles Fothergill'.

Names

As a general rule, anyone who pronounces their surname differently from the way in which it is spelled ('Fanshaw' for 'Featherstonehaugh', 'Chumley' for 'Cholmondeley', 'Mawlborough' for 'Marlborough' and so on) is a snob. The exceptions are one or two ancient aristocratic names ('Ponsonby', for example, which was originally pronounced 'Punsonby') corrupted by recent, demotic usage. Similarly, the owner of Woburn is perfectly entitled to pronounce his home as 'Wooburn'. The possessor of a name whose pronunciation is in doubt may naturally insist on correct usage. On the other hand, to make a fuss about this is snobbish. 'Burn*ett*, we call it,' Anthony Powell remembered the novelist Ivy Compton-Burnett instructing him, 'in an absolutely freezing voice.'

There is nothing inherently snobbish about double-barrelled surnames. Here in the twenty-first century, they are far more likely to be the result of an unmarried couple compromising on what to call their children than the reminder of a status-enhancing raid on the Victorian marriage-market. On the other hand, excessive self-deprecation in their use, as in The Honourable James Beresford de la Poer Hardy-Jones, who prefers his letters to be addressed to 'J. Jones Esq.', is probably an example of inverted snobbery.

Similarly, no Christian name is snobbish *in itself*. As with a title, a military rank or an advanced degree, any imputation of snobbishness lies in the use to which it is put. Modern snobs are much more likely to declare themselves by way of their attitude to other people's names rather than their own. This tendency is especially marked in the long tradition of amused middle-class disapproval of certain working-class Christian names, which can be traced back at least as far as the late Victorian era. The famously bleak short stories of the Norfolk farmer's wife Mary Mann (1848–1929), for example, set in a rural economy blighted by the agricultural depression of the 1890s, feature several poverty-stricken children whose parents have given them such socially exalted, and by implication unsuitable, names as 'Randolph' and 'Evangeline'.

If the late Victorian middle classes were amused by the idea of working-class children being named after cabinet ministers and duchesses, then their early twenty-first century equivalents are more likely to laugh at names that seem to glory in their naffness. Thus any non-working-class person who finds any of the following names *ipso facto* funny is a snob: Wayne, Bradley, Tyler, Ryan, Jason, Kayleigh, Charleen, Jordan (both sexes). For purposes of historical comparison, the 'joke' working-class names of forty years ago were Dawn, Sharon, Tracey, Mandy,

Gary and Kevin (with the exception of the children of Irish peers, as in 'The Hon. Kevin Pakenham').

In the same way, any non-upper-class person who finds any of the following names *ipso facto* funny is also a snob: Peregrine, Gervase, Marmaduke, Hector, Jonty, Oenone, Loelia, Ariadne, Gavin, Inigo, Perdita, Xantippe, Fenella, Arabella. Naturally, given the relative elasticity of modern social demographics, it is possible for certain socially insecure middle-class people to be snobbishly amused by one or two of the standard upmarket middle-class names, for example, Jeremy, Nigel, Simon, Giles, Felix, Henrietta.

Hatches, matches and despatches

The average newspaper 'Births, Marriages and Deaths' column is, naturally, a miasma of snobbery. As with the use of titles, several distinctions apply. It is not, for example, snobbish to give your children what might be thought fanciful names that they may well consider a burden in later life. Snobbishness consists of playing up the circumstances of their birth to create an aura of exceptionalism, thus: 'To Tarquin and Calliope Fitz-Alan, a daughter, Tallulah Petal Goldilocks, born on Christmas Day on the Isle of Mull, under a horned moon, welcomed by a regiment of swooping owls and the sound of bagpipes, a sister to Ethelred and Godwin' is snobbish.

It is also snobbish to laugh at the death or 'In Memoriam' announcements in local newspapers, particularly if they contain poetry.

Notes and Further Reading

Unless stated, the place of publication is London.

1. The Snob Defined

For Andrew Mitchell and 'Plebgate', see the *Daily Telegraph*, 24 September 2012. The circumstances of Emily Thornberry's resignation were reported in the *Guardian*, 20 November 2014. On David Mellor's encounter with the taxi-driver, *Independent*, 25 November 2014. Thackeray's memory of his time at Cambridge can be found in 'On University Snobs', originally published in *Punch*, 1846–1847, later reprinted in volume form as *The Book of Snobs*. All quotations are taken from *The Works of William Makepeace Thackeray, Volume XIV: The Book of Snobs and Sketches and Travels in London* (1879).

On current interpretations of the word 'snob': Zoe Williams, *Guardian*, 24 July 2015; Lynne Mortimer, *Eastern Daily Press*, 27 July 2015; Memphis Barker, *i*, 4 August 2015. For snob 'statements': Michael Jopling, quoted in Alan Clark, *Diaries: In Power 1983–1992* (1993), 17 June 1987; Stephen Glover, quoted in a *Guardian* article by Simon Kelner commemorating the final print edition of the *Independent*, 26 March 2016; Dame

Janet Vaughan, quoted in Charles Moore, *Margaret Thatcher: The Authorized Biography: Volume I: Not for Turning* (2013), p. 47; Paul Weller, quoted in Steve Malins, *Paul Weller: The Unauthorised Biography* (1997), p. 171. For Richard Rees on Orwell, *George Orwell: Fugitive from the Camp of Victory* (1961).

For Isaiah Berlin, see Henry Hardy and Mark Pottle (eds), *Affirming: Letters 1975–1997* (2015). On Robbie Williams, Louise Wener, *Different for Girls: My True-Life Adventures in Pop* (2010), pp. 288–90. Simon Raven, quoted in Michael Barber, *The Captain: The Life and Times of Simon Raven* (1996), p. 87. On the 'inverted snob', Professor Alan S. C. Ross, 'U and Non-U', in Nancy Mitford (ed.), *Noblesse Oblige: An Enquiry into the Identifiable Characteristics of the English Aristocracy* (1956).

2. Heroes and Villains: Katie Price, Lord Prescott and Others

For a summary of Lord Prescott's career, see 'The Passing of Prescott', *Independent*, 10 May 2010.

3. The Great Snobographer

For Thackeray generally, see Gordon N. Ray, *Thackeray: The Uses of Adversity 1811–1846* (Oxford, 1955) and *Thackeray: The Age of Wisdom 1847–1863* (Oxford, 1958), and D. J. Taylor, *Thackeray* (1999). All quotations from *The Book of Snobs, The Works of William Makepeace Thackeray, Volume XIV: The Book of Snobs and Sketches and Travels in London* (1879). The letter to Edmund Yates of 13 June 1858 is reproduced in Gordon N. Ray (ed.), *The Letters and Private Papers of William Makepeace Thackeray: Volume IV: 1857–1863* (1946), pp. 89–90.

The Snob in Action I: Ralph Straus

Most of the information about Straus is taken from Alec Waugh, 'Ralph Straus', in *My Brother Evelyn and other Profiles* (1967), pp. 96–104.

4. Best Sets

On the attitudes of the Krays towards social class, see John Pearson, *The Profession of Violence: The Rise and Fall of the Kray Twins* (revised paperback edition, 1983). For Arthur Harding, see Raphael Samuel, *East End Underworld: Chapters in the Life of Arthur Harding* (1981). For the interrogation of Ridley and Latimer, Keith Thomas, *The Ends of Life: Roads to Fulfilment in Early Modern England* (Oxford, 2009).

There is a wide-ranging discussion of the nature of Victorian social protocols in Andrew St George, *The Descent of Manners: Etiquette, Rules & The Victorians* (1993). For Thomas Carlyle, see *Sartor Resartus* (1836). The anonymous mid-Victorian definition of etiquette is quoted in St George, p. 47. The details of Victorian dress styles are taken from C. Willett and Phyllis Cunnington, *Handbook of English Couture in the Nineteenth Century* (1959). For the Fougasse cartoon, see Alec Waugh, *A Year to Remember: A Reminiscence of 1931* (1975), p. 81. The *Punch* skit from 1862 is reproduced in St George.

Anthony Powell's trip to Holloway and the 'Pooter country': *Journals 1982–1986* (1995), p.139. For his memories of A. G. Lewis at Duckworth, *To Keep the Ball Rolling: The Memoirs of Anthony Powell: Volume II: Messengers of Day* (1978), pp. 10–12. On Earl Beauchamp and the Lygon family, see Paula Byrne, *Mad World: Evelyn Waugh and the Secrets of Brideshead* (2009). Arthur Benson's diary entry of 8 June 1925 is quoted in David

Newsome, *On the Edge of Paradise: A. C. Benson Diarist* (1980), p. 377. For information on King's College, Cambridge, in the early 1880s, see Newsome and Michael Cox, *M. R. James: An Informal Portrait* (Oxford, 1983).

Brian Howard's 'My Lords and Gentleman' speech: Marie-Jaqueline Lancaster, *Brian Howard: Portrait of a Failure* (1968), p. 202. John Carey remembers his time at Christchurch in *An Unexpected Professor* (2014). For John Prescott and Anthony Eden: D. R. Thorpe, *Eden: The Life and Times of Anthony Eden First Earl of Avon, 1897–1977* (2003), pp. 553, 555.

5. Noblesse Oblige

Tom Driberg, quoted in Alan Watkins, *Brief Lives* (1982), p.24. For Anthony Powell's view of Mrs Thatcher, see his *Journals 1982–1986 (1995)*, p. 142; on Evelyn Waugh, ibid., p. 201. Powell writes about Andrew Cavendish, Duke of Devonshire, in his *Journals 1987–1989* (1996), p. 218. For James Lees-Milne on Deborah Cavendish, Duchess of Devonshire, see *Ceaseless Turmoil: Diaries, 1988–1992* (2004), pp. 100–101. Patrick Hamilton is quoted in Sean French, *Patrick Hamilton: A Life* (1993), pp. 206–7.

The Snob in Action II: Mrs Thatcher and Her Critics

The majority of the remarks about Mrs Thatcher can be found in Charles Moore, *Margaret Thatcher: The Authorized Biography: Volume II: Everything She Wants*, pp. 635–72. For Angela Carter's assessment, *New Statesman*, 3 June 1983.

6. The Pockthorpe Factor

For Anthony Powell and 'Welshness', see his *Journals 1990–1992* (1997), p. 124. Orwell's essay 'Notes on Nationalism' is reprinted in Peter Davison (ed.), *George Orwell: The Complete Works: Volume XVII: I Belong to the Left: 1945* (1998), pp. 141–56. Thackeray's 'Memorials of Gourmandising', W. M. Thackeray, *A Shabby Genteel Story and Other Writings* (1993); 'The Second Funeral of Napoleon', *The Works of William Makepeace Thackeray*, vol. XXII. *The Paris Sketchbook*, ibid., vol. XVI. The 'England versus France' diptych is reproduced in Taylor, *Thackeray*, p. 167. Kingsley Amis recalled his encounter with Carson McCullers and her maid in *Memoirs* (1991), pp. 200–201. On de La Varende and Normandy, Theodore Zeldin, *France 1848–1945: Volume II: Intellect, Taste and Anxiety* (Oxford, 1977), pp. 72–3.

Such, Such Were the Joys is reprinted in Peter Davison (ed.), *Orwell: Complete Works: Volume XIX: It is What I Think: 1948–1949*, pp. 356–87. For the letter to Anthony Powell, *Volume X: A Kind of Compulsion: 1903–1936*, p. 484.

On the Merseyside accent, see Paul Farley's 'Archive on Four' programme *Learn Yerself Scouse*, first broadcast on BBC Radio Four, 28 March 2015. For the Beatles's social background, Ian McDonald, *Revolution in the Head: The Beatles' Records and the Sixties* (rev. edition 1997). The history of Pockthorpe is entertainingly outlined in Rosemary O'Donoghue, *Norwich, an Expanding City 1801–1900* (Norwich, 2014), pp. 149–53.

7. Two Snob Portraits: J. L.-M. and 'The Beast'

For James Lees-Milne, see *Ancient as the Hills: Diaries 1973–1974* (1997), *Through Wood and Dale: Diaries 1975–1978*, *Ceaseless Turmoil: Diaries 1988–1992* (2004) and *The Milk of Paradise: Diaries 1993–1997* (2005); and Michael Bloch, *James Lees-Milne: The Life* (2009).

For Dennis Skinner, see his autobiography *Sailing Close to the Wind: Reminiscences* (2014). There are interesting glimpses of the young MP in Susan Crosland, *Tony Crosland* (1982).

The Snob in Action III: W. G. Grace

Most of the information about Grace is taken from Simon Rae, *W. G. Grace: A Life* (1998), but see also David Kynaston, *W. G.'s Birthday Party* (1998).

8. Snob Lingo

For Peter Fleming, see Duff Hart-Davis, *Peter Fleming: A Biography* (1974). For the proportion of upper-class people in Attlee-era Britain and Professor Margaret Stace's Mass Observation survey of 1948–51, Arthur Marwick, *British Society Since 1945* (1982, rev. 1990), ch. 2. For Raymond Mortimer on Holroyd's *Lytton Strachey*, Frances Partridge, *Good Company: Diaries 1967–1970* (1994), p. 105.

9. 'These people ought to be shot': The Future of Snobbery

Orwell's *The Lion and the Unicorn: Socialism and the English Genius* is reprinted in Peter Davison (ed.), *Orwell: Complete Works: Volume XII. A Patriot After All. 1940–1941*, pp. 392–434. Evelyn Waugh, preface to *Brideshead Revisited* (revised edition 1960), p. 10. Simon Raven, 'Perish by the Sword', in Hugh Thomas (ed.), *The Establishment* (1959).

For the Conservative MPs of the 1950 intake, see *The Times Guide to the House of Commons* (1950). On Anthony Crosland, see Susan Crosland, *Tony Crosland* (1982). The portrait of Paul Johnson from which these quotations are taken appears in Watkins, *Brief Lives*, pp. 79–84. Janet Street-Porter's article about the Man Booker Prize was published in the *Independent*, 13 October 2008.

The Snob in Action IV: Beau Brummell

For Brummell, see Ian King, *Beau Brummell: The Ultimate Dandy* (2005), and also Virginia Woolf's essay 'Beau Brummell', reprinted in *The Common Reader: Second Series* (1932), pp. 148–56.

10. In Defence of the Snob

Orwell remembered the incident of the ladder in an 'As I Please' column for *Tribune*, 26 May 1944, reprinted in Peter Davison (ed.), *Orwell: Complete Works: Volume XVI: I Have Tried to Tell the Truth: 1943–1944*, pp. 230–32. For Matthew Arnold and Sir Daniel Gooch, *John Gross, The Rise and Fall of the Man of Letters* (1969), pp. 54–5.

The Snob in Action V: Tom Driberg

The portrait of Driberg draws on Watkins, *Brief Lives*, pp. 20–28, and Francis Wheen, *Tom Driberg: His Life and Indiscretions* (1990).

The Progressive Snob: Henrietta Crabbe

'Eborebelosa' and one or two of Henrietta's comments about him are borrowed from Malcolm Bradbury's novel *Eating People is Wrong* (1959).

Sporting Snobs

For Alec Waugh and the MCC blazer, see *A Year to Remember*, pp. 80–81. Martin Amis's *Observer* essay, 'Darts: Gutted for Keith', is reprinted in *Visiting Mrs Nabokov and Other Excursions* (1993).

A Note on Names and Titles

For a full account of the circumstances of William Golding's knighthood, see John Carey, *William Golding: The Man Who Wrote Lord of the Flies* (2009), pp. 484–5. Anthony Powell's remark about Ivy Compton-Burnett was made to the author. The best of Mary Mann's short stories are collected in *Tales of Victorian Norfolk* (Bungay, 1991).

Acknowledgements

I should like to acknowledge the influence of several books that touch, directly and indirectly, on the behaviour and historical importance of the snob. Naturally, the most important is Thackeray's *The Book of Snobs*, but valuable information was also to hand in Stephen Potter, *Lifemanship* (1950), Geoffrey Gorer and Ronald Searle, *Modern Types* (1956), Nancy Mitford (ed.), *Noblesse Oblige: An Enquiry into the Identifiable Characteristics of the English Aristocracy* (1956), Simon Raven, *The English Gentleman* (1961) and Ann Barr and Peter York, *The Official Sloane Ranger Handbook* (1982).

Earlier (and shorter) versions of 'Film Snobs', 'Sporting Snobs' and 'The Broadhursts and Lucy' were originally included in the 'Life as We Know It' feature in the *Independent on Sunday*'s now sadly defunct *New Review* magazine. Part of Chapter 2 derives from a profile written to mark the subject's retirement from the House of Commons, *Independent*, 10 May 2010. I am grateful to EIS Media for permission to reproduce this material.

Especial thanks to Mike Higgins, Robert Epstein, Gordon Wise, Andreas Campomar, Claire Chesser and Howard Watson.